E. Power Biggs, Concert Organist

E. POWER BIGGS,
Concert Organist

BARBARA OWEN

INDIANA UNIVERSITY PRESS

Bloomington and Indianapolis

© 1987 by Barbara Owen

MANUFACTURED IN THE UNITED STATES OF AMERICA

Library of Congress Cataloging-in-Publication Data

Owen, Barbara.
  E. Power Biggs, concert organist.

  Bibliography: p.
  Includes index.
  1. Biggs, E. Power (Edward Power), 1906–1977.
2. Organists—United States—Biography. I. Title.
ML416.B5309 1987   786.5'092'4 [B]   86-45743

ISBN 0-253-31801-7

1 2 3 4 5 91 90 89 88 87

for Peggy,
because it is her book, too.

When the artist is alive in any person, whatever his kind of work may be, he becomes an inventive, searching daring, self-expressing creature. He becomes interesting to other people. He disturbs, upsets, enlightens, and he opens ways for a better understanding. Where those who are not artists are trying to close the book, he opens it, shows there are still more pages possible.

It seems to me that before a man tries to express anything in the world he must recognize in himself an individual, a new one, very distinct from others.

—*Robert Henri,* The Art Spirit *(1923)*

Contents

ILLUSTRATIONS

PREFACE

My first acquaintance with E. Power Biggs was shared with thousands of other radio listeners back in the 1940s and 1950s. That led to my buying his early Columbia long-playing records and attending his recitals whenever they came within attending range. When I finally met him personally, at an American Guild of Organists convention in 1956, I was already a full-fledged Biggs fan. In fact, I still am.

From that time on, our paths crossed often. I had the pleasure of working with him on occasional projects, and the distant E. Power Biggs of the record jacket and concert stage became the familiar "Biggsie," frequently encountered in the audience at Boston-area musical events and Guild meetings—not to mention parties, no small number of which were held at the large Victorian house on Highland Street, hosted by his charming and capable wife, Peggy. Familiarity with Biggs by no means bred contempt; it bred affection and a very healthy respect for his remarkable power of organization and the prodigious amount of high quality work this enabled him to turn out. It also bred an abiding admiration of his determination to stand up for his ideals and even go quite far out on a limb for them. We owe him a lot for that alone.

I always felt that Biggsie must have had a particularly high fidelity crystal ball hidden away somewhere. His guesses and predictions with regard to trends and directions were uncannily accurate a very high percentage of the time. Of course, it is anyone's guess how much he himself had to do with making some of them come to pass.

And I think he expected that someone would write his biography after he was gone. As I began to sort through the mountain of information left behind by a very busy and useful life, I started finding some markers left by Biggs himself, mostly from the period in the 1970s, when his health was beginning to decline. The first was a notebook full of biographical jottings dated 1971, with "B. Owen" written at the top. There is no mystery concerning their origin. In 1971 I was asked to write an article on Biggs for the periodical *Music,* and I of course called Biggs to ask for suggestions. He then proceeded to outline the salient points of his career (with commentary) in one of his notebooks, and then called back ready to answer my questions. But I never actually saw the notebook until much later. With typical thoroughness Biggs had sketched out more than I had asked for, and all of it was extremely useful.

In 1973 he put down, ostensibly for publicity purposes, a full outline of his career and those events to which he attached the greatest importance. In the same year, in response to a request from John Fesperman for material on the Busch-Reisinger Museum organs, he taped some of his recollections of these instruments. According to Fesperman, the taping was his own idea, and Biggs seemed to enjoy doing it, for he rambled on well beyond the immediate subject matter, again giving valuable insights into his own perspective on his career. Finally, there are the autobiographical articles written between 1975 and 1977—the Cunningham and Koussevitzky reminiscences, and his account of his recording career—which were published just before and just after his death. All these writings give important clues to what Biggs thought was important and meaningful in his life and work, and I have tried to steer my biographical course by Biggs's own guideposts.

This is all by way of saying that credit has to be given to Biggsie himself for providing, in his usual prescient manner, direction and information for this posthumous biography. Equal credit is also due to Peggy Biggs, without whose help, encouragement, criticism, and general collusion the whole undertaking would not have been possible. In fact—let's face it—it was *her* idea, first gently hinted at while the two of us were on our hands and knees attempting to bring order to a chaotic jumble of papers, scores, notebooks, clippings, and programs piled up on her livingroom floor during the summer of 1980. Having lived most of her life with a consummate "idea man," it was perfectly natural that she should be capable of some rather good ideas herself.

Of course many others contributed to this book, not the least in the area of encouragement, and I fervently hope that they will pleased with the result. Special thanks are due to Andrew Kazdin and Eileen Hunt, who, along with Peggy, read the first draft and offered many helpful corrections and suggestions; to John Fesperman of the Smithsonian Institution and William Parsons of the Library of Congress; to Gail Hennig, librarian of the Longy School; to Allen Kinzey for information on various Aeolian-Skinner organs; to Dirk Flentrop for reviewing chapter 13; to Wesley A. Day, Daniel Pinkham, Robert Covell, Mary Crowley Vivian, and many others for personal recollections of Biggs in the period before I knew him; to Elizabeth Coolidge Winship for giving permission to use excerpts from Elizabeth Sprague Coolidge's correspondence; to Columbia Masterworks for granting permission to use Andrew Kazdin's discography and other copyrighted material; and to the Boston chapter of the American Guild of Organists for assisting with copying costs.

E. Power Biggs, Concert Organist

1 | *Jimmy Biggs*

Early in September 1930 a young English organist strode down the gangplank of an ocean liner and onto the streets of depression-wracked New York. He had no job or, apparently, any real prospect of one, but he had come to stay. For the next few weeks he pounded pavements and knocked on doors, eating at the Automat—where a sandwich or a piece of pie could be had for a nickel—and staying at the YMCA for 75 cents a night.

The previous year he had made a chaotic and financially unrewarding tour of the United States, consisting largely of one-night stands in small towns, followed by a single New York recital; nonetheless he was almost completely unknown in a country where audiences equated organ concerts with the flamboyant orchestral transcriptions of his charismatic countryman Edwin H. Lemare or the melodious platitudes of the "millionaires' organist," Archer Gibson. This young musician's style—personal as well as musical—was conservative. His assets were a solid conservatory training under some outstanding teachers, considerable raw talent and capacity for work, self-confidence of a quite realistic sort, and a seemingly unshatterable optimism.

Edward George Power Biggs was born on March 29, 1906, in the sign of Aries, to Alice Maud Tredgett and Clarence Power Biggs of Westcliff-on-Sea, a small town east of London. His father was an auctioneer, his mother the daughter of a farmer. As far as can be determined, the family was not a particularly musical one.

In 1907 the Biggses moved to Ventnor on the Isle of Wight, partly in an attempt to restore Clarence Biggs's health, which had been undermined by tuberculosis. There they took in paying guests in a rambling Victorian house named Highport Towers, which was well supplied with smooth banisters, hidden cupboards, and other diversions for an imaginative (and perhaps sometimes lonely) child. The sea breezes and Alice Biggs's Christian Science convictions notwithstanding, Clarence Biggs died only two years after the move, leaving his widow to cope with both the boardinghouse and an active three-year-old son.

At the age of seven, Jimmy Biggs (his unwieldy full name temporarily bypassed) entered Hurstpierpoint College, a "public" (i.e., private) school in Sussex, where, among other extracurricular activities, he played soccer and began taking piano lessons. During his summers at Ventnor he had ample opportunity to observe the many boats that passed the Isle of Wight on their way from Southampton to France. His interest in them led to the compilation of a notebook titled, in a youthful but firm hand, "Notes on Model Boats." In it are a number of clippings and photographs of ocean-going vessels, the latter possibly taken by young Biggs himself, plus businesslike comments on the various classes of boats.

The end result of this rather mature (for an eleven-year-old) piece of research was a 31-inch model of a liner, which he admitted was "not very easy to build except in large sizes as it is impossible to put in much detail." In determining the size of his model, however, some compromise must have been necessary: "A 4 ft. model liner is about the best size as it is possible to put in a good bit of detail yet the boat is not too big & heavy to carry to the water." Nonetheless, "great attention should be given to the deck fittings." Electricity is recommended over steam for motive power, and "speed should not be aimed for." The resulting model, powered by a tiny electric motor, and now in the possession of Peggy Biggs, is a very creditable piece of youthful craftsmanship. The deck fittings are all there in some detail, and it is indeed "not too big & heavy to carry to the water."

Young Jimmy Biggs probably spent a good deal of his spare time tinkering with things. In his teens, he often spent summers at Wiggie, a farm owned by family friends. One of his duties there was feeding the chickens, but at some point a conflict arose between the timing of this chore and his newfound love of tennis. He cannily resolved the problem by inventing an automatic chicken feeder. The chicken feed was placed in a pan atop the device, which was turned by a spring activated by an old alarm clock. All Jimmy had to do was to load the pan and set the alarm clock, and he could be off playing tennis for the rest of the afternoon, knowing that the feed would be scattered to the biddies at the appointed time.

Jimmy Biggs's stay at Hurstpierpoint encompassed the years of World War I. During that time he took his music lessons, participated in sports and school plays, studied hard (excelling in mathematics and science), and, toward the end of his school days, joined the Officers Training Corps, or Cadets, where he did well in miniature range musketry. He was rated by Captain Pocock as "a keen cadet who left before developing into a leader." When he graduated from Hurstpierpoint at the age of sixteen he had earned a good recommendation from headmaster A. H. Coombes with regard to his behavior and scholarship.

Biggs may have already given up his piano lessons, and certainly he gave no indication of seeking a musical career at the time of his graduation. Instead, he headed directly toward the kind of work a boy who liked tinkering and who excelled in mathematics and science might be expected to pursue. Shortly after leaving Hurstpierpoint, Jimmy Biggs entered into an apprenticeship with an electrical engineering firm in London.

The active musical life of London must have exercised a powerful stimulus on the young man from Sussex, for at the age of eighteen Biggs began studying music again. This time it was not piano, but organ. His teacher was J. Stuart Archer, who was organist of a large Christian Science Church in London (which Biggs may have attended) and was also well known as a recitalist. Archer saw sufficient promise in the apprentice engineer to recommend that he audition for a scholarship at the Royal Academy of Music. This Biggs did in the spring of 1926, shortly after his twentieth birthday. He was award-ed the Thomas Threlfall organ scholarship, but he agonized all summer as to whether it was really to be his, since he felt that he had played the audition piece (the slow movement from Rheinberger's Sonata No. 7) "not particu-larly well."

Entering the Academy in the fall, Biggs studied organ, at Archer's recommendation, with George Dorrington Cunningham, then at the height of his career as a concert organist. He also studied piano with Claude Pollard and Welton Hickin, and harmony with J. A. Sowerbutts, but it was Cunningham—who, in the words of Reginald Whitworth, was beloved "not only for his supremely fine playing but also for his delightful and unassuming per-sonality"—to whom Biggs turned as a role model and who appears to have been a powerful determinant in his choice of a career.

In a memoir written near the end of his life and published posthumously in *Music*, Biggs recalled his influential teacher, who was, "first of all, and by the style of his playing, a concert organist." Cunningham was himself an Academy graduate who had achieved early fame through his weekly recitals on the famed Willis organ in London's Alexandra Palace, where he played reg-ularly until the organ was silenced by World War I. In 1925, when Biggs began studying with him, Cunningham had just been appointed municipal organist to the City of Birmingham, a position he held in addition to that of organist to the University of Birmingham, and was only teaching one day a week at the Academy. In his article, Biggs comments on the backbreaking schedule this necessitated for Cunningham:

> At the crack of dawn every Thursday, he would take the two-hour train trip from Birmingham to London (let's hope the dining car coffee was hot!), arriving early, and would teach right through the day. Quite often he would then give a London recital in the evening, returning late that night to Birmingham.

I was always conscious of the considerable privilege of being one of his pupils. But it was only later, when I, too, came to give lessons, that I realized what devotion and sacrifice of his own work such days must have cost him. Only later does one realize how precious and irreplaceable is the element of time.

Archer's recommendation of young Biggs to Cunningham was fortuitous in every way, for the two had much in common, and Biggs found in his teacher a man with whom he could identify, both musically and intellectually. Reginald Whitworth, writing in *The Organ* for July 1933, makes some observations about Cunningham that could well have applied to Biggs himself later on in his career:

> Mr. Cunningham is not a believer in organ transcriptions, except as relief items used in order to obtain variety. He plays many of his programmes from memory, and has frequently played various organ concertos under our distinguished conductors. As many of his recitals are broadcast, his influence upon organ playing is incalculable. He is continually receiving letters of thanks and appreciation from listeners both at home and abroad. This work must of necessity possess a high educational value. Unspoiled by success, Mr. Cunningham has preserved a delightful modesty, which, with his other great gifts, has won for him many friends and admirers.

And, according to Biggs, "Cunningham was not only a great player, he was also a great teacher." To the end of his life, in both his teaching and his personal practice habits, Biggs adhered to the basics laid down by Cunningham; not dogmatically, for that was not his nature, but rather because these techniques worked and produced a desired result. These concepts are important to the understanding of Biggs's own thought and practice, and the following is his own summary of them:

> His [Cunningham's] own playing projected a wonderful sense of accent, a splendid ongoing rhythm. This rhythm was by no means metronomic; it was plastic and flexible. The secret (though "the secret" is no secret at all) was his sensitivity to note duration and his finger control of the organ key, disciplined by his piano technique.
> He had the gift to teach this to his pupils. He gave his students a method of work—a key—but of course one had to open the door oneself. He insisted on much piano practice. It was in any case obligatory to study the piano with one of the piano professors, as a "major" equal to the organ.

Cunningham practiced what he preached with regard to the piano, as is evident in an incident related by Biggs. When the organ in Birmingham City Hall failed just before one of his scheduled organ recitals, Cunningham coolly switched to the piano, giving from memory an impromptu program that included music by Brahms and Beethoven and was favorably received by the critics.

For the learning of most compositions Cunningham recommended a "divide and conquer" process. For finger sprightliness, one practiced the manual parts first on the piano. On the organ, one started with the pedal part alone. Naturally, in the process all fingerings and footings were to be puzzled out and pencilled in.

Having attained fluency at pretty nearly the right tempo in each of the three parts, one started to put them together—perhaps even in the three easy stages of pedal and left hand, pedal and right hand, and then all three.

Cunningham wished his pupils to avoid becoming mired in slow "organy-like" practice—trying to swallow the animal whole, so to speak. He wanted an ongoing rhythm right away, along with the notes, and though the above three-part breakdown seems a long way around the bush, one actually learned a piece very quickly that way.

A fault had to be worked out until it could be played correctly at least three times consecutively. It was a good idea, Cunningham thought, sometimes to begin one's practice period with the last section, and work section by section to the beginning of a piece. Then one's right-through performance seemed to take on a certain freshness. (This incidentally is a useful idea to try with one's choir.) If to this practice approach one added contrapuntal, harmonic and form analysis, the music seemed to become almost automatically set in the fingers and memory.

Cunningham recommended that certain pieces should be worked on and worked on until thoroughly memorized for the formation of concert programs. Other compositions—"Sunday music" if you like—could be thoroughly studied but left to play from music. Playing from memory does not by itself assure a fine performance, although certainly it can add flare and excitement.

A very succinct summary of some of these precepts is found in a notebook entitled "Organ Notes," dating from the time Biggs began his studies under Cunningham. On the very first page, under the heading "Organ Technique," he wrote, "Always practice pieces in 'ultimate units,' & gradually build up phrases, & then sentences & so on. Then you don't get fed up & wonder why on earth you can't do the thing properly." A page later he noted that "The feel of the time or pulse is more important than anything else. . . . " Further on, one finds additional proof of the importance Biggs (and his teacher) placed on rhythmic flow: "If registration cannot be changed without breaking the rhythm, then don't change it."

In the spring of 1929 Cunningham made his only concert tour of the United States and Canada, winning high critical praise in New York, Philadelphia, Seattle, San Francisco, Los Angeles, Toronto, Ottawa, and Montreal. Biggs recalled that Cunningham found "the Americans wonderful, the country magnificent, and many of the organs terrible." The positive parts of this observation doubtless outweighed the negative in Biggs's mind, and it may well be that it was this that first stirred his interest in pursuing a career outside his homeland.

At the end of Biggs's first year at the Royal Academy, Cunningham rated his punctuality and industry as "excellent," commenting that Biggs had "made a capital start." Welton Hickin, his first piano teacher, found him "an intelligent student and thoughtful." Despite this obvious devotion to his studies, Jimmy Biggs led a social life like that of most other college and conservatory students. He lived at 84 Warwick Gardens, Kensington, near the Academy, Royal Albert Hall, and the Victoria and Albert Museum. He was an avid attendant at concerts of all kinds—symphonic, choral, operatic, student recitals, and "school shows." He was still an enthusiastic tennis player, and he attended all the R. A. M. dances. That he did not lack for company at these functions is obvious from the list of young ladies (with phone numbers) kept at the back of his date books. But his winning of the Hubert Kiver Organ Prize in 1927 shows that his social life did not interfere unduly with his practicing.

It was not long after receiving this honor that Biggs, though still a student, began to be involved in professional musical activities. His first public performances had been in student concerts, but the pieces he played show that he had already attained an impressive level of proficiency. In a student concert given in February 1928 at Duke's Hall, he played Dupré's Prelude and Fugue in G minor, and at a similar concert given on May 31, he performed the Allegro Vivace from Widor's Symphony No. 5. His skill on the piano matched his achievements on the organ, for barely a week later, on April 5, he took part in a joint "Pianoforte and Song" recital in Leighton House, where his piano solos included Schubert's Fantasy in C Major ("The Wanderer"), De Falla's *Ritual Fire Dance,* and Liszt's Rhapsody No. 6.

In the fall of 1928 Biggs was appointed a "sub-professor" at the Academy and was chosen to play two concertos for organ and orchestra under Sir Henry Wood. He also did some broadcasts for the BBC and a recital in Queen's Hall, the latter apparently on fairly short notice, but reviewed in *The Referee* for November 25 as "a remarkably brilliant performance." In 1929, in student concerts at Duke's Hall, he performed the Finale from Vierne's Symphony No. 1 in January and two movements from Reubke's Sonata in C minor in June. In July he again played the Widor Allegro Vivace at the Academy's prize distribution ceremony in Queen's Hall. He also began playing full recitals in London churches in this year; and programs survive from concerts given in the churches of St. Paul, St. Mary-le-Bow, and St. Dunstan-in-the-East. From these we find that, in addition to the virtuoso pieces already mentioned, Biggs had also mastered the rest of Widor's Symphony No. 5, Bach's Fantasia and Fugue in G minor, and Liszt's monumental Fantasia and Fugue on "Ad nos, ad salutarem undam." In between these big works he sandwiched smaller pieces by Wesley, Bach, and Vaughan Williams; transcriptions from Schubert and Haydn symphonies; and transcriptions of piano works such as MacDowell's *A. D. 1620.*

Biggs also held a few church positions. One was at the Third Christian Science Church on Curzon Street, where he auditioned in January 1928—and from which he was fired. Another may have been St. Columba's Church of Scotland on Pont Street in Belgravia, for he is thought to have made his first gramophone recording there (possibly for H. M. V.)—of the Scottish church service. A recital program of February 3, 1929 identifies him as organist of Chiswick Parish Church. In 1929 and 1930 Biggs also served as the piano accompanist of the London Select Choir, which participated in a Delius Festival under Sir Thomas Beecham in the summer of 1930.

During Biggs's conservatory years his name appears in a variety of forms. On some notebooks dating from his first year at the Academy, he wrote it "E. G. Biggs," and in the 1927 Prize List the Threlfall scholar is "Edward G. P. Biggs." On various concert and recital programs it is variously "E. G. Power-Biggs," "Edward Power Biggs," and "Power Biggs"—almost as though he were trying out different styles. But by 1929 his name appeared consistently as "E. Power Biggs," and so it remained for the rest of his life.

The year 1929 began in a flurry of activity as Jimmy Biggs approached the end of his student days. It also saw the beginning of a brief but ardent romance between him and Joan Boulter, an attractive vocal student at the Academy. For the rest of the term she was his regular companion at boat races, R. A. M. dances, operas at the Old Vic, plays at the Embassy Theatre, and "talkies." Occasionally Biggs let his romantic ebullience spill over onto the pages of his date books, as on May 23, when he scrawled "A gorgeous day of brilliant sunshine—Joan darling!" It takes very little imagination to conjure up a picture of two high-spirited young music students strolling hand in hand in the warm spring sunshine of Kensington Gardens, Regents Park, or some similar idyllic spot.

However, in that final term of Biggs's studies at the Royal Academy of Music there were also serious matters concerning the future to be settled. Biggs approached Sir John McEwan, the principal of the school, about the possibility of staying on as a teacher. McEwan had probably heard similar requests before. His reply was both fatherly and sensible: "We hate to lose any of you, but you must go out in the world, go anywhere. Of course, come back later if you like."

But there were other options to be pursued. On January 21 a notation in Biggs's date book reads, "Meet Davies at 1:45 at Finsbury Pk. St." The individual Biggs met at the Finsbury Park tube station was Rhys Davies, a Welsh baritone associated with a small touring group known as the Cambrian Concert Company. Its other members were Jeannette Christine, soprano, and David Owen Jones, "Business and Field Manager," but it lacked a keyboard player. Biggs was probably aware that the group was a second-rate affair that played largely to small-town audiences wherever Jones could scare up a one-night stand. But more important to him was the fact that the group had scheduled a six-month tour of the United States in the fall of 1929, and he signed on as a kind of utility man—organist, pianist, and accompanist.

For the rest of the term Biggs was occupied in studying for his final examinations, but he also found time to play some recitals, carefully hoarding the reviews for future use. He took the examinations in June—in organ, piano, harmony, ear training and accompaniment—earning good marks on all of them. July was spent with his mother at Wiggie, and no doubt Biggs found a bit of time for playing tennis.

In August he was back in London, accompanying the Select Choir, playing more recitals, collecting addresses of American organists, checking out boat fares, equipping himself with a new wardrobe, and, of course, practicing. He also prudently had a publicity flyer printed up, replete with endorsements from G. D. Cunningham and Sir Henry Wood, favorable excerpts from reviews, and a photo of a coolly confident young musician in his best double-breasted suit. Biggs had accepted what was probably the most intriguing of the seemingly limited options open to him. Two months after his graduation from the Academy he made ready to embark on his first transatlantic concert tour.

2 | *The Cambrian Tour*

> After a jolly nice send off from Euston (thanks to the gang!) arrived at Liverpool in good time. Had tea in state in guard's van—there was plenty of room there. No one spoke the whole way up, though I wanted some of the chocolate the person opposite had; & I'm sure she wanted my Punch (Vivian's present). . . .

The "send off" from London's Euston Station occurred on September 20. In addition to F. Vivian Dunn (now Sir Vivian Dunn, conductor of the Light Music Society) and others from Biggs's R. A. M. "gang," Alice Biggs was on hand to see her son off on his adventure. A little poem that she gave him—and that he kept among his personal papers to the end of his days—suggests that she realized that she probably would not be seeing much of her "darling boy" from this time onward.

For the only time in his life, possibly at the instigation of his mother, Biggs essayed to keep a diary. Consisting of loose-leaf pages in a small student's notebook, it chronicles the first four months of his American tour, September through December 1929, and provides us with an opportunity to experience the world of a 23-year-old English organist, just graduated from the Royal Academy of Music, as he sets out—as the storybook tales always begin—to seek his fortune.

Biggs's goal in Liverpool was the ocean liner *Adriatic*, which, to his impatient chagrin, was in no hurry to leave. "A policeman said it was too windy for the Adriatic to come out of dock yet—suppose it might blow the funnels off or ruffle the bosun's hair." Biggs had to spend the night at the North Western Hotel, and the "queer dreams" he reported having were probably due to his excitement. He met Rhys Davies the following morning, and they went to the Gladstone Dock, where the *Adriatic*—"not as big as I expected"—was berthed. On board, Biggs gloated over the fact that he had been given a bigger cabin than Davies, begged a deck chair, and had lunch "opposite a very interesting young girl who looks likely for future reference." Discovering that the ship would not depart until evening, Davies sought to kill time by going to a football match, "but they take up the gangway at 3 o. c. &

we are all prisoners." Nothing daunted, the travelers explored the ship and took tea, and Biggs was "most delighted and pleased" to receive six cables from his London chums, including one from Owen Le P. Franklin, a fellow Cunningham student who had visited America himself a year or so earlier.

The *Adriatic* finally got under way around noon of the next day. It soon passed the Irish coast and sailed into the open sea, which was becoming rough. Biggs preferred deck games to the lounge, where "people sit around and look at each other and make each other feel sick," but he retired early and woke the next morning feeling "rather queer" and not inclined to more than a "very microscopic lunch." The following day it was Davies's turn to get seasick, while Biggs was feeling fit enough to enjoy both the good food and the company of two young ladies from Philadelphia.

A few days later the ship reached the Gulf Stream (which "must surely be quite warm, & nice to jump into") and Biggs "got licked" at shuffleboard. He spent the rest of the day writing letters as the weather turned foul, eventually working up to a howling gale. "There is a movie this evening & community singing afterwards. The movie is very feeble (they all are!) & the other falls flat. But the storm was the best (& quite sufficient) entertainment for the day!"

On the morning of Monday, September 30, the *Adriatic* passed the lightship, and a rum runner was observed. Despite poor visibility, Biggs was on deck as the ship sailed into New York Harbor:

> As we get near the sky scrapers emerge out of the mist. It is a pity it is not a clear day, but the way the sky line looms through the mist is rather fine. . . .
> We move more slowly now, & the sky scrapers come into view. It is really a magnificent sight! We pass the Statue of Liberty & gradually edge into dock. This N. Y. skyline is alone worth crossing the Atlantic to see!

On clearing customs Biggs and Davies went ashore, where they met Jeannette Christine and checked into the Manger Hotel. Afterward the three musicians took a stroll down Broadway:

> The signs are wonderful—the trams are not! The shops vary very much—the roads are in a bad condition—I remember how I have read that it seems as if they are in the middle of rebuilding bits here and there & that they never finish anything for long. Well, it's just like that.
> [Broadway] is not very broad & doesn't seem to have the dignity of say Regent Street, or Piccadilly. We went down to Times Square station & that looks as if it were built in a hurry & never properly finished. Not anywhere near say Bond St. or Piccadilly Circus.
> But it was a poor evening & it was raining; so I daresay it was not a good time to see the place. Probably tomorrow will alter my thoughts a lot!

The following morning, after breakfasting at the Automat, Biggs went to the Aeolian studio to arrange for practice time. He noted in passing that Fifth Avenue was "a bit better" than the previous night's scenery. The Cambrians regrouped to take in a movie and have lunch, after which Biggs headed for the Wanamaker Store, which then had a large concert hall containing one of the city's most notable organs. The store was closing as he arrived, but he left a note for Dr. Alexander Russell, the resident organist. He then telephoned T. Tertius Noble and also left a message for Lynnwood Farnam. Armed with a letter of introduction from Cunningham, Biggs had lost no time in contacting perhaps the three most influential organists in the city.

At day's end Biggs was, understandably, "jolly tired" and still puzzled by the anachronisms of New York. He was appalled to learn that New York policemen had to buy their own uniforms, and he considered the subways poorly built.

> But by gum! you realize London is not so bad after all! There's a certain dignity and beauty about London which New York lacks entirely, & on the other hand, New York has pep, go, zip, or anything you like which is reflected in the buildings everywhere & which London hasn't.

The following day, Biggs practiced at the Aeolian studio, arranged for piano practice at Steinway Hall, and proceeded to Grand Central Station ("Now! here is a station! A terrific hall of marble"). He took a train to Boston, apparently for the sole purpose of visiting the Christian Science Mother Church and meeting its organist, Mr. Adams, who did not particularly impress him. Possibly he was hoping to make a useful contact, but perhaps he was simply fulfilling a promise to his Christian Scientist mother.

On October 4 Biggs finally made contact with Farnam and had lunch with him (including corn on the cob, "priceless stuff"); later in the day he met Noble, who impressed him as "very nice." The next day, after rehearsing with Jeannette Christine, he looked up Dr. Russell, who, as luck would have it, was hosting a party for the Parisian organist Marcel Dupré and his wife. Farnam was also present, and "Mrs. Russell was giving out cocktails (naughty woman!)"—for these were Prohibition days. After a "ripping dinner" the musicians in the party retired to the Church of the Holy Communion, where Farnam and Dupré played some of the latter's latest compositions until the small hours. The occasion was a stroke of pure luck for young Biggs, and he was by no means unappreciative of it: "Now I had a ripping evening, killing, so to speak, several birds with one stone; & Dr. Russell seemed pleased, giving hopes of a Wanamaker show, & I think Farnam is a very nice & decent chap indeed."

On October 6 the Cambrians journeyed to the First Presbyterian Church of nearby Bridgeport, Connecticut, to give their first concert.

> The organ is a three manual by Howard. The wind is awful & full organ is a
> hopeless mess. Has its good points however. Got some practice at last—thank
> goodness! Now this concert shows me that [Owen Le P.] Franklin was quite right!
> It is practically impossible to explain & still more impossible to write, in fact it is
> unbelieveable in many ways!

The next day's concert in The Bronx was no less perplexing: "A funny concert.
It was an appreciative crowd and yet a difficult one—I believe I did not play
anything popular enough for them."

Biggs played the following day on a Hope-Jones organ in "jolly bad
condition" in Hanson Place Baptist Church in Brooklyn. (He was considerably
more impressed with Pennsylvania Station: "It's like a Cathedral! With a Ford
transcontinental plane there.")

On October 9 he cut some player rolls at the Aeolian studio, a new
experience for him:

> It is the same sensation as making a gramophone record, the same precipice
> walking sensation. The first record was not very satisfactory because the pedal was
> too heavy. The second was better but with some bad patches of wrong notes.
> However there it is for the present until next April. Perhaps they can graft different
> parts of the roll together.

Unfortunately, there is no evidence that Biggs's only player rolls were ever
issued.

On October 10 the group took to the road in earnest. Biggs made
admiring note of the beauty of the New Jersey marshes at evening as they made
their way to Burlington, to perform in a church where "the verger took great
pains to show me the stop for the chimes!" Still enjoying the Indian summer,
they proceeded to Frankford, Pennsylvania, to face an audience of "about 60
or 65 in a church holding 1,500" and which didn't clap.

> There were no programs, I played the Widor 5th—Moonlight—Le Cygne—
> Air & Gavotte—Vierne 1st. [The organ was an Estey,] two manuals and for its size
> an excellent affair [but] I wonder when (or—perhaps—if?!) I am going to have a
> *decent big* organ! One worthy of the Reubke and the [Dupré] G minor!

Biggs's education with regard to small-town American audiences and
organs was only beginning, for the nature of the Cambrian Concert Company's booking system precluded the possibility of prestigious locations, good
publicity, or large organs. Bookings were in fact made on a very hit-or-miss
basis by Jones, who traveled a few days ahead of his troupe, drumming up
business wherever he could (generally in small churches and high school
auditoriums) and notifying the musicians by cable or letter of their forthcoming engagements.

Before leaving the Philadelphia area, however, Biggs made one more contact of possible future value. Dupré and other European notables had made debut recitals at the Philadelphia Wanamaker Store, which boasted an even larger organ than the New York store ("You can walk around inside the console just as you might walk about in an ordinary *organ!*") Biggs met Mary Vogt, the incumbent organist, and George Till, the organ builder for whom the care of the mammoth instrument was a full-time job. He also just missed a sold-out performance of the Philadelphia Orchestra at the Academy of Music, much to his chagrin. ("My God! Am I going to hear no music but my own for 7 months!! I must get a radio or something. It's awful!!") Philadelphia seems to have pleased Biggs, though; he thought it might "make a very pleasant home."

The next stop was Chester, Pennsylvania, where "the organ is a Moller & is marked 'Op. 3409.' A 2 decker and just about the three thousand four hundredth & ninth organ too many! But not bad as organs go—so far!" He fared little better at a Presbyterian church in Wilmington, Delaware, where "Owen Jones had written that there was a 'good organ'; & by gum, it's so dashed good it's just about the limit. A wretched little two manual by Hook & Hastings (Op. o probably) . . . and the program has been made out including the E minor, Widor 6th, Vierne, Jarnefelt." Despite all this, the concert went well and was well attended, an extra bonus being the meeting of a "charming Miss Mason" afterward.

The travelers continued southward, playing in Baltimore ("A very nice two manual Moller") and in Washington, where the first three-manual organ of the trip turned out to be another elderly specimen in dubious condition. But Biggs managed to get in a bit of sightseeing in the capital with a shipboard acquaintance—unfortunately accompanied by her mother! From there the Cambrians made their way through Maryland and Virginia, where Biggs took note of historical sites and the difference between the sprawling southern towns and the "just-so" English villages with which he was familiar.

In Richmond, the group "provided an introductory half an hour before a service in the evening—not very interesting." But the informality of Protestant services in the South, where people often applauded points in the sermon ("as if the ministers offered their goods in competition with the movies over the road"), struck Biggs as "curious" but "far more vital than the hushed voices and scrapings of the C[hurch] of E[ngland]."

Norfolk provided Biggs with a "fine 4 manual Hall," but in Newport News he was "frightfully annoyed because the blanked pistons on the organ don't work." En route to Suffolk the musicians stopped to pick some cotton for a souvenir, to the amusement of the field hands; but when they arrived Biggs had to cope with an organ in which "some dashed notes on the pedals stick on." In Washington, North Carolina, despite a build-up from Jones about the "important engagement & rare opportunity at the Women's Club," Biggs was faced with "a perfectly awful piano & a quite decent organ by Hall with the choir out of action & notes striking right & left!" Town and concert were rated "a flop," and Jones's judgment was seriously questioned.

Up to this point the three Cambrians had been giving a concert every night; Friday, October 25, was their "day of glorious freedom," although they had to spend a good deal of it on a bus. Still, the weather remained fine, and Biggs was restored to an optimistic mood. Somewhere in North Carolina between Goldsboro and Raleigh, he was moved to poesy by the "coloring of the cotton fields & the constantly changing silhouette of trees":

> The golden sun swings down into the pines,
> And the sky flames up.
> The cotton fields are bathed in blue and purple.
> The red & yellow trees & shrubs
> Take on the fiery rainbow of the sun,
> And as the globe sinks down the sky
> A pageant comes and passes.

Good weather stayed with the musicians as they continued southward, and Biggs even acquired a mild sunburn. In Raleigh he was taken aback when the newspaper asked them to write their own review: "If this is the accepted procedure over here, the notices won't have much value." A social evening following a good concert in Raleigh revived everyone's spirits, and Biggs's were bolstered even more on the following day after a concert at a women's college in Greensboro: "There were a whole crowd of jolly girls round the organ seat (ahem!). And they seemed to like the organ & piano very much (also, ahem!). It was too bad that they had to be in bed by 10 o. c."

On October 30 the papers were full of bad news from the New York Stock Exchange, but a young and idealistic Biggs took a dim view of the whole capitalist system: "What a silly system it is. One man ploughing a field is doing more than all these wretched people with their buying and selling of the so-called 'right' to take as fat a percentage as they can of other peoples work." Throughout his whole life Biggs was a firm believer in working—usually very hard—for a living, but in later years he did temper his opinion of the stock market sufficiently to invest in it himself.

But whatever may have been happening on Wall Street on that October day, it was business as usual for the hard-working Cambrians, whose concert in High Point, North Carolina "went well." Another good performance followed in Lexington, where the musicians were invited to take part in some enjoyable Hallowe'en festivities. Then they were off to Gaffney High School and "perhaps . . . the biggest flop we've had!" Although the weather suddenly turned rainy, the concerts improved, the one at Converse College being exceptionally good, and with an appreciative audience containing a "charming lot of girls."

The tour was definitely having its ups and downs. After the good concert at Converse, Biggs was disappointed to learn that it had not been reviewed for the papers. His mood was not improved by having to play a full recital to a packed house the next day on an organ that was "the WORLDS WORST. Unless you hold down a note for 30 seconds it doesn't speak at all!" The rain continued as the trio headed into Georgia, where they saw Stone Mountain and gave a good concert in an Athens church with a three-manual Austin organ, although "Miss C. was deplorable." Biggs's opinion of the Cambrian soprano was not too high at the outset, and it diminished as the tour wore on.

By November 12 the Cambrians were in Texas, and Biggs's recollection of the individual concerts was beginning to blur. His comments on the route through Alabama had more to do with places than with concerts, and the apathy of the audiences puzzled him more and more. About the only real enthusiasm encountered was in the colleges.

Toward the end of November the Cambrians doubled back to Florida via "a lot of dud bus rides," one of which stranded them in a place with the memorable name of Rising Fawn en route to Chattanooga. There they performed at the Baptist Church ("with one of these silly 'windy' organs"), and Biggs learned that this was "the place where [Edwin H.] Lemare has been City Organist until they kicked him out a week or two ago." The popular Lemare had settled in the United States some time before and had held several municipal organists' positions. Biggs probably would not have minded such a job himself, and it appears that he made some discreet inquiries about the newly vacant position.

Back in Athens, Georgia, Biggs enjoyed the luxury of a Steinway piano in his hotel room, and the Methodist Church proved to have a good organ. Cold weather had set in in earnest now, but the musicians received a warm welcome in Decatur, where, however, "Miss C. made a mess of a program." Fair concerts to good houses were given in various Mississippi and Tennessee towns, and the month ended in Arkansas, where neither the towns nor the concerts were particularly memorable. In Little Rock Biggs whiled away his boredom talking to the soda fountain girl in the Hotel Marion.

As December opened, the Cambrians moved from Arkansas to Oklahoma—"interesting country to come through but not very musical." In Tulsa, which "dispenses with traffic lights, & the autos look after themselves," Biggs played a four-manual Aeolian organ, and in Sapulpa, "a curious Estey organ, 3 manual, with a sort of typewriter control; you touch a button and it lights up, & touch it again & the light goes out, very easy to handle." Then on to Oklahoma City, where Jones made his appearance, apparently for the first time: "So this is Jones! Davies and I discuss him afterwards."

Jones accompanied the group to Norman, where they played at a college with "an excellent piano & a good 3 manual Hillgreen Lane organ. The show went well (to a smallish but nice crowd) & impressed Jones no end! He's quite a decent chap, but plainly incompetent!" Halfway through the tour was probably not the best time to make this discovery, and the next night's concert in Oklahoma City could hardly have improved Biggs's morale either: "A rotten show to a flop of an audience, just like a crowd of sheep to play to. Jones sings a solo, & Miss C. makes a mess of Hear Ye, Israel. Wretched organ."

On December 16 Jones saw his troupe off on the bus for the long ride to Dallas, where, despite cold and snow, they gave a "jolly good concert . . . to a rather small audience." The next concert was called off because of bad weather, and the days preceding Christmas found them at a church in Fort Worth where they did not feel particularly wanted. The weather improved on Christmas Day, but the Cambrians' concert left something to be desired, and after Christmas their spirits must have hit an all-time low. The 26th found Jeannette Christine in bad financial straits, trying to scare up more concert dates, and on the 29th Biggs wrote in exasperation, "Miss C. is in a real tight corner now, and so are we, damn it! This blanked thing must stop!"

As the year ended, so did the diary. Biggs had a free day on Sunday, December 29, in which he went to the movies, did some letter writing, and organized his belongings. The following day he played a "piano only" concert to a good audience in Vernon, and on the last day of the year the trio left Texas for Frederick, Oklahoma, where they gave "a fair show to a fair crowd who gave about a nickel apiece!"

> Really sorry to leave Texas, I wish I had "done" it as intended; for it has a nice atmosphere & individuality. Had a letter from Jones today, with suggestions of being a bit "mutual" about the losses. Miss C. tries to evade us when we cross-examine her a bit over supper. We went to the movies & saw the "Aviator"—a 11:30 show & came out in 1930! Well! Well!

The year 1929 had come to an end, but the Cambrian Concert Company's tour ground on, and Biggs continued to make occasional notes in his new 1930 date book. By mid-January the Cambrians were in Kansas, and February was spent largely in Illinois, where Biggs found little to comment on beyond a "pretty little organ" in Lawrenceville. March saw the Company's progress through Ohio; by April they were back in Pennsylvania and then worked their way through central New York. Biggs's occasional notations concerning large, new, or simply "good" organs were not just idle scribblings. Next to the most promising ones he marked a large X, presumably for reference when planning future tours.

At last, on May 2, Biggs arrived back in New York City. The Cambrian Concert Company, having given 190 concerts in 24 states for whatever "take" they could get, was disbanded, but Biggs had business of his own to attend to before returning to England. On May 3 Biggs and Davies, perhaps in the hope of extracting some wages from him, spent the afternoon looking for the elusive Jones, but presumably did not find him. Biggs, having been promised a concert by Alexander Russell, spent most of the ensuing week practicing at the Wanamaker's and at Farnam's church. He visited T. Tertius Noble again, and made the acquaintance of George Kemmer of St. Bartholomew's Church.

On Wednesday, May 14, Biggs played what was billed as his "New York debut" at the Wanamaker Auditorium. His ambitious program included Reubke's *Sonata on the 94th Psalm,* some short Bach transcriptions, Liszt's Fantasia and Fugue on "Ad nos, ad salutarem undam," a Haydn transcription, Samuel Wesley's Air and Gavotte, the Allegro Vivace from Widor's Symphony No. 5, Dupré's Prelude and Fugue in G minor, and the Finale from Vierne's Symphony No. 1.

Biggs spent the remainder of the month renewing contacts, job hunting (apparently with little success), attending concerts, and "sorting ends" before his return to England. On May 22 he went again to Boston and thence to Portsmouth, New Hampshire, where on May 25 he played a recital in the North Church. On May 30 he made a final round of his new friends in New York—Kemmer, Noble, and Farnam—and by early June he was back in London. The Cambrian tour had been a near disaster financially, but Biggs had made some important contacts and had seen a rather large chunk of the United States. Despite the somewhat checkered nature of his experiences, there is little doubt that he had liked much of what he had seen.

3 | *Newport*

To whom it may concern.

This is to testify that I have known Mr. J. P. Biggs intimately for a good many years, and that I know him to be a man of excellent character in every way.

G. D. Cunningham.

One of Biggs's first acts upon returning to London in June 1930 was to procure another letter of reference from his former teacher. Cunningham continued to be his supporter and friend but seems to have assumed that Biggs's actual first name was Jimmy!

During July Biggs went to a Royal Academy of Music social and dance, visited friends, attended a performance of Wagner's *Die Walküre,* and took a few final organ lessons. On August 21 he attended a "Prom" concert at Queen's Hall with a dozen or so of his old classmates, who afterward inscribed his program with such sentiments as "Cheerio!" "Good Luck," "Dash it!" and "O. K. by me!" Two days later Biggs again boarded a liner bound for New York, apparently with no firm prospect of a job—and at the height of the depression.

Of the ensuing month we know nothing. Without doubt Biggs was busy cultivating the contacts he had made the previous spring, and he later gave credit to T. Tertius Noble for suggesting that he apply for a church position that was open in Rhode Island. On September 27 he arrived in Newport; on October 19 he was hired as organist and choirmaster of Emmanuel Episcopal Church there; and four days later he gave a well-attended recital on the church's Welte-Mignon organ. He needed little practice for this—the selections were all "war horses" from the previous year's tour—and the press reported that "In every way the concert was delightful and was a happy introduction for this new organist, whose pedal technique is most remarkable, if not quite flawless."

On October 29 Biggs took the Fall River Line steamer to New York. The following day he made arrangements for another Wanamaker Auditorium recital. He also paid visits to Ernest Mitchell, organist of Grace Church, and Bernard LaBerge, who was then the leading manager of concert organists in

Alice Maud Tredgett Biggs with "Jimmy," ca. 1906

Biggs at 14, 1920

A passport photo of Biggs, ca. 1930

Biggs on the beach, Newport, ca. 1931

the United States. A church position was a reliable means of putting bread on an organist's table, but from the start Biggs's plans had a broader scope, and he lost no time in implementing them.

He by no means neglected his musical duties at Emmanuel Church, however. On November 1 his choir gave a "special musical service" consisting of choral works and solos by Bach, Schubert, Handel, Mendelssohn, and Rheinberger, and a month later it presented the first half of Handel's *Messiah*. In January 1931 Biggs inaugurated a series of monthly sacred music concerts, and in March he performed Bach's *St. Matthew Passion* to a packed house, earning a favorable notice from the press:

> Last evening's presentation was a revelation to the huge congregation which completely filled the church.
> Mr. E. Power Biggs, organist, gave a most creditable performance. His playing left no doubt of his ability in the command of the organ, and the other departments, of soloists, chorus, and instrumental direction.

Despite all this ambitious activity, Biggs found time to attend concerts in New York (including those of the New York Philharmonic and the American debut recital of the blind Parisian organ virtuoso André Marchal at Wanamaker's) as well as in Boston. He was always genuinely interested in hearing the music made by his fellow musicians. Unlike many of his colleagues, he could often be found at organ recitals, and he thoroughly enjoyed orchestral and chamber music concerts as well.

While Biggs was not the first English organist to choose the United States as his home—Lemare and Noble immediately come to mind—the question might arise as to why he did so, and at so early a stage in his career. Although he remained an Englishman to the marrow of his bones in countless ways, his background differed from that of the average British organist. Most of them reached the organ bench via the time-honored Anglican choirboy route, but Biggs grew up in a family of nonconformist religious affiliation, attended a secular school, and did not even begin his organ studies until at an age when most of his contemporaries were already holding church positions. Because of this his outlook, doubtless reinforced and encouraged by Cunningham, differed considerably from that of the majority of his peers, who assumed without question that a career as an organist was a career within the church—with perhaps a little teaching and concertizing on the side. Some doubtless were temperamentally and intellectually suited for this life; others were not, but were trapped by their early conditioning into accepting its inevitability. Some, like Cunningham and Lemare, were fortunate enough to secure one of the relatively scarce municipal organists' posts, or an equally rare full-time teaching position. But no organist, on either side of the Atlantic, made his or her living exclusively as a free-lance concert artist.

Historically, of course, the organ has always had its secular side. The great Renaissance, Baroque, and Romantic organs of Europe, even when housed in churches and cathedrals, had a secular as well as a sacred function. Sweelinck entertained the burghers of Amsterdam with his variations on popular songs even though the organ of the Oude Kerk stood silent during the preaching services of the Calvinists on Sundays. Buxtehude, patronized by the wealthy merchants of Lübeck, staged concerts at St. Mary's Church for the business-men who thronged that port city, and DuMage, Dandrieu, and Balbastre entertained with their *Noëls* the Parisians who thronged their churches in the hours before the Christmas *messe de minuit.*

From the second half of the nineteenth century onward, great organs were built in concert halls, town halls, and educational institutions, and the line between the sacred and secular uses of the organ became more sharply defined. Recitals were still given in churches, but the church organist's functions were more and more restricted to playing at services and training the choir. Organ-ists employed by concert halls were expected to play not only the standard literature but also accompaniments, trivial pieces, and transcriptions of orches-tral works. Between the demands of the church on one hand, and a seem-ingly debased public taste on the other, how was an organist to serve pure music?

This dichotomy appears to have troubled the mind of young Biggs as he pursued his seeming destiny as a church organist in the small New England city of Newport. Although he had come to America because he believed it offered wider opportunities for pursuing a concert career, he must at times have questioned the wisdom of his choice. Certainly the times were not propitious. The depression had caused a noticeable decline in patronage of the arts; the Carnegies, Duponts, and their ilk were now much less inclined to donate organs to concert halls and churches or to finance the concerts of those who played them. In 1920 Edwin H. Lemare had enjoyed an enviable standard of living as the highest paid organist in the world; by 1930 he was out of work and out of money, his savings having been wiped out when the stock market crashed. Only the organists of the large urban churches continued to live in any real comfort, and many of them had suffered salary reductions.

One such full-time church musician was T. Tertius Noble, formerly of York Minster in England. For some years he had been securely ensconced as organist and choirmaster of the prestigious St. Thomas's Church in New York, where he presided over a large and active music program. Here was a man, the child of a musical family, who had spent his youth on the organ bench of Bath Abbey and had taken his first church position at the age of fourteen, a man who had come the traditional Anglican route. Although he was almost the same age as Lemare, he had comfortably weathered the economic upheaval that had destroyed the fortune and health of his contemporary and compatriot.

Noble contributed some recollections of his long career to the March 1931 issue of *The Diapason;* the article included a paragraph describing the circumstances surrounding the composition of his well-known seven unaccompanied anthems:

> I well remember composing the first, "Souls of the Righteous." After having played morning, afternoon and evening services on Sunday at [York Minster] I walked home with my wife, and after the evening meal sat in a comfortable chair with my feet on another. Thus I pondered the beautiful words, and very soon ideas poured forth on my manuscript paper. The anthem was written in less than half an hour. . . .

It appears that these words touched a very raw nerve in Biggs. Possibly with a letter to the editor in mind, or perhaps just to get something off his chest, he took pen in hand:

> Did he really believe this—that the "souls of the righteous" are actually "in the hand of God" etc. If so, does he ever read anything of present day thought in investigation? And if he reads it can he disprove it? Certainly not! Then why does he choose to ignore it? Why! because that comfortable study in which he was sitting and that comfortable dinner just inside him are a direct result of his passive acceptance of whatever emanates from the pulpit; or is printed in the prayer book. He must swallow all this literally (though he certainly can't swallow the bible literally—or he'd be a revolutionist!)
>
> Is not the position of Dr. Noble typical of the whole of the organist's profession? I suppose their vacant stares in the "Diapason" are no worse than the pudgy faces one sees in any professional journal. But is the organist allowed any intellectual life? Can he really believe in what he is doing? No! A few virile ministers in exceptionally lucky circumstances can modify and improve their circumstances, but an organist cannot do this!
>
> What can an organist do except get a position in a church? Practically nothing. A mere handful find positions as city organists and as recital organists. Herein lies the great disability of the organ—it is a mere prostitute to the church— bought for so much to attract people to the orthodox teaching.
>
> Will residence organs help? Will there be a number of organists who will become known as artists; and who will achieve the popularity in broad musical circles of a Paderewski? I doubt it. For one thing, a good piano anywhere will suffice for the rendering of the entire piano literature; but a residence organ, unless it is a very unusual one, will not be an adequate medium for 90% of the organ repertoire. "The Swan" by S[aint] S[aëns] would be the most popular piece; and Vierne's Symphonies would be impracticable.

In 1931 Noble was 64 years old and a veteran of 50 years on the organ bench, some of which were, by his own admission, "not altogether easy." But he obviously loved his work and probably did believe what he heard from the pulpit and read in his prayer book. His long years of service to church music had earned him his comfortable fireside. Biggs, on the eve of his 25th birthday, writing in his spartan quarters at 21 Bull Street in Newport, stewed in a confusing cauldron of youthful idealism, artistic frustration, driving ambition, and half-formed plans for his future. The generation gap between these two musicians was too great to be easily bridged. Having vented his feelings on paper, Biggs seems not to have submitted the result for publication, perhaps out of recognition of his own debt to the kindhearted Noble, or because he realized that no real good could come of having it appear in print. Very possibly he felt better for having written it, though—and he saved the manuscript.

Then too, he may have reconsidered after reading further in Noble's article, where the venerable organist of St. Thomas's Church bursts out somewhat unexpectedly with:

> Oh, ye organists who play services daily in the cathedrals and churches of England and elsewhere, get away from the smell of the organ loft! Write other music than hymns and spiritual songs; even write jazz, play jazz, write comic songs. It all helps to broaden one's view of life. There are too many strait-laced organ grinders today.

Now *there* was a sentiment with which Biggs could readily identify.

During the summer of 1931 Biggs taught the organ courses at St. Dunstan's College of Sacred Music, a privately endowed summer school in Providence. He also entered a sand tennis tournament at Newport Beach and was rather soundly beaten by one Jerry Mahoney, who, according to the local sports reporter, used his "Vines-like service and slashing attack" to quell "the trans-Atlantic invader in straight sets."

Toward the end of the summer Biggs gave two concerts with other instrumentalists in Newport and in nearby Middletown. All indications are that the soloists—Edward Murphy, horn, and Karl Zeise, cello—were summer visitors whom Biggs had recruited. Zeise, a member of the Philadelphia Orchestra who later joined the Boston Symphony, was to appear with Biggs on several subsequent occasions.

By the fall of 1931 Biggs had adopted a system of scheduling all his choir rehearsals, lessons, and other church-related activities toward the end of the week, leaving the early part free for concert-going, practicing, and trips to New York, where, among other things, he continued negotiations with manager Bernard LaBerge. Concerts continued to be programed at Emmanuel Church, and Biggs enjoyed an active social life. He was popular with his choir singers, who had established a custom of scrambled-egg parties following rehearsals in which even Biggs, never renowned for culinary expertise, took his turn with the skillet. To his bass soloist, a house painter with the improbable name of

Daniel Boone, he confided his continuing frustration with trying to combine a concert career with that of a small-town church organist.

That Biggs aspired strongly to the concert field there was no doubt whatever. He spent most of his free time working diligently toward this end—gathering names for his mailing list, printing publicity flyers and press releases, saving reviews in a scrapbook. Even while attending concerts by other musicians, the improvement of his own programs was on his mind. During a recital given at Boston's Trinity Church in January 1931, he sketched out some thoughts on recital planning on the back of the program:

1. Short but interesting classic
2. Big Bach work
3. Big work (say Liszt—Reubke)
4. Scherzo piece (Haydn)
5. Tuneful melody
6. Another interesting big work
7. Scherzo (Bee's wedding)
8. Big work (1st Vierne Finale)

Biggs was now under LaBerge's management and was regularly obtaining recital engagements, including the promise of another important New York concert. Newport, for all its congeniality and obvious appreciation of Biggs's work, was simply not the best base of operations for a concert artist. Although Biggs had been pursuing possible job openings in New York, it was in the Boston area that the first promising opening occurred.

Early in 1932 Biggs accepted the position of organist and choirmaster at Christ Church in Cambridge. He played his last service in Newport in early February, but that was preceded by two or three "farewell" recitals and a "special service." Although the newspaper reviewer found some fault with Biggs's pedaling in his first Newport recital, it was reported of the postlude to the "Special Service" (Handel's Concerto No. 2) that "the pedaling, the crisp, almost jolly phrasing, made the organists who remained to hear it happy." Emmanuel Church was loath to give up its energetic young organist, and the *Parish Leaflet* published a warm testimonial to Biggs's work during his relatively short tenure:

It has been difficult for those who have had the privilege of enjoying, week after week, the excellent work of Mr. Biggs, to face the fact that he is leaving us on February 15. . . . We shall miss him greatly, and he may always be sure of a warm welcome from his Newport friends. He has worked hard and conscientiously and leaves us with two well built-up organizations, in the church choir and the church school choir, as well as with the memory of those recitals and special services through which he brought inspiration and joy to many grateful listeners.

4 | *Building a Concert Career*

We are very happy to welcome to his first Sunday services in Christ Church, Mr. E. Power Biggs, our new organist and choirmaster. He comes to us from Emmanuel Church, Newport, where he has had splendid success. . . .

Thus did the Christ Church bulletin for February 21, 1932 welcome Biggs to Cambridge. His new church, a staid wooden colonial period edifice, was located a few blocks from Harvard Square and just across Cambridge Common from Harvard Yard. Many members of the Harvard faculty and student body could be found in its pews on Sundays. Christ Church's organ, an electrified two-manual Hook & Hastings buried in a chamber, was undistinguished and somewhat past its prime, but that did not discourage Biggs from immediately scheduling organ recitals. The Friday following his first service he prefaced the 5 P.M. Lenten service with works by Handel (the same concerto the Newporters had praised), Bach, Mozart, and Reubke, following it up with a full evening recital on March 3.

As at Emmanuel Church, Biggs took his duties seriously, and he soon set about upgrading the church's musical equipment, which, judging from the following plea in the church bulletin for April 3, was rather badly in need of help:

We need a Victrola for the Parish House which can be used in training the Choir. Mr. Briggs [*sic*] would like to play records of some of the great choirs to our Choir. We also need a music stand, and we are still plaintively asking for a piano. In fact, if anyone has anything musical, except a saxophone, which is no longer needed by him, the Church would like to be allowed to consider receiving it as a gift.

Presumably Biggs got his Victrola and piano, and he wasted no time in getting his choristers into shape. By the fall of the same year the Christ Church choir presented a full performance of Handel's *Messiah*.

In the spring of 1932 Biggs gave another Wanamaker recital in New York, as well as programs in Brooklyn and Princeton. He programed some new repertoire for the Wanamaker concert, including a Bach transcription, a Karg-

Elert work, the Saint-Saëns Fantasie in E flat, and a Debussy transcription. An anonymous "admirer" in the audience sent Biggs the following pencilled note anent the Debussy, which must have amused him, for he pasted it into his scrapbook with his press notices: "My dear Mr. Biggs—I had formerly thought that the selection from the Petite Suite was a Ballet. I do not think that a Ballet, and particularly one by Debussy, should be played as a March by Sousa."

Spring also marked the beginning of Biggs's acquaintance with an attractive French pianist, Colette Lionne, an honor graduate of New England Conservatory and a former pupil of Harold Bauer. Suddenly tennis matches and boat races again began to appear in Biggs's social calendar.

On August 31 Biggs played a recital at a joint convention of the National Association of Organists and the Canadian College of Organists in Rochester, New York. Actually it was only half a recital, shared with Ruth Spindler of Garnett, Kansas. But Biggs's portion was well planned to show off what he could do: an arrangement from Bach's Cantata 147 and W. T. Best's transcription of the Air and Variations from Haydn's Symphony in D Major, sandwiched between two tried-and-true showpieces, the Reubke *Sonata on the 94th Psalm* and the Finale from Vierne's Symphony No. 6. A successful concert at a convention was certain to lead to further engagements, and one may be sure that Biggs was well aware of that. Reviewer Stewart Sabin of the *Rochester Democrat and Chronicle* bestowed some rather faint praise on Miss Spindler, but showed no restraint in commending Biggs's technique, musicianship, and handling of the instrument. In closing he stated that "Mr. Biggs gave one of the outstanding recitals, short as was his program, which this writer remembers in Rochester."

Biggs's out-of-town concerts were balanced by some nearer to home. The Boston/Cambridge area provided an ideal arena for his talents and a far wider audience than did Newport. But as in Newport, Biggs enjoyed playing concerts with other musicians and exploring a repertoire largely ignored by other organists. In June he gave an organ and cello program at Christ Church with Karl Zeise, and in the fall he was engaged by the Church of the Covenant in Boston's Copley Square to do a series of five concerts. The last of these, given early in 1933, included Biggs's first known performance (from manuscript) of Howard Hanson's Concerto for Organ and Orchestra. In the spring Biggs, Colette Lionne, and Walter MacDonald collaborated in a program for organ, piano, and horn that was given at both Christ Church and the Church of the Covenant. By this time Biggs's interest in the French pianist had progressed beyond the merely professional. In May he and Colette became engaged, and in June they were married.

Thanks to LaBerge, Biggs was now securing concert engagements in cities such as Philadelphia, Cincinnati, and Chicago, as well as at St. Thomas's

Leo Sowerby, Colette Lionne, and Biggs, ca. 1940

Church in New York (proving that he was still on good terms with Noble). In the fall of 1933 he also played to full houses at his former church in Newport and on the recently completed Aeolian-Skinner organ in Harvard's Memorial Church.

It did not take Biggs long to become involved in the musical life of Cambridge. In addition to his work at Christ Church, in the fall of 1932 he was engaged to teach music history and organ at the Longy School, a position he held for a number of years. Conscious of his lack of a university degree, he also enrolled as a special student at Harvard. It is said that it was G. Donald Harrison, the organ builder, who told Biggs that if he aspired to a college teaching position he would find an academic degree useful, but that if a concert career was his chief goal, he was wasting his time. The point was well taken. Biggs knew quite well what he wanted to do, and his student phase was very brief.

Those who knew Biggs only in later years regarded him chiefly as a performer, but in these young years he was very much a teacher as well, and he remained so until the pressure of recording and concert work eventually drove all other professional activities from his life. As with everything he essayed professionally, his teaching system was well thought out and planned in considerable detail. He gave equal attention to students of both lesser and greater gifts, but the latter received all the support and encouragement of which Biggs was capable. A letter in the Longy files, written in 1935, shows his interest in one such student, Wesley Day, who "has done so well that I think both he and his parents will be considering the possibilities of a career in music when he graduates from high school next summer." Biggs had already aided young Day in getting a scholarship and in securing a paying position as a church organist, but he was now concerned about where this gifted student would find the money to finance his higher education.

Wesley Day did indeed continue his musical education, becoming in time a highly respected church musician in Philadelphia. In his early studies with Biggs at Longy, Day's lessons always began with piano work—scales and repertoire—before going to the organ, where he was introduced to a wide range of Bach's works as well as those of pre-Bach and Romantic masters. Biggs—like his own mentor, Cunningham—was clearly a teacher who encouraged independence in his pupils. Day recalls:

> He seldom assigned fingerings but insisted I work them out according to good principles and be able to explain them satisfactorily. Similarly with registration; we discussed basic sounds and their characteristics, singly and in combination, but then I had to register for myself according to those outlines. He was quick to approve at any good ideas I had, and gentle in correcting my many blunders.

Day obviously made rapid progress, for in the final year of his study with Biggs he was assigned the entire Symphony No. 5 by Widor, a formidable task for a high school senior. Further, Day was not to bring the work to Biggs until he had completely learned it. Then he would have to defend his choices of tempo, registration, and interpretation, "but one reason he would not accept— that I did something because *he* did it that way!" This was creative and concerned pedagogy, and the student rose to the challenge: "He so encouraged me to find my own personality, scary tho' it was at the time." Biggs obviously worked his best students hard, but there was also a lighter side to the student– teacher relationship. Often after lessons, Biggs and this self-described "typical scrawny teenager" would, in Day's words, "go across the street to a drugstore and have an ice cream soda, for which I was never allowed to pay!"

As the years went by, the pressure of Biggs's growing concert and recording schedule made it necessary for him to restrict his teaching at Longy to a small group of advanced students, until in 1951 he had to give it up entirely. From that time on he held no permanent teaching position but often taught summer courses at such widely separated places as the Organ Institute in Methuen, Massachusetts, and Pomona College in California. A class outline from one of these summer sessions, dating from the 1960s, shows that he had not departed significantly from the procedures recalled by Day and other early students, or, for that matter, from the precepts laid down by G. D. Cunningham. Piano practice was still regarded as essential, including scales and arpeggios. So were good practice habits, consciousness of agogic accent, slow practice for accuracy (but fast practice for rhythm), breaking down long works into sections, and working on new pieces one line at a time for fingering and pedaling.

Perhaps Biggs did not teach long enough, or in a prestigious enough institution, to have left behind a galaxy of notable former students. But Wesley Day, among others, went on to make a mark on the musical world; and Mary Crowley, a scholarship student whom Biggs always regarded as one of his best, had a short but distinguished career as a recitalist. Others became good church organists and teachers; and two, David Gifford and Walter Hawkes, became organ builders. Many of Biggs's former Longy students kept in touch with him after leaving the school, and during World War II Biggs regularly corresponded with those in the armed services. All seem to have held Biggs in affection as a teacher and friend who gave them a solid background in their craft and was ever willing to help in the furtherance of their careers.

Biggs's professional activities were on the increase in the early 1930s, but he still found time to attend many recitals and concerts. One notable performance was given by the legendary Gunther Ramin of St. Thomas's Church in Leipzig, and Biggs had the opportunity of meeting him. But not all visiting artists were of Ramin's stature. English organist Edward d'Evry, "sometime examiner" for the Royal College of Organists, played so badly that during the concert Biggs scribbled on his program, "How can he have the nerve to *fail* anyone?" As the performance wore on, he apologized to his companion (probably Colette), "I'm terribly sorry I dragged you to this! But we had better stick it out for sake of appearances." All hope of escape having obviously fled, there was the final wry observation that "There will, of course, be EN-CORES!"

In January 1934 Biggs played three consecutive Wednesday evening recitals at the church of St. Mary the Virgin in New York, then a center of avant-garde organ playing under the aegis of Ernest White. A recital in February at Harvard's Memorial Church included an unpublished chorale prelude on Tallis's Canon by T. Tertius Noble, Reubke's *Sonata on the 94th Psalm*, and Handel's Organ Concerto No. 10. Biggs repeated the last two pieces in a program given in the same place in November—perhaps by request? In April he gave two concerts in Canada, one of them for a chapter of the Canadian College of Organists, and both earned good reviews. At this point in his life Biggs was still playing recitals from memory, and that may explain the frequent repetition of some of the larger and more-demanding works. In later years, while still conceding that memorization was good discipline and had "audience value," he also observed that it "does seem to lead to restricted repertoire" and was "often a waste of time." And time was always of great importance to Biggs.

In Biggs's boy choir at Christ Church there was a lean, dark-haired and bespectacled little nine-year-old with a considerable fondness for music. His ambition, at that point in his life, was to become a jazz trumpeter. His mother had given him a diary for Christmas, and his entry for January 2, 1935 read: "I went to choir practice. Mr. Bigs wasn't there." The choirboy's name was Charles Fisk; Biggs was to encounter him again, much later, and would play with delight and approval the organs built by his former young chorister.

The reason "Mr. Bigs" was not at choir practice on that wintry day was that he had just been fired. According to Biggs, the firing was "one of the best things that ever happened to me. Realized you can't train choir, practice boys choir, etc. etc. & find enough time to develop as a player." The loss of the church position did of course mean some loss of income, but he still had his students at the Longy School, and LaBerge had recently booked him on his first transcontinental tour of the United States to take place in January and February 1935. The long absence it necessitated may have been part of the church's reason for dispensing with his services, but it may also have had something to do with Biggs's refusal to comply with the rector's request that he add the reading of the early service to his duties—with no additional wages.

The tour was truly transcontinental but a far cry from the Cambrian affair of five years previous. The concert locations were, for the most part, prestigious ones; remuneration and accommodations were suitable, and in most cases adequate practice time was provided between concerts. In addition, every concert was reviewed, and the reviews were without exception favorable. The first recital was in the First Methodist Church of Fort Worth, Texas, where critic Clyde Whitlock waxed enthusiastic over Biggs's pedaling, phrasing, and musicianship, calling the program "a masterly performance which may go down among the concert traditions of the city." In an interview in the *Fort Worth Star Telegram,* Biggs defended the use of the organ as a concert instrument: "The organ contains a vast range of orchestral color; a vast literature for concert use. It is certainly good for something besides an accompaniment to hymns or the Wedding March from Lohengrin."

Following a concert in San Antonio, Biggs headed for California. On February 3, he gave a program at the University of Redlands in the afternoon and another in the evening at the First Presbyterian Church of Pasadena. Of the latter, Roland Diggle, in a review for *The Diapason,* wrote, "Mr. Biggs played with sureness and understanding and his tempo control and phrasing were those of a master organist who had the certainty of his convictions." On February 9 the Canadian College of Organists sponsored a recital at Centenary College in Hamilton, Ontario, where, according to the local newspaper, "the organ came into its own under the hands of Power Biggs." Biggs's next stop was the Church of St. Andrew and St. Paul in Montreal, and there he earned a review that indicated that he was getting a point across: "Mr. Biggs's playing is scholarly and straightforward, eschewing all extraneous effects of decoration and color. He contents himself generally with exposing the simple beauty of the music." Biggs underlined these words, something he did only rarely.

From this point onward hardly a year was to go by without at least one tour to distant points. Shortly after his return from Montreal, on February 26, 1935, Biggs gave a recital in Harvard's Memorial Church. He performed, for the first time in its entirety, a work he was later to popularize—Leo Sowerby's Symphony in G. He had played the "Fast and Sinister" movement in Montreal, but the reviewer there dismissed it as being "made up of uncomfortable discords and not much else." The impression made by the complete Symphony on the perhaps more sophisticated *Boston Evening Transcript* reviewer was more favorable. He praised the work's "melodic wealth," "rhythmic vitality," and "deftness of harmonic and contrapuntal technique" and was equally impressed by the performance:

> The brusque rhythms, the smashing dissonances, the abrupt harmonic transitions of the symphony came with clear incision from Mr. Briggs [*sic*]. His own musical temper seems well matched to that of Sowerby's Symphony. His trick of stressing brief phrases, his willingness to depict sharply differentiated moods with extremes of dynamics, his crowding of note on note, phrase on phrase, all brought into startlingly sharp relief Sowerby's music.

While Biggs seems not to have minded at all his dismissal from Christ Church, his absence from Sunday-morning commitments proved only temporary. In May 1935 he became organist and choir director of the Harvard Congregational Church of Brookline (now Brookline United Parish). This church differed from the two he had previously been associated with in that it was not Episcopalian. As part of a "non-conformist" denomination, its services and theology were perhaps more palatable to Biggs than those of the Anglican tradition, which he never seemed to have cared for. In addition, his duties there were lighter, consisting of one Sunday service and the rehearsal of an adult choir, plus weddings, funerals, and whatever concerts he wished to prepare. A further attraction was unquestionably the church's 1932 Aeolian-Skinner organ, a sizable four-manual instrument showing the influences of both Ernest Skinner and G. Donald Harrison, which admirably met Biggs's needs for a suitable practice, teaching, and recital instrument. Presumably the church also had a more lenient attitude toward the occasional protracted absences that his concert commitments entailed (and for which Biggs always provided a well-qualified substitute).

The fall of 1935 found Biggs on another brief tour of Canada, playing in Toronto, Guelph, Kingston, and Ottawa, again with excellent reviews. The

Guelph Daily Mercury for November 26 gave his concert a full banner headline, praised the brilliance of Biggs's execution, and stated that "Seldom does one hear a program containing so many big works and rare indeed is the man who can carry us through them without a dull moment. But such is he—this young man Mr. Biggs." In January 1936 Biggs concertized in Washington, D.C.; in February he was off to the West Coast again, for a somewhat more extended tour, which included Claremont, Stockton, and Redlands colleges; Grace Cathedral in San Francisco, and several churches in Oregon—all again to favorable notices. On his return he gave a recital in his new church in Brookline under the auspices of the Massachusetts (now Boston) chapter of the American Guild of Organists; and in April, sponsored by the local Bach-Brahms Society, Biggs gave his first recital in Methuen, Massachusetts, on an organ with which he was subsequently to have a long association, as teacher, performer, and recording artist.

In 1863 a large organ was imported for the old Music Hall in Boston from the German firm of E. F. Walcker & Cie.; its walnut casework, made in New York, was a triumph of Victorian extravagance. To make way for an enlarged symphony orchestra, the "Great Organ" was removed to storage in 1883. It remained there until 1897, when it was purchased by Edward F. Searles of Methuen, a wealthy widower with artistic and musical interests who was heir (via his late wife) to the Mark Hopkins railroad fortune. Searles owned, among other extensive properties, his own organ factory, where he proceeded to have the "Great Organ" reconditioned and rebuilt. Because no public place in Methuen was large enough to house the organ, Searles hired the noted architect Henry Vaughan to design a classically oriented brick auditorium next to the organ factory, and there, in 1909, the "Great Organ" was installed. For a while hall and organ were used for both public and private concerts, but after Searles's death in 1920 the place became a deteriorating white elephant in the hands of his heirs. In 1931 the organ builder Ernest M. Skinner, soon to separate from the Aeolian-Skinner Company in Boston, purchased the property, largely to have use of the organ factory. But the hall and the organ were to some extent resuscitated as well and made available to local musical interests.

In 1936 Biggs became one of the first organists to give a concert in the reopened hall, and included on his program was the premiere of a set of variations by Skinner's longtime friend Wheeler Beckett. That summer Biggs, recognizing the unique possibilities of the situation, organized a study course during July in which he gave classes, private lessons, and recitals, with Skinner giving lectures on the design and construction of the organ.

Biggs played recitals weekly during July, performing a wide range of literature from Bach and Handel to Dupré, Elgar, Karg-Elert, and Vierne. Also included was a work by his old acquaintance Lynnwood Farnam, who had

Biggs in Methuen Memorial Music Hall, 1936

died suddenly in the fall of 1930. Biggs saw to it that the organ and the summer school received proper publicity. He was doubtless responsible for a feature article in the *Christian Science Monitor* for July 15, complete with pictures of both the organ and Biggs. At the end of the summer, Biggs gave two more recitals; reviews in the *Lawrence Daily Eagle* hailed Biggs as "A player of wide talents, both in musical taste and technical finish."

In the fall Biggs gave concerts on the large City Hall organ in Portland, Maine, and at All Saints' Church in Worcester, Massachusetts. In an interview in the *Worcester Daily Telegram* for November 12, Biggs expressed his usual optimism for the future of the organ. It was not, he emphasized, "on the way out," and he predicted "a bright future for the organ. The competition of electrical-instruments . . . has had its effect in bringing out new interests, new tonal colors in the modern organ." In a lighter vein, he allowed that he did not even object to a little jazz on the organ ("very jolly"), but it ought not be overdone: "too much jazz on the organ is pathetic."

Events were indeed pointing to a brighter future for the organ in America. In Cleveland, the builder Walter Holtkamp and the organist Melville Smith were experimenting with the revival of certain time-honored tonal and visual aspects of the organ. In the summer of 1936, even as Biggs was participating in the renaissance of the "Great Organ" in Methuen, G. Donald Harrison, technical director of the Aeolian-Skinner Company, was touring the historic organ lofts of Europe with Carl Weinrich, a young organ teacher from Westminster Choir College. In less than a year's time Biggs himself would assume a key role with regard to these forward-looking developments in the American organ world.

5 | The Germanic Museum Organ

The so-called classic organ designed by G. Donald Harrison, in the Germanic Museum of Harvard University, was really just a lucky accident.

So said Biggs in 1973 in a taped interview with John Fesperman of the Smithsonian Institution. Things were not, of course, quite that simple. One must take into account the fact that Biggs always had an uncanny knack for making the best possible use of "lucky accidents."

G. Donald Harrison, an English builder formerly with Henry Willis of London, came to the Skinner Organ Company of Boston in 1927 at the age of 38. The Skinner firm had achieved prominence in a period when organ tonal design was strongly influenced by the concept of orchestral imitation, but organists' tastes were beginning the long swing away from a transcription-oriented literature and back to the more traditional idiomatic organ repertoire. Harrison represented this more eclectic approach as it was practiced in England, and at the time he came to Boston his tonal concepts were not so much classical as they were anti-orchestral.

Because of financial difficulties, control of the Skinner firm had slipped from its founder's hands, although Ernest Skinner remained with it in a position of responsibility. With regard to tonal matters, however, Harrison rather quickly rose to a position at least equal to Skinner's; and while a number of organs built in the early 1930s (including that in Biggs's Brookline church) showed the influence of both men, ideological conflict between them was inevitable. The rift between the two widened in 1932, when more and more customers insisted on having Harrison draw up the tonal scheme and supervise the finishing of their instruments. And Skinner strongly disapproved of the direction in which Harrison's tonal work was heading.

Arthur Hudson Marks was a wealthy amateur who then held the controlling financial interest in the company; he had consolidated it with the organ division of the Aeolian Company in 1931 under the name of the Aeolian-

Skinner Company. In May 1932 Marks wrote a strongly worded letter to Skinner mandating that henceforth Skinner and Harrison were each to have full control of the organs they themselves sold but were not to work together on the same organ. Marks, a shrewd and tough-minded businessman, was beginning to favor the more avant-garde Harrison. Biggs, although on the periphery of the conflict, also cast his lot with Harrison, whose tonal ideals were closer to his own than were Skinner's. The following year the dictatorial Marks, irritated by mounting friction with Skinner, demoted him and appointed Harrison technical director. In 1935 Skinner, realizing his cause was lost, left the firm for good.

This reshuffling of the hierarchy of the firm left Harrison solely in charge of its tonal policies. Bit by bit, he experimented with what would come to be known as his "American classic" concepts, incorporating his adaptations of French reeds and German mixtures and mutations into certain influential organs built in the years immediately following Skinner's departure, notably those of the Church of the Advent in Boston, Groton School, St. Mary the Virgin in New York, Westminster Choir College, and All Saints' Church in Worcester.

Although born and reared in England, Harrison had never studied the organs on the Continent. He set out to do just that in the summer of 1936, in the company of Carl Weinrich, who, like Biggs, was concerned about broadening the organ repertoire. According to Biggs,

> [Harrison] had come back with a number of ideas he wanted to put into practice. In those years, business was rather slack at the Aeolian-Skinner Company, and Harrison proposed to use some of the free time to plan and build a small organ to be used as a demonstration model, and this was to be put up in a small room at the factory.

The organ, Aeolian-Skinner's Opus 951, was begun in December 1936. The plans were labeled "Baroque organ—Experimental," and the completed instrument was, as Biggs indicated, intended as a studio organ for the firm's Dorchester factory. A lot of the parts making up the organ were odds and ends found around the premises, the console being a legacy from the old Aeolian operation. Most of the pipes were new, however, and were made largely to standard Harrison scales and construction, although a few stops were made to new experimental specifications, notably, some of the flutes. The Pedal 16' Bourdon was a "stock" set, and the Pedal Posaune 16'/Trompete 8' unit was a reject from the Westminster Choir College Chapel organ of 1934. There seems never to have been any consideration of casework for the instrument.

In his few years of residence in Cambridge, Biggs had become thoroughly familiar with Harvard Yard and its surrounding buildings, including a little stucco-and-masonry museum on the corner of Kirkland and Divinity streets that would have looked more at home in Heidelberg than in Cambridge. Although presently known as the Busch-Reisinger Museum of Germanic Culture, it was referred to in those pre-World War II days simply as the Germanic Museum. It was donated to Harvard by a midwestern brewer and houses a tasteful collection of antique and modern art works by German masters. Immediately inside the main entry is a barrel-vaulted exhibition hall with a gallery at one end and a replica of the Golden Gate of Freiberg Cathedral at the other—and superb acoustical properties. Biggs was not the first to recognize the room's potential for musical performance. He himself noted that William King Covell and Edward Gammons, two recent Harvard graduates who were also avid organ enthusiasts, had already observed that it would make an ideal location for an organ.

Biggs's first reaction, on hearing of Harrison's experimental organ, was that it should be in a more accessible location than the Dorchester organ factory. Ever one to follow up his ideas with action, Biggs "took the rather large liberty of suggesting the idea to Dr. Charles Kuhn, Curator of the Museum. He was very sympathetic, but of course remarked that there was no money available." Biggs also approached officials of the nearby Fogg Museum, with the same result.

> So it was really just the most fortunate coincidence of several factors that I was able to suggest through Donald Harrison and Bill Zeuch, who was Vice-President of Aeolian-Skinner, why not put that organ in the Germanic Museum, at any rate, say for a year, on loan. See how it sounds; it would certainly sound much better than in a small room at the factory.

Kuhn was agreeable to Biggs's idea, even though it required the removal of an ancient boat from the gallery of the Great Hall.

One wonders if Biggs or Harrison ever paused to notice the quotation from Goethe on the front of the tower, high above the Museum's doors: "Es ist der Geist der sich den Koerper baut" (the spirit makes an embodiment for itself). Surely if anything in the Museum merited the distinction of being the embodiment of a spirit or an idea, it was the organ that, piece by piece, entered those doors during the spring of 1937.

The organ was a curious hybrid. It possessed Aeolian-Skinner's standard "pitman" windchests and electro-pneumatic action. Most of its pipes were of standard scales, metal composition, and construction, voiced by contemporary techniques with close nicking and small-to-medium toe-holes. The wind system was Aeolian-Skinner's normal aggregation of small, spring-loaded reservoirs, and the two-manual console, with its tilting stop-tablets arranged on slanted jambs, was originally intended for a small stock model Aeolian residence organ. Yet the stoplist combines north and south German features from the seventeenth and eighteenth centuries (including the then almost unheard-of Krummhorn), and the wind pressure was, for those days, uncommonly low—2 1/2 inches in the manuals, 3 inches in the Pedal. There was no enclosed division, no tremulant. The nomenclature was German, even to the *Hauptwerke* and *Positiv* manual designations. Although innocent of casework, the organ was located not in the usual hole-in-the-wall chamber but high in the gallery, speaking directly out against the reflecting masonry walls down to the hall below. Seen in the light of previous and subsequent history, it was transitional in every sense of the word—a creation with a curious personality all its own, linked to both past and future. Biggs liked it.

Despite the threat of delay due to increased activity at the Aeolian-Skinner factory in February, construction of the organ was in its final stages by March. Everyone agreed that it ought to have a name, but there was no consensus on what that ought to be. Harrison suggested "Baroque Organ," but Biggs took exception on the grounds that the adjective, "while signifying excellence to the organ student, suggested merely frills and gewgaws to the public." Other suggestions were "Classical Organ," "Bach Organ," and "Organ built in the Classical Manner." "Classic" was the adjective that ultimately came to be associated with it; probably it was Biggs's preference. The "Baroque" designation was left to fall on a similar but smaller instrument that Harrison built in 1939 for Carl Weinrich's studio at Westminster Choir College—the similarity extending even to the recycled Aeolian console. Although this particular instrument began life burdened with the grandiose title of "Praetorius Organ," it was later referred to by students simply as "The Baroque."

Articles on the new Germanic Museum organ, complete with interviews of Biggs and Harrison, appeared on March 27, 1937 in both the *Christian Science Monitor* and the *Boston Evening Transcript,* the former with pictures of Biggs, Harrison, and the organ pipes. Ample references were made to the "back to Bach" aspect and the dawning realization that the orchestrally imitative organ was a dead end as far as classical literature was concerned. Yet the use of electro-pneumatic action and modern voicing techniques was defended, at least by Harrison. At that time such a compromise was in fact quite justifiable. The cover of this particular Pandora's box had only been cracked open; very little was yet known about the manner in which all the components of the historic instruments interacted musically, nor was the true sophistication of their design and construction recognized. Some of the earliest European attempts to reproduce a historic instrument were done more in the spirit of archaeology than of musicianship, and the results were singularly unappealing. In retrospect, Harrison's unabashed hybrid had more artistic integrity and certainly had more appeal. In a very real way it broke the first ground for the enlightened reproductions that ultimately appeared in the 1970s and 1980s.

The Germanic Museum instrument had three very important factors in its favor: good placement, good acoustical environment, and a good stoplist. The first two gave warmth and immediacy, and the third, with its broad spectrum of pitches, gave color and clarity. Emerson Richards, writing in *The American Organist,* characterized the Positiv, with its varied flutes and mutations, "a color organ in which hues of so vivid a character are possible as to almost shock those accustomed to the smoother and more sophisticated colors produced by the average modern organ." Richards also observed that the instrument did not rely on dynamic extremes for its effectiveness:

> The softest stop is the Spitzfloete and yet it is not, in reality, very much softer than the Principal. All the stops are within the same power range and the actual variety of timbre in the various voices is limited to flutes and Diapasons. Yet in combination there seems to be almost endless tonal variety, due, apparently, to the mixing ability of every voice. . . . [One can draw] apparently impossible combinations without disastrous results.

Richards derided those who would call such an organ cold and colorless because it did not contain some of the familiar orchestral sounds: "It is all color—unimagined color, brilliant, vivid hues in endless variety. And if we have robbed Peter we have paid Paul because there are new tone-colors equally as beautiful as those supplanted. . . ."

Two identical opening recitals were given by Biggs on April 13 and 18, 1937, consisting of music by Bach, Handel, and d'Aquin. Alexander Williams, in the *Boston Herald* for April 19 stated confidently that "Another round in the battle for a just and perfect performance of Bach has been conclusively won." Decrying cinema organs and the orchestral transcriptions of Bach's organ works then enjoying considerable popularity, he praised the "brilliant skill" and "perfect taste" of Biggs's performance. "The effect . . . of listening to that organ played with such knowledge and ability was electrifying. The harpsichord requires some mental adjustment before its qualities can be appreciated; but the immense superiority of this organ is under no such handicap."

The *Christian Science Monitor* was likewise complimentary, its reviewer moved by the "spirit of simplicity and unity" in the Bach and Handel performances. "The beautiful tone of the instrument, lighter in texture, sweeter and more mellow than that of the average instrument built according to modern specifications, was yet capable of grandeur." At this time it was still believed in most quarters that a good acoustic was a dead acoustic, and the same writer was somewhat bothered by the reverberation of the hall; he also found Biggs's playing of Bach's Fantasy and Fugue in G minor "somewhat rushed and breathless."

One of the most discerning reviews was written by Moses Smith of the *Boston Evening Transcript,* who was evidently a habitué of Biggs recitals—he compared the Museum performances with performances of the same works heard on other organs:

> It was apparent as soon as he had begun the Allegro of the Vivaldi Concerto that the greater clarity of parts resulting from the structure and materials of the new organ was no mere boast on the part of the designer, G. Donald Harrison. The polyphonic development was far clearer than it is on the typical contemporary instrument. . . . The voices were more sharply contrasted.

Smith took exception to only one thing: the solo combination used by Biggs in the Adagio of the Vivaldi Concerto. From Smith's description it was apparently a "gapped" combination of an 8' flute and one of the 2 ⅔" stops, in which the mutation stop was a bit too strong to blend completely with the fundamental. One wonders if this criticism was what prompted Biggs to use flutes in the same passage in his subsequent recording of the work.

T. Scott Burhman, editor of *The American Organist,* measured the newspaper coverage of the organ and Biggs's concerts at a total of 155 column inches ("undoubtedly . . . a world record of newspaper attention to any such event in the organ world"). It was capped by an editorial by Alexander Williams in the *Boston Herald* for April 26, entitled "The New Classical Organ: a Victory for Bach." Williams was fully aware that the Harrison instrument was not a copy or a reproduction of an actual "Bach organ" but rather "an original instrument, modelled on the best examples of the 18th century and suitable for playing the great music of Bach's period and earlier." Edward B. Gammons concurred with this assessment in the May issue of *The Diapason,* calling the organ "the most satisfying musical medium for the interpretation of classical music that the writer ever hoped to hear." Emerson Richards observed in *The American Organist* that even with "its obvious limitations and necessary shortcomings . . . it displays a vitality and resourcefulness that are amazing." A significant observation of Richards's was that "The musicians came to hear the music, not the organ," for, after all,

> The organ is only the instrument. The music's the thing. And through this instrument we have revealed to us a music so new, so arresting, and so alive that we cannot believe it is the same old stodgy, uninteresting and decadent set of notes that have been running through the fingers of our organists since the middle of the last century.

During the summer of 1937 Biggs held another teaching session at

Celebrating the tenth anniversary of Biggs's naturalization, 1947

Methuen Music Hall, similar in content to the previous year's and including four Sunday afternoon recitals. Biggs's expense account for this venture—with outlays of $145.00 and receipts of $173.65—indicates that it was not a particularly profitable activity, although it doubtless resulted in some publicity and contacts that, as Biggs knew, would very likely bear future dividends.

Up to this point in his career Biggs was frequently referred to in the press and in his own publicity releases as an "English" or "Anglo-American" musician. In September 1937 he formally became an American citizen, an event whose anniversary he celebrated regularly for several subsequent years.

In the fall Biggs announced a series of twelve recitals comprising the complete works of Bach to be played on the Germanic Museum organ between November 1 and April 11. He was not the first American organist to undertake this ambitious project; that distinction belongs to Lynnwood Farnam, who accomplished it in 1928. But Farnam had to make the best of the orchestrally conceived Skinner organ in the Church of the Holy Communion as his medium. Biggs had the advantage of a far more congenial instrument for the purpose. In the November 1937 issue of *The American Organist* he described his project:

> I have spent much time on plans for the recitals and I have experimented a great deal with different ways of arranging the material. I believe the arrangement finally adopted has a certain logic, while keeping plenty of variety. This plan presents the chorale preludes that Bach arranged according to his own group-ings—the Orgelbuechlein, the Eighteen Great, the Clavieruebung—while the pre-ludes and fugues follow a rough chronological order. The close attention of the audience to the stiffest sort of program has been remarked by everyone; I believe it is going to continue.
>
> In between the two halves of the Bach concerts . . . I am to go on tour. I'm very anxious that these Bach recitals shall not label me a "specialist." I revel in all organ literature and play Sowerby, Vierne, Widor, Karg-Elert, etc. with as much gusto as J. S. B.

Biggs's mention of Vierne and Widor had special significance: both of these French Romantic masters, along with Clarence Eddy, one of America's finest exponents of "orchestral" playing, had died earlier in the year. Indeed, the year 1937 might well be called been a turning point in twentieth-century organ history.

The Bach series was a success. It drew standing-room paying audiences and earned more good reviews for Biggs as well as more fame for Harrison's instrument. The *Boston Globe* critic stated that "With the conclusion of this exhaustive series, Mr. Biggs indisputably places himself among those making the most magnificent contributions to the Boston musical season. . . . " The *Boston Evening Transcript* reviewer praised Biggs's articulation, expressed a bit of concern over an occasional "tendency to hurry," but felt that "in the larger works requiring passion and grandeur . . . Mr. Biggs really made his zeal for Bach most manifest."

In March 1938 Emerson Richards commented on the record attendance at the Bach series, wryly observing,

> I did not say that organists came to the recitals but the music-lovers did. Speedily followed by the music critics. Since the result was both unexpected and unprecedented and threatened to devaluate Mr. Biggs' standing in the eyes of the organists, this brilliant young recitalist did everything possible to cut down the size of his audience. He fed them the Trio Sonatas and the more austere of the Great Contrapuntalist's works. But the musicians still packed the galleries, remained for the last note and applauded.

By December, the editor of *The American Organist,* still keeping count of Biggs's newspaper footage, had totted up a record 370 column inches.

Biggs performed regularly on the new organ, but he also welcomed visiting recitalists. Ernest White and Edward Gammons gave early programs at the Germanic Museum; and in October of 1937 Marcel Dupré, whom Biggs first met almost by accident while on the Cambrian tour, gave a recital that included an improvisation. Unfortunately Dupré does not mention any of the events of his seventh American tour in his autobiography, but Biggs himself recalled that he seemed not to care much for the organ. Other Europeans who played the Harrison instrument during its first few years of existence included Fritz Heitmann, a noted German Bach player, and Susi Hock (now Lady Jeans), a prominent early music advocate.

In January 1938 Biggs made a transcontinental tour, completing the Bach series upon his return. In April his church choir combined with William Zeuch's choir from First Church in Boston for a performance of Bach's *St. Matthew Passion*. In the summer Biggs and Colette took a vacation trip abroad—Biggs's first ocean crossing since he came to the United States in 1930. Before the trip, Biggs had contacted various English friends, including his first teacher, J. Stuart Archer. He sent Archer some of the publicity on the new organ and his Bach series, to which Archer responded in a letter of July 14:

> I was very interested in reading about your Bach recitals—what a prodigious undertaking—and the Bach specifications on which you played. Harrison has done splendid work in reviving interest in the so-called "baroque" instrument. There is no doubt that for Bach playing that is the sort of thing you want. Since the middle of the last century the tone of the diapasons began to thicken. Willis never yielded to this—but Walker began to use absurdly large scales—and Hope-Jones introduced leathered lips. Many people liked the tone—they called it the "Cathedral roll"—but, unfortunately—this Cathedral roll refused to mix with upper work—and stood away like oil from water.
>
> I saw Harrison when he was over last year. He hasn't changed much. I am wondering about you—you look thinner—at any rate in the face. . . . I have been looking at your programme and press notices again today—and feel I should like to have heard you play Bach on that organ. You must tell me how you registered. I wish we could have an instrument like that over here. Willis could tackle the job—& then we could get you to come over & give the series over again.

Biggs renewed many British acquaintances on his trip but apparently played no recitals. He and Colette visited relatives in England and France and did such "tourist things" as climbing the towers of Notre Dame in Paris, and in general it was a true vacation.

Nineteen thirty-eight was proving an eventful year, and before it was over Biggs had made his first commercial American phonograph recordings, using the new organ: a five-record album entitled *A Bach Organ Recital* and a single disc containing a movement from a Handel Concerto and one of d'Aquin's

Noëls. The recordings were issued by Technichord, a small Brookline firm run by H. Vose Greenough, a recent Harvard graduate who had previously made some amateur recordings of some of Biggs's concerts. The old Technichord 78s, collector's items today, created something of a stir when they were first issued, and they got good reviews. In the February 1939 issue of *The American Organist,* editor T. Scott Buhrman observed:

> It is only in the past few years that records of organ playing such as this have been available; what a prize to have them now. He who finds his audience does not like Bach, will do well to buy these Bach albums and learn why. Here we have Bach as Bach should be, and we can each of us for himself readily compare and find out what he lacks to make Bach as vital and living as on these records. Is this album enjoyable as music or is it merely instructive? The answer depends on one's taste; I think there are few albums of any kind that make a stronger musical appeal or provide more enjoyable music for educated listeners.

G. Donald Harrison apparently concurred with Buhrman's evaluation and promptly put the records to a very practical use. Writing to W. King Covell in April of 1939, he observed that

> [The records] were quite a help to me on my trip South. I was able to play them to many prospects and gave them some idea of how an organ sounded built to classical lines. It convinced many of them that such an organ need not be all top, which is the usual criticism.

Although the five two-sided 78 rpm discs in the Bach album contained only four complete works—the Concerto in A Minor, the Trio Sonata in E flat, the chorale prelude on "Wachet auf," and the Prelude and Fugue in E flat—there was much variety within these narrow bounds, and virtually every facet of the organ's resources was shown off to advantage. Small wonder that Harrison found it useful as a demonstration record.

The Germanic Museum organ was, in its way, just as vital to Harrison's professional development as it was to Biggs's. It had provided Harrison with a laboratory in which to test his newly formed concepts of classical tonal design as well as some beneficial publicity. In an article in the *Germanic Museum Bulletin* for March 1938, he described some of these concepts and especially stressed the importance of clarity—a property already noted by several reviewers—in the interpretation of polyphonic music. Recalling the organs heard on his European tour two years previous, Harrison observed that "clarity and transparency of tone are the most striking characteristics of the organs of the seventeenth and eighteenth centuries" and added that "an attempt has been made to recapture these desirable qualities in the Germanic Museum instrument." Harrison's experimentation did not end with the installation of the instrument; despite Richards's opinion that the 8' Principal was "a beauty," Harrison rescaled this stop and the 4' Principal two notes smaller early in 1938.

From its installation in the Germanic Museum until its sale in 1958 to Boston University, Harrison's "classic" organ was inextricably entwined with Biggs's recital, radio, and recording career. It remained the property of the builder for some time, however. In 1940, the Aeolian-Skinner firm, needing money, tried to sell it. The asking price was $8,000, and a group of people in the Harvard community, led by Taylor Starck, attempted to raise the sum from alumni contributions, in order to donate the organ to the university. Perhaps because of this effort, and perhaps also because of the hardships occasioned by World War II, the organ remained undisturbed for another seven years. In the fall of 1947 the organ fund committee abandoned its task, having raised only $1,323.30. The university still declined to purchase the organ (of which they had had the free use for a decade), but by this time it had become so well known through Biggs's broadcasts that it seemed unthinkable to remove it. It became obvious to Biggs that if he wanted to continue to use it he would have to purchase it himself, and so he did.

In 1973, 36 years after the organ was built, and two years after its destruction by an arsonist while in the auditorium of the Boston University School of Fine Arts, Biggs could still speak appreciatively of the 1937 organ— with only the mildest of criticisms and perhaps a faint tinge of affection:

> All in all, the organ was quite playable; it sounded extraordinarily well— bright tone, outgoing, very persuasive. Of course the bland voicing did not give the organ any articulation, and the electric action would have precluded any control of chiff, had there been any chiff. As a whole, the ensemble sounded very well when the hall was empty. When the hall had people in it, and the acoustics were cut down, one tended to hear the mutations as separate lines. But at the time, these limitations were not so apparent; one rejoiced in the forward-sounding tone, unhampered by enclosure. It took a little while for the lessons, both positive and negative, taught by the instrument, to be learned. Still, all in all, the effect in the museum was new and striking.
>
> It lived its life, 1937 to 1971, in a period in which it was possible for its useful influence to be greatest. . . . I am enormously grateful to G. Donald Harrison, to Dr. Charles Kuhn, to James Fassett, and to others, for all the wonderful opportunity that the instrument represented.

6 | *Champion of New Music*

> Then two things happened. It became possible to put in the
> organ at the G[ermanic] M[useum]. And Leo S[owerby] wrote a
> concerto for me. K[oussevitzky], who was interested in new
> ideas, programmed it. Perfectly awful organ. . . .

In his autobiographical notes of 1971, Biggs thus linked his interests in both
old and new music. In 1938 he not only completed his Bach series at the
Germanic Museum but also gave the premiere performance, with the Boston
Symphony Orchestra under Serge Koussevitzky, of Leo Sowerby's Organ
Concerto in C. It was not the first such performance for Biggs; in 1933 he
had premiered Howard Hanson's Concerto for Organ and Orchestra. His interest in the music of Sowerby was also not new, for he had done much to popularize that composer's ambitious and controversial Symphony in G for
organ solo.

In the last magazine article he ever wrote (*Music*, March 1978), Biggs
related the genesis of the Sowerby Concerto:

> When I came to the United States, I brought from Sir Henry Wood a promise
> that if I could turn up a large-scale concerto for organ and orchestra by an
> American composer, preferably a new work, Sir Henry would program it at the
> Queens Hall "Proms." Quite brashly, I wrote to Leo Sowerby, the Chicago
> composer—then at the height of his fame—asking if he would write such a piece.
> He replied that he would think about it, but made no commitment. However,
> within a month or two a postcard arrived saying that the first of the three
> movements had been sketched out.
>
> Just at that time, fate took a hand. The Boston Symphony Orchestra was
> playing in Chicago, and at a luncheon Dr. Koussevitzky happened to be sitting
> next to Leo Sowerby. "And what are you writing now," inquired Koussevitzky.
> Sowerby described his piece. "Fine," said the conductor. "I will play it, but I must
> have the *first* performance. And *you* will be the soloist."

When the time for the performance approached, however, Sowerby recommended that Biggs be the soloist, and Koussevitzky engaged him on the
strength of Sowerby's word. But the hoped-for Queens Hall debut never
occurred. It was not until after World War II that Biggs performed the

Sowerby Concerto in England—and then not under Wood at Queens, but under Malcolm Sargent at Royal Albert Hall.

The premiere performance of the Sowerby Concerto in C was given by the Boston Symphony Orchestra on April 22, 1938. Biggs had planned to perform the work from memory, but as it turned out the console was placed so close to the viola section that he could not adequately hear the rest of the orchestra, so for safety's sake he had to use the score. The "perfectly awful" organ was the large 1901 George S. Hutchings instrument in Symphony Hall. One of the first significant organs with electro-pneumatic action to be built in America, it had never had a really major overhaul, still had its original Skinner-type "bat wing" console, and was rapidly approaching senility. Biggs described its tone as "woolly." Considering that Sowerby conceived most of his organ music for the elderly Austin organ he played in St. James's Church, the Concerto was probably not totally unsuited to the resources of the Symphony Hall organ. And, as reviewer William Zeuch observed in *The Diapason,* "The bravura passages flashed brilliantly despite the archaic instrument. . . ."

Sowerby was present, there was a full house, and the critics were pleased. Alexander Williams of the *Boston Herald* found the new composition "a brilliant and effective work . . . which neither scorns virtuosity nor exploits it for its own sake." He admired the middle movement, but expressed concern that the work required "closer attention than the average Symphony Hall patron is willing to expend." Moses Smith of the *Boston Evening Transcript* found portions of the work "difficult to grasp," also favored the more melodious middle movement, and observed that the organ occasionally "waged an unequal battle with the orchestra." The seemingly more sophisticated *Boston Daily Globe* reviewer, however, saw Sowerby essentially as subsequent generations have classified him—"a moderate among present-day American composers"—and found his new composition "vigorous and healthy, harmonically up-to-date yet neither cacophonous or confused." These sentiments were echoed by William Zeuch in *The Diapason,* who also mentioned a detail that may explain the popularity of the middle movement: it opened with an exposition for organ solo, "played by Mr. Biggs on the 8-ft. Gedeckt, with tremulant, on the Swell." The player was not forgotten in the reviewers' preoccupation with the new music. Described as a "consummate artist," Biggs was praised for having "surmounted the difficulties of the score with ease and taste." The Sowerby work became an important part of his concerted repertoire, and he later performed it with other major orchestras, including those in Chicago and Cincinnati. Unfortunately, he was never able to record it.

Biggs continued to encourage the composition of new works and introduce them to concert audiences. Five years later he was responsible for the

Biggs at his Cambridge home, 1940s

writing of Walter Piston's Prelude and Allegro for organ and strings, which received its first public performance with the Boston Symphony Orchestra under Koussevitzky on October 29, 1943. The actual first performance, however, had occurred two months earlier on a radio broadcast from the Germanic Museum, played by Biggs and a group of Boston Symphony string players conducted by Arthur Fiedler. The Piston work, which is dedicated to Biggs, became one of his favorites, and was the first contemporary concerted piece he recorded. It was recorded in Symphony Hall and issued as a 78 rpm RCA Victor disc in March 1947, the only record ever made by Biggs in collaboration with Koussevitzky. Another Piston work was the Partita for violin, viola, and organ, commissioned by Elizabeth Sprague Coolidge and inspired by some of her favorite passages from Carl Sandburg's *The People, Yes.* It was premiered by Biggs at the Coolidge Auditorium of the Library of Congress in Washington, in October 1944.

In an article in the June 1945 issue of *Church Music Review,* Biggs listed some of the more notable new works that had received their initial performances in his concerts and radio broadcasts. Besides the Piston and Sowerby works, they included Howard Hanson's Concerto for organ, string orchestra, and harp, Roy Harris's Chorale for organ and brass, Quincy Porter's *Fantasy on a Pastoral Theme* for organ and strings, and two additional Sowerby works, *Classic Concerto* for organ and string orchestra, and *Poem* for viola and organ. Daniel Pinkham's Sonata No. 1 for organ and strings might also have been included, as it was premiered on a radio broadcast early in 1944. All these works are by American composers, but Biggs also gave the first American performances of European compositions such as Marcel Dupré's *Heroic Poem* for organ and brass and Francis Poulenc's durable and popular Concerto for organ, strings, and timpani.

Biggs's CBS radio program, begun in 1942, provided even more opportunities for the performance of new solo and concerted music than did the concert hall. However, the size of the budget and the length of the programs precluded large symphonic works while encouraging performance of more-accessible short works involving small ensembles or solo instruments. By 1947, the fifth year of the broadcasts, Biggs's repertoire of new music had grown impressively. In addition to works by the composers mentioned above, Biggs had aired pieces by Gardner Read, Ned Rorem, Alec Templeton, Emil Kornsand, Cecil Effinger, Ellis Kohs, Robert Noehren, Rayner Brown, and Seth Bingham, among others. Bingham in particular took up the challenge of Harrison's Germanic Museum organ and produced *Baroques,* a suite of five pieces for solo organ in quasi-antique style. Dedicated to Biggs and published in 1944, it gained considerable popularity with performers during the heyday of the "American classic" organ.

While Biggs was not alone in encouraging the writing of new solo organ music, his active interest in ensemble music was almost unique among his peers. In a 1945 *Musical America* article, he pointed out that conductors such as Serge Koussevitzky and Eugene Goossens recognized that "the combination of organ and orchestra has an immediate and direct appeal to the public" and that, besides "attracting listeners beyond the circle of organ fans," the organist himself benefited musically from the association, particularly in the areas of articulation and phrasing.

> Certainly every orchestra throughout the country, where there is an organ in the hall, owes it to its public to present first-hand [the literature for organ and orchestra], and the pick of this deserves to be played by organists with far greater frequency than is sometimes the case.

Conductors were supportive of Biggs's cause and interested in the literature. In a letter dated May 4, 1944, Pierre Monteux commented on works by Piston and Sowerby (probably the Prelude and Allegro of the former and the *Classic Concerto* of the latter):

> I must say that I was more interested in the Sowerby, which, for me is more personal, more original than the Piston, although this one was very good, if a little conventional [in its] treatment of the organ. . . . Sowerby is most interesting, because it [does] not suggest anything religious, it is really a concert work that I would be delighted to present in San Francisco if we had a real organ in the opera house. . . .

Alas for both Monteux and Biggs, it was not until 1983 that a real organ appeared in a San Francisco concert hall.

Monteux's high regard for Sowerby's music was obviously shared by Biggs, for despite the fact that a large portion of his prolific output was written for church use, Sowerby was also capable of producing secular works totally free of the taint of "churchiness." In some unpublished notes jotted down shortly after Sowerby's death in 1968, Biggs recorded his impressions of the man:

> Leo Sowerby was obviously devoted to the church, to composing music for the church, and to his many pupils. His time was carefully organized. One might say that he gave too much time to teaching, but that was his way. Certainly there are countless pupils greatly indebted to him.
>
> Meeting LS, you would not suspect him to be the highly imaginative and original genius that he was.
>
> His musical idiom, as we all know, was essentially "romantic modern." His concepts of the organ (as an instrument) were based on the large Austin in St. James' Episcopal Church in Chicago. Brevity of composition was never his style.
>
> As a person, LS gave the appearance of being reserved, though this changed to greater assurance in later years. He had a wry and engaging sense of humor. It is perhaps a pity that throughout the long years of his best orchestral writing he made no effort to promote the works with conductors or orchestras. (However, Koussevitzky did perform some of LS's symphonies and piano concertos.) Nor did LS choose to be involved in musical politics generally. Some substantial support from managers or press, influential in the whole field of music, could have

obtained for LS far greater currency of his works during his most creative years.

Of course, LS has always had countless performances and admirers in church circles, but that is not the field in which I knew him.

Biggs's former student, Wesley Day, is the source of an anecdote relating to Sowerby's lack of brevity. Following Biggs's premiere performance of Sowerby's Suite for organ and brass at an American Guild of Organists' convention in Houston in 1952, Biggs remarked to Sowerby that the Suite was a very fine composition, but rather long. Whereupon Sowerby is said to have replied, "I know, I know, but everything I write seems to get longer and longer!"

Biggs remained a lifelong friend of Sowerby's and a staunch promoter of his secular compositions. With Louis Speyer he premiered Sowerby's *Ballade* for English horn and organ on his radio program; William Primrose was Biggs's collaborator when *Poem* for viola and organ was broadcast on Easter Sunday 1942 from the Hammond Castle in Gloucester, Massachusetts (then the home of the moneyed and eccentric inventor, John Hays Hammond). In 1952 Biggs played the West Coast premiere of Sowerby's *Concert Piece* with the Pomona College Orchestra, and in 1958 he gave the first performance of his *Festival Musick*.

Biggs summed up his indebtedness to Sowerby in his contribution to "A Symposium of Tribute," a memorial to the composer published in the October 1968 issue of *Music:* "How can a mere player repay a composer for such gifts? Leo Sowerby was a great artist, a great man, and a wonderful friend." There was no false modesty in Biggs's opening statement. He stood in awe of very few things, but the art of musical composition was one. Having made a few ineffectual attempts at composition in his student days, he early concluded that he had no gift for it, and, with the exception of a short "Spoof Bach Suite" (written for one of the lighter moments of the 1950 national American Guild of Organists convention), he made no further attempts.

Biggs first became acquainted with the organ music of Charles Ives when the composer was in his declining years, although the work Biggs was to popularize belonged to Ives's youth. Biggs recalled that "the composer obligingly dug out the music from a pile in a barn . . . in Connecticut. The score had remained undisturbed for almost half a century." The music was, of course, the Variations on "America," written when Ives was but sixteen years old. Although the idiomatic concept of the work owes a lot to sundry popular variations on "God Save the Queen," by composers such as Rinck and Lemmens, it also contains much that is pure Ives, with definite intimations of things to come. When one realizes that it had its first performance (by young Ives himself) in 1891, the atonal interludes and other idiosyncrasies appear even more remarkable for their daring.

Charles and Harmony Ives, in their correspondence with Biggs, shared recollections of early performances of the variations. The pedal part in the last movement was, according to Ives, "almost as much fun as playing baseball," and he likened the fast manual changes at the end of that same variation to the give-and-take of the Battle of Bunker Hill. In a letter written shortly before Biggs's first radio performance of the Variations in July 1948, Harmony Ives added some further background:

> Mr. Ives father would occasionally play with him but always insisted that the 4th variation be omitted because it was, in his opinion, a kind of polonaise which had no place in our country and also because it was in a sad minor key. The Brass Band joining in and the loud pedal variations were considered more appropriate.
>
> Sometimes when [the tune of] America would appear to their ears some of the listeners would join in even if occasionally it made the boys go marching down the aisles. Usually, as he remembers, many of the boys had more fun watching the feet play the pedal variations than in listening to the music.

Biggs's association with the Ives Variations by no means ended with that first radio broadcast. Although Biggs admitted that the piece "seemed like a joke at first," it ended up becoming "almost a classic" and remained a popular item in his recital repertoire. He played it only once in Canada, however. On that occasion one of the critics, like Queen Victoria, was "not amused," condemning the piece as a tasteless parody on the British national anthem. Biggs took the hint and never played it north of the border again. But he recorded the work twice, in 1959 and 1969, and continued to program it in recitals. It was his performance of the Ives Variations at the opening of New York's Lincoln Center in 1962 that inspired William Schuman to make his well-known orchestral transcription of the piece.

In 1949 Biggs edited the Ives Variations for Mercury Music, along with a short hymn-prelude on "Adeste Fidelis." The latter has some of the characteristics of certain other Ives works, such as the short song on the hymn tune "Serenity." According to Ives, the high, soft chords at the beginning and end of "Adeste Fidelis" "should be like distant sounds from a Sabbath horizon."

Biggs maintained cordial relations with all the composers whose works he performed, and he was always anxious that his performance meet the composer's expectations. With a writer such as Sowerby, who was himself an organist and thoroughly familiar with the organ idiom, it was merely a matter of the two agreeing on tempi and dynamics. Other composers had to be encouraged to familiarize themselves with the organ. When Roy Harris took the trouble to try his work on a nearby organ, he found the complex harmonic structure of the full organ sound perplexing. This led to revisions, concerning which he wrote to Biggs in August 1943:

> After trying a large organ out here, I decided that the more advanced harmonies do not have the luster that they should have on an organ, and I have, for that reason, tried to use a more basic kind of harmony so that the overtones which are so rich on the organ will not get too mixed up in the upper partials. . . . As a matter of fact this medium is quite difficult to write for because of the harmonic implications which you must accept with the medium, if you want to write something which has body and mood.

The resulting work was Chorale for brass and organ, which Biggs subsequently performed on a radio broadcast, and it was not the last piece Harris would write for the organ.

Biggs first performed Poulenc's Concerto with the Boston Symphony under Charles Munch on November 14, 1949 (at a benefit concert for Dr. Albert Schweitzer's African hospital). In preparation for a planned recording of the work, he corresponded with the composer during the summer of 1949 concerning its interpretation. Poulenc was delighted with the idea ("Quelle joie pour moi d'apprendre que vous avez l'intention d'enregistrer mon Concerto pour Orgue et orchestre . . ."), especially if the conductor was to be Charles Munch, whom Poulenc felt would provide the necessary pungency and lyricism ("le mordant et le lyricisme necessaire"). While Biggs did in fact record Poulenc's work that year, for some reason it was not with Munch and the Boston Symphony, but with Richard Burgin and a smaller group dubbed the "Columbia Symphony Orchestra." The solo timpanist, violist, and cellist were all members of the Boston Symphony Orchestra, however.

In response to Biggs's request, Poulenc wrote twice giving his suggestions for performance. The second letter went into considerable detail, but the first gave a nice overview of Poulenc's concept:

> Forget Haendel—play very much in the French style, pompous, gay, and pungent (pompous in the introduction)—the two andantes shouldn't drag, strictly in time, no rubato—the solo cadenza should be very allegro and sprightly—Land squarely on the big chords (G minor) with an extreme violence (timpani dry and firm)—the final Allegro should be very rhythmic (very fast) and sprightly, in contrast to the serene and poetic conclusion—but why do I tell you all this—I am sure that it will be marvelous. [Translation by Eileen Hunt.]

In his 1945 *Church Music Review* article, Biggs had made a point of noting that the new concerted works were in the mainstream of a distinguished musical tradition that encompassed Handel's organ concertos, Mozart's "Epistle" Sonatas, and the Romantic concertos of Rheinberger:

> These compositions represent an enrichment and rejuvenation of the repertory that may have far-reaching effects. Composer and public are experiencing a renaissance of interest in the organ. Instead of being an instrument removed—the Pope in isolation—the organ may be once again restored as a medium of expression for all creative spirits and a joy to all people as it once was in the days of Bach and Handel.

Sowerby remained one of Biggs's favorite writers, but other contemporary composers whose works Biggs played in broadcasts and concerts in this period included Richard Purvis, Parks Grant, Ronald Arnatt, H. Leroy Baumgartner, Myron Roberts, Aaron Copland, Philip James, Mario Castelnuovo-Tedesco, Everett Titcomb, Searle Wright, Herbert Fromm, Gershon Ephron, Normand Lockwood, and Paul Hindemith. Some of them were fellow organists, but among the others were established composers who had written little for organ until encouraged to do so by Biggs.

Biggs did not wait for the composers to come to him. More often he went to them with requests for new works, and just as often they delivered. Sometimes it was necessary for Biggs to come to the aid of a composer struggling with the peculiarities of an unfamiliar instrument, as when he suggested registrations for Copland's *Preamble*. Occasionally a well-meaning composer unfamiliar with the organ idiom would unintentionally throw Biggs a curve, as Castelnuovo-Tedesco did in 1953, when he wrote an overly pianistic fugue that was nearly impossible to perform on the organ. Writing to the composer, Biggs tactfully opened with, "I wonder if I dare venture a few comments on the OPUS! The suggestions are the result of some hard practicing, in an effort to prepare the Toccata for broadcast next fall, and for the next season's programs." He then plunged into the heart of the problem:

> The Toccata itself is fine, and the Aria also. But the problem in the Fugue is to make it sound well on the organ. Two aspects make this rather hard—the very frequent crossing of parts, and the very high writing at times. It sounds very well on the piano, and theoretically it ought to go well on the organ. But actually it's very hard to find registrations on two manuals that balance, and it's particularly difficult to make the upper register of the organ sound well if played at all forte.
>
> I wonder if you have any ideas and suggestions? I've been experimenting in putting certain passages down an octave, but I don't believe any one section will do the trick. Is it possible do you think to bring the Fugue writing generally more to the middle of the keyboard, and to make it playable on one manual? I know this is a tall order, and that players are supposed to perform music just as composers write it,—yet it would be almost impossible to take the piece on tour in this form, and I do hope you have the magic wand handy.

Castelnuovo-Tedesco took the criticisms graciously. Part of the trouble, it turned out, lay in the fact that the composer had based his fugue on Biggs's name! While he did not think it possible to make it all playable on one manual, he nonetheless made a number of revisions, and Biggs did perform the work.

Composers respected Biggs's opinions and often solicited his advice. When Normand Lockwood invited suggestions on improving the balance in a work for organ and brass, performed in 1952, Biggs offered the following insights:

> I think your comments on the way the work sounded result from the characteristics of organ tone. Actually an organ doesn't really create a lot of sound, and is easily covered by other instruments. This is just as true with much larger instruments than the Germanic Museum instrument. Antiphonal contrast of the instrumental ensemble and organ is always effective, in the Handelian manner, but as soon as the brasses all combine with the organ they tend to drown it out, except for full organ percussive-like chords.
>
> I've noticed this to be true in other works where one, two or three contrapuntal lines on the organ tend not to hold their own against the orchestral fabric. On the piano they would sound through impact.

In this case, however, Biggs advised against making any changes in the score. Since it was the nature of the instruments involved that produced the imbalance that was bothering Lockwood, Biggs felt the work would still be effective left as it was.

An impressive array of new compositions were first heard on Biggs's weekly radio programs from 1942 to 1958. New works also found frequent place in his touring programs, and from time to time he performed large concerted works with symphony orchestras, but it was the radio programs that provided the major showcase for the shorter works. The composers, especially the less known and the younger ones, responded with genuine gratitude to this exposure of their music—and occasionally with amusement, as when Castelnuovo-Tedesco was surprised to hear a little scrap of a composition he had written for a Christmas card used as a fanfare to open Biggs's program one Sunday morning.

When the radio programs ended, so too did Biggs's need for a more extensive repertoire. His efforts went increasingly into recitals, where a limited number of pieces would suffice for a lengthy tour, and recordings, where old music was simply more salable than new. Several modern favorites, including Poulenc's Concerto in G minor, Copland's Organ Symphony, Piston's Prelude and Allegro, Barber's *Toccata Festiva* and Sowerby's Organ Symphony in G major, were in fact recorded by Biggs at various times, and there is every indication that he would have liked to expand the list. But while his interest in new music was undiminished and he never turned down the opportunity to premiere large new compositions, the series of recordings on historic instruments that Biggs commenced in the 1950s led to a recording and performing repertoire that consisted largely of earlier music. There is little question, however, that the increased output of solo and concerted organ music by American composers during the 1940s and 1950s was in no small measure due to Biggs's encouragement and to his willingness to program new works.

7 | *Red Seal Recording Artist*

I had heard of Mr. Biggs, but was not at the time acquainted with his playing. When he approached me in an in-
terval of a recording session with the Boston Symphony with an
invitation to hear the baroque organ [in the Germanic
Museum], I was candidly more interested in the instrument than
I was in Mr. Biggs. I readily accepted his invitation, after which I
was more interested in Mr. Biggs than the instrument. We made
arrangements then and there to record with him and the
Germanic Museum organ, and shortly afterward I put before
the artist certain long-range projects which I am happy to see
are being moved forward.

Charles O'Connell was director of Victor Red Seal Records from 1930 to 1944
and later chronicled his experiences in *The Other Side of the Record,* published
in 1949. In it appears the above description of the circumstances that led to
Biggs's being engaged, in 1939, as an exclusive artist with a major recording
company. O'Connell could on occasion be acidly critical of the foibles of many
of the performing artists he worked with, but his relationship with Biggs was
always cordial. He lauded Biggs as "a scholar, a virtuoso, and an artist of the
first rank. . . . One can believe that Bach himself was such an organist." His
one criticism was not of Biggs the organist but of Biggs the driver ("a nerve-
wrecker"). Biggs, who had managed to overturn his first car in a ditch while
still in Newport, had had a decade to acquire the legendary skills of the typical
Boston driver by the time O'Connell met him. While he was never involved in
an accident more serious than the typical Bostonian "fender bender," his
image as a driver was probably not enhanced by his penchant, even at the
height of his career, for driving superannuated autos until they almost literally
fell apart.

Most of the 26 recordings made by Biggs for Victor—all 78s—were done
at the Germanic Museum. A few, mostly of works demanding a larger instrument of more Romantic resources (as well as one involving the Harvard choir),
were recorded across the street on the 1934 Aeolian-Skinner organ in Harvard's Memorial Church. Still others, which combined organ and orchestra,
were recorded on the old Hutchings organ in Boston's Symphony Hall.

In recollections taped in 1973, Biggs described the making of his first Victor recordings at the Germanic Museum, early in the fall of 1939:

> After recording the Boston Symphony one day, Victor brought over their machines. These were the old wind-ups; they had heavy weights which had to be cranked up, and which in their downward fall, turned the cutting table. Needles cut into a heavy platter of soft wax. You had one go at playing a piece, and just possibly a second or third. But that was that; you had to choose. And you heard no playback, for to play the wax would have been to ruin it for later pressing.

As soon as his contract with Victor was signed, Biggs produced the first of his long series of "Five Year Plans" for future recording projects. This one was divided into three sections: repertoire, suggestions for order of recording, and suggestions for album series and publicity. The repertoire section was chronological and ranged from pre-Bach to contemporary. A lot of concerted music was included for a wide variety of instrumental combinations, and below Sowerby's Concerto for Organ and Orchestra Biggs wrote: "A SUPERB WORK, WHICH SHOULD BE RECORDED AT THE FIRST OPPORTUNITY." Neither Victor nor, later, Columbia ever rose to the challenge that the large Sowerby work presented, but even in the last year of his life it appeared on a list of future projects in the last "Five Year Plan" Biggs submitted to Columbia, touching proof of his convictions concerning the work's worthiness. Victor did, however, record Sowerby's Symphony in G for organ solo, which appeared as an album in 1942.

Biggs's plans were peppered with his own ideas for the promotion of his recordings. An emphasis on "name" composers—Bach, Brahms, Handel, Mendelssohn, Mozart, Liszt—was suggested because they "are already known to record fans, and in many cases this completes their composition listing in the catalog." And a series on modern American composers "could be done with appropriate patriotic fanfare." Organ records would make "a particularly great gift for music lovers," many of whom, Biggs theorized, had never heard a really good organ first hand. But "church associations" should be avoided in publicity, and the organ should be treated as a "straightforward musical instrument." Biggs knew the value of the visual, and for accompanying photos he recommended multiple keyboards, pipes (they "lend themselves to very striking shots"), candid shots of recording sessions, and pictures of "other musicians with the instrument, thus relating it to the stream of music as a whole."

From the beginning, Biggs, unlike most other artists, wrote most of his own jacket notes and promotional material. Much of the latter could be found in the *RCA Victor Record Review* during the 1940s. The purpose of the publication was, of course, to "plug" new Victor releases, but in his articles Biggs usually managed to do more than that. Biggs the missionary and teacher continually appear side-by-side with Biggs the record salesman.

A good writer of prose, Biggs had a talent for succinctness and a nice instinct for the right proportion of anecdote and erudition needed to sustain a reader's interest. In a 1944 article entitled "The Organ Comes into Its Own," Biggs entered a plea for restoring organ literature to the organ, citing with mild condemnation an unnamed "eminent conductor" (presumably Stokowski) who "has raided this musical storehouse for his orchestral transcriptions. . . . There is nothing obscure about fine organ music. It is as colorful and as full of interest as that for the orchestra." In the course of his short article, he whetted the reader's interest in organ music of the classical, Romantic, and contemporary periods, mentioning, by way of examples, three of his own recent releases—Bach's *Orgelbüchlein,* Reubke's monumental *Sonata on the 94th Psalm,* and Sowerby's Symphony in G major. Of course his articles helped to sell Victor records. But they also helped to "sell" organ music, and Biggs's brief commentary on each work (as well as his jacket notes) was intended to educate the listener painlessly.

In a 1946 article entitled "Organ Music—from Hydraulis to Bach," Biggs summed up the colorful early history of the organ in nontechnical language (including a simple and understandable description of organ-pipe physics) and rounded it out with eye-catching illustrations taken from old prints. He seemed a bit concerned, however, that the average music lover might be put off by "early music" and "baroque organs." The latter term was beginning to be bandied about a bit too freely for Biggs's taste, since it was tending to polarize both music lovers and organists into "pro" and "anti" camps. In an obvious (if low-key) attempt to pour a bit of oil on the troubled waters, Biggs concluded:

> With the present day renaissance of organ building, people frequently inquire about the distinctive characteristics of a "baroque" organ. Really there are none, at least none in the sense that would set such an instrument apart. The progressive trend to design modern instruments on eighteenth century tonal lines has resulted in such organs being nicknamed "classic" or "baroque." The adjective is actually superfluous, since such instruments are simply good organs, a parallel to any modern violin which succeeds in recreating the sound of a Stradivarius.

While such appeals to reason may have helped to broaden the outlook of the music-loving public, they seem to have had less effect within Biggs's own professional circles. Two years later, under direct attack from a minor music critic who had dismissed organs such as the one in the Germanic Museum as "museum pieces," as well as from the organ builder Ernest M. Skinner, who deplored the recent trends of his former company (by this time known as

Biggs and curator Emmanuel Winternitz examining an early positive organ,
Metropolitan Museum of Art, New York, 1942

Aeolian-Skinner, and under the direction of Biggs's friend Harrison), Biggs
retaliated feistily in *The Musical Digest* for March 1948: "Does Mr. Skinner
think that everyone is out of step but himself? Does he really believe that the
fine art of organ building came to full flower in himself and the instruments he
built? And that others are now engaged merely in tearing down that perfection?" With inexorable logic, Biggs then proceeded to defend Harrison's tonal

concepts, put Skinner's "orchestral" philosophy in its proper historical perspective, and, coincidentally, to demolish the critic ("Perhaps it's rather hard on Mr. Gunn to introduce the eloquent writing of Robert Schumann. . . ."). Gunn, who damned the harpsichord as well as Harrison's organs, was also, it turned out, a proponent of orchestral transcriptions of organ music. Biggs seized the opening and administered his knockout punch: "The poor organ, he claims, is not worthy of its own literature!"

In his recordings during the Victor years, 1939-1947, Biggs took pains to keep his repertoire as eclectic as that of his recitals, which were gradually increasing in frequency in the late 1940s, and his broadcasts. There were, of course, large helpings of Bach (notably the *Orgelbüchlein* and *Art of Fugue,* the latter in Biggs's own organ arrangement), Handel, and other Baroque composers such as d'Aquin, Corelli, and Felton; but there were also Mozart, Reubke, Dupré, Sowerby, and Piston. Several recordings of concerted music were made with the Fiedler Sinfonietta, a chamber orchestra made up of Boston Symphony players under the direction of Arthur Fiedler, which also made occasional appearances on the radio programs. And one recording, the last on the Victor label, was not made on the organ at all, but on the celesta. It was of music which would later be recorded again under very different circumstances—Mozart's little Adagio and Rondo for glass armonica.

Recording was by no means Biggs's only activity in this period. There were the weekly broadcasts to prepare, recital tours, teaching, church work, and a newer enterprise, the editing of music. During the 1940s H. W. Gray published Biggs's realization of Bach's *Art of Fugue* as well as his famous arrangements of Bach's "Sheep May Safely Graze" (used for many years as theme music on his broadcasts and referred to by Biggs simply as "Sheep") and "Jesu, Joy of Man's Desiring." His music editions were often closely related to his recordings. In 1942 Victor released Biggs's performance of William Felton's Concerto No. 3 in B flat, and in the same year his arrangement of the Andante from that work was issued by Gray.

Biggs's editions also began to appear in other publishers' catalogs. In 1947 Mercury Music Corp. published his *Treasury of Early Organ Music,* which quickly became a standby among church organists and is still in print. In it were a number of works by seventeenth- and eighteenth-century composers popularized by Biggs in broadcasts and recitals. In 1943 B. F. Wood published his edition of Bach's Fugue in C Major (BWV Anh. 90), nicknamed the "Fanfare" fugue and long a Biggs recital staple. Although it is not usually included among Bach's authentic organ works (it is thought by some to have been conceived for the pedal harpsichord), it was always convincingly performed as such by Biggs.

During the early 1940s World War II placed restrictions on both travel and cultural activities, and the conversion of the organ factories to war production resulted in a moratorium on organ dedication recitals; yet Biggs continued to record, teach, broadcast, and maintain a fairly active if somewhat reduced recital schedule. In the fall of 1940 he gave a series of Bach recitals on the Aeolian-Skinner organ in St. Paul's Chapel of Columbia University in New York City, and during the summer of 1941 he took part in the Boston Symphony Orchestra concerts at Tanglewood. Many of the recitals he gave in 1942 and 1943 were in the greater Boston area or in a relatively nearby location such as Middlebury, Vermont. In 1944 Biggs participated in the famous Bethlehem (Pennsylvania) Bach Festival, and he premiered Walter Piston's Partita for organ and strings in Washington.

During this period Biggs's marriage to Colette Lionne had become increasingly troubled, and in 1944 it ended in divorce. But Biggs was never without female companionship for very long and was soon seen in the company of a tall, attractive chestnut-haired young woman who sang alto in his choir at the Harvard Congregational Church. In March 1945 Biggs was in Chicago for a performance with the Chicago Symphony when he heard that the government was considering drafting unmarried nurses. He lost no time in telephoning a certain nurse in Brookline, who responded by boarding the next train to Chicago, where she and Biggs were married by a justice of the peace. The Army thus lost a skilled and compassionate nurse, but in Margaret Allen—better known as Peggy—Biggs gained a witty and energetic companion who would come to play an increasingly important part in the development of his career.

Biggs's 1945 concert schedule carried him not only to Chicago but also to Montreal, St. Louis, and Raleigh (where a critic called his playing "both regal and vigorous"). Some of his appearances were becoming annual events, including those at Tanglewood, the Bethlehem Bach Festival, and the concerts of the Société Casavant in Montreal. For the Casavant program in October 1946 Biggs brought along Boston Symphony trumpeter Roger Voisin, a frequent collaborator in broadcasts and Boston-area concerts. Early in 1947 Biggs embarked on his first transcontinental tour since before the war. In Los Angeles, the *Times* reviewer observed that his "virtuosity and genius for effective registration were expected, but equally appreciated were his finesse, his cleanness of fingering, and his minimizing of the overwhelming forte qualities of the modern organ." On the four-manual 1915 Austin organ in the Mormon Tabernacle in Salt Lake City Biggs played a largely Romantic program that included Liszt, Karg-Elert, and Reubke, as well as a chorale prelude by the host organist, Alexander Schreiner. Other stops on the tour included Louisville, Naperville, Nashville, Birmingham, and Syracuse. Later in the spring Biggs, with Roger and René Voisin, presented a concert of music for organ and trumpets as part of the Spring Festival of the Massachusetts chapter of the American Guild of Organists. Mary Crowley, one of Biggs's most promising pupils, also performed in this series of concerts.

The last few records Biggs made for Victor contained a considerable amount of music that he would record again later in his life, notably, some of the Mozart Sonatas, recorded at Symphony Hall in 1945 with the Fiedler Sinfonietta. In 1946 he recorded a varied group of Bach works and Dupré's Variations on a Noël at Harvard's Memorial Church. His last Victor records were released in March and June 1947, after which RCA decided that it was no longer feasible to renew his contract as an exclusive artist. Nothing daunted, Biggs, who already had tenuous connections with the Columbia enterprise via his broadcasts for CBS, appeared at the office of Goddard Lieberson, vice president of Columbia Records, armed with another "Five Year Plan" for new recording projects. Lieberson is said to have responded "Why not!" and Biggs's recording career thus continued virtually uninterrupted.

8 | *On the Air*

Knowing your interest in everything musical and particularly in any new or unfamiliar music . . . I venture to write to
you about a fairly ambitious project. . . .

In 1942 Biggs approached arts patron Elizabeth Sprague Coolidge with an idea
that he had been considering for some time. His initial contact with Mrs.
Coolidge had occurred in the spring of 1940, when he was engaged to perform,
with the composer as soloist, Marcel Grandjany's *Fantasy Choral* for harp and
organ at the Library of Congress in Washington, D.C. Mrs. Coolidge had
commissioned the work; Biggs liked it and persuaded her to sponsor an
additional performance in Cambridge. That concert grew to involve not only
Grandjany but eleven members of the Fiedler Sinfonietta in a program that
included the *Fantasy Choral* as well as Grandjany's *Aria* for harp and orchestra, a Handel concerto, and Poulenc's Concerto for organ, strings, and timpani. It was given at the Germanic Museum on February 24, 1941 to an audience
that "just packed the Museum to the limit." It cost Mrs. Coolidge $600, a tidy
sum in those days.

In his highly diplomatic letter to Mrs. Coolidge, Biggs outlined an even
grander project. How long he had been thinking of it is not known, but he later
stated that it had had its genesis in discussions with CBS music director James
Fassett, well known to the radio audience of his day for his "Invitation to
Music" program and his weekly commentaries on the Sunday afternoon
broadcasts of the New York Philharmonic.

Biggs stated his case with the astuteness of a trial lawyer. "As you know,
the organ literature is second only to that of the orchestra and string quartet,
and yet it is practically unknown to the public at large." Citing musical
examples over the whole range of the literature, and deploring the fact that
some of Bach's organ works were known only through orchestral transcriptions, Biggs came to the point in his third paragraph:

It has seemed to me that the radio offers a perfect medium for bringing such
music, played on a good organ, to the public; and that while the orchestral and
instrumental repertoire has been well represented on radio programs for some

years, the organ literature has been completely neglected. In fact—the organ has been thoroughly abused and discredited in its use on the radio. With the technical progress of broadcasting, as of recording, organ tone can now be transmitted faithfully, and the time seems ideal for a really striking series of organ concerts, covering the finest compositions of the very large repertoire. Such programs would have the originality of presenting a completely new aspect of musical life.

Biggs had been doing some groundwork on this project; in the letter he also mentioned that he had discussed it with representatives of the networks, noting that he had already played a successful radio concert from the Hammond Castle in Gloucester, Massachusetts. In closing, Biggs sketched out six experimental radio recitals—"though this can easily be expanded to eight or ten if circumstances permit."

"Your plan interests me enormously," replied Mrs. Coolidge. But she requested more information about the financial aspect of the proposed broadcasts and wondered if they might originate from the Coolidge Auditorium at the Library of Congress rather than from the Germanic Museum. This suggestion did not appeal to Biggs, who knew that the organ in the Coolidge Auditorium was an undistinguished orchestral instrument by Skinner, buried in a deep chamber. In response, he tactfully expressed doubts "that the organ possesses the necessary characteristics for transmission" and cited the extra expense of weekly travel to Washington.

Biggs had been making his own investigations and reported to Mrs. Coolidge that while the NBC Blue Network would provide the air time, it was unwilling to pay the cost of a telephone line to transmit the broadcast to the nearest radio station for network pickup. He also hinted that the network officials favored his choice of the Germanic Museum and the nearby Memorial Church as points of origin for the programs. Mrs. Coolidge balked. While she still liked the idea of the broadcasts, she continued to press for the Washington location, where there were, apparently, no line charges, and where the tab could be picked up by the Coolidge Foundation.

Biggs capitulated—temporarily. He dutifully went to Washington, where he discussed matters with Harold Spivacke of the Library of Congress and allowed that the organ there might be serviceable after all. But Spivacke encountered difficulties in negotiating with the Blue Network and opened discussions with Columbia (CBS) about the project. Biggs must have picked up the reins again at this point, for by September he was able to write Mrs. Coolidge:

> This fall Columbia has revised its Sunday morning timetable, and out of our negotiations there comes from them an offer of a weekly program from the Germanic Museum in Cambridge. It would be from 9.15 to 9.45, coast to coast. I

am of course very interested, for their proposal of "an extended period" provides a wonderful opportunity to perform the best of the organ literature on the air.

This time there would be no line charges, and although the Washington location would have to be given up, Biggs wondered if Mrs. Coolidge would still be willing to lend her patronage to the project—there was still a little matter of $50 per concert for "remuneration of the player." Biggs enclosed a program outline for the first ten concerts. It was an ambitious undertaking, in which Biggs's knack for programing was evident. There was something for everyone, from Bach, Handel, Purcell and d'Aquin, through Haydn, Mendelssohn, and Schumann, to Guilmant, Alain, Vaughan Williams, and Sowerby, with a premiere performance of Richard Arnell's Sonata for Organ thrown in for good measure.

While Mrs. Coolidge still did not understand why something could not have been worked out in Washington with CBS, she was (doubtless to Biggs's great relief) "not at all sorry to have these concerts take place in Cambridge." Fortunately she had a fondness for Harvard; while she did not think that the Coolidge Foundation could be involved in the revised project, she was willing personally to underwrite the broadcasts as her own gift to the university. With her letter came a check for $500 to cover the cost of all ten concerts.

At 9:15 on the morning of September 20, 1942, via CBS's Boston affiliate, WEEI, the voice of James Fassett came over the airwaves to thousands of radios nationwide:

> This is the first of a series of ten organ recitals given by Harvard University through the generosity of Mrs. Elizabeth Sprague Coolidge. The organ used is the baroque instrument designed by G. Donald Harrison in the Germanic Museum of Harvard University, now a school for Chaplains of the United States Army. The player, at the invitation of the University, is E. Power Biggs, and this series of concerts will present much of the finest organ literature, and particularly the "great" Preludes and Fugues of J. S. Bach.

Response was immediate. Before the first month of broadcasts was over, fan letters had begun to arrive at CBS headquarters in New York from all over the country. They came from a music librarian in Washington, D.C; a nun in West Virginia; the Organists' and Choir Directors' Guild of Evansville, Indiana; organ students at Western Maryland College; servicemen who heard the program on Armed Forces Radio; and numerous ordinary music lovers, including one determined soul in Victoria, B.C., who had to get up before six on Sunday mornings to hear the program. The Rev. Arthur R. McKinstrie, Bishop of Delaware, probably spoke for the majority of hearers when he wrote, "The general public has been exposed to mediocre organ playing via the radio. Here is an opportunity for people to know what real organ playing sounds like."

In early November Mrs. Coolidge wrote to Biggs,

> We are enjoying your broadcasts so much, and are hearing so many pleasant things about them, that I am wondering whether the Columbia people could arrange to give another series and how the idea would appeal to you. If it could be done in the same way, I should be very glad to help to the same extent that I did this year for producing another ten concerts.

Of all the letters Biggs received, this one was doubtless the most gratifying. Within a week he had drawn up another series of ten programs to send to his benefactor. He also forwarded some of his fan mail to Mrs. Coolidge, who was impressed by its "unusually sincere and discriminating" nature. In January she volunteered to finance a third ten-concert series.

Up to this point the broadcasts had presented only solo organ works, and, despite the two ten-week extensions, it still had no real prospects for permanence. In March 1943, Biggs, emboldened by listener response and the continued interest of Mrs. Coolidge and James Fassett, proposed some important changes: that the series be continued in the standard thirteen-program network format, and that music for organ with other instruments be added. This of course meant an increase in the financial commitment of both CBS and Mrs. Coolidge. The latter responded with a guarantee of $1,600 for the quarter, and Biggs began to write to some of the composers he knew, such as Sowerby, Harris, and Piston, requesting new works of moderate length for organ and small ensemble. Earlier composers were by no means neglected. For his Easter Sunday program Biggs engaged the Stradivarius Quartet and the Bach Cantata Club for a performance of two Sonatas and a *Missa Brevis* by Mozart.

Unfortunately, the programs could not continue on quite such a lavish scale. Immediately following the Easter program word came from CBS that it was cutting back on its financial involvement in the program, and Mrs. Coolidge was reluctant to pick up the slack. In order to stay within their budget Biggs and his collaborator, Arthur Fiedler, had to substitute programs involving fewer instrumentalists for some of those originally planned.

During the next quarter (again partially funded by Mrs. Coolidge) Biggs found it prudent to alternate solo and ensemble programs. This format continued, with minor variations, into 1944, and Mrs. Coolidge had joined the ranks of Biggs's radio fans to the extent that she complained to the CBS management when, for a brief time, the program was "bumped" from her Washington, D.C., station. And she continued to contribute to the funding.

By 1945 Biggs's program had become a permanent feature of CBS's classical music offerings, along with the New York Philharmonic, the Budapest String Quartet, and the Beethoven Trio. Biggs had become a respected member of the CBS radio "family," one who could be relied upon to be on hand when needed. Such an occasion was described by Biggs in a letter to Mrs. Coolidge dated April 18, 1945:

> Many thanks for your kind Easter message. Only part of the Easter Day program was carried up here, but we have made up for lost time during the past week. On Thursday evening CBS asked me to stand by, and during the next three days we went on the air six times. Of course, the organ has a wonderful literature for such an occasion, and I was most happy to play, for it seemed the least one could do. I hope perhaps you may have heard one or more of these programs. They were all of Chorale Preludes and other music of Bach and the Chorale Preludes of Brahms, and were carried on all CBS stations. One short period, immediately following the one minute of silence at four o'clock, went out over all four networks, to an estimated seventy million people!

The occasion was the death of Franklin Delano Roosevelt, a man whom Biggs admired. In defiance of union rules, Biggs tried to donate his services for the broadcasts, prompting a slightly exasperated letter from Fassett explaining why this was not possible ("The simple fact is that we are not allowed to accept your services gratis") and suggesting that Biggs might wish to donate his fee to charity.

It is important to remember that the Biggs broadcasts were born in the early years of World War II. Travel was restricted, and wartime finances, gas rationing, and blackouts all conspired to discourage the promoting and attending of concerts. While most homes had a phonograph, often of a rather primitive sort, records were a luxury in those years and were not produced in anything approaching the quantity and variety one finds today. But virtually every home, no matter how poor or remote, had a radio. And on that radio one could listen to regularly scheduled live classical music broadcasts.

Many of these programs—the opera, the symphony, the chamber music, and, of course, Biggs—were not commercially sponsored. They maintained high standards and had no need to pander to anyone's ideas of popular taste. Biggs was well aware that this cast him in the role of tastemaker. An interviewer for *Newsweek* (April 22, 1946) quotes Biggs as saying, "The public be damned. Go ahead and play something that is good—and the public will follow right with you." It was a blunt statement, but a high compliment to the public's taste. Biggs could not have made it or played the kind of music he played, had he not had an unshakeable faith in the innate good taste of his audience.

And the public never let him down. For sixteen years it listened faithfully while he played all sorts of early and contemporary music that the public was not supposed to like, most of it on organs that many of his colleagues did not like. Indeed, in its appreciation and acceptance of both Biggs's music and the Germanic Museum organ, the humble radio audience was often several giant steps ahead of the organ-playing profession which, with a few notable exceptions, tended to be defensively conservative during the 1940s. Many professionals grudgingly acknowledged Biggs's status only because it was quite impossible to ignore it.

Radio, Biggs quickly found out, is not the same as a concert tour, where one can play the same program in each city. In his *Newsweek* interview, he likened radio to a hungry mouth: "It has one piece of steak and it is ready for the next." Over the years Biggs proved that he was capable of feeding that demanding maw, and what it got was mostly good tasty steak, sometimes accompanied by a crisp salad or even an occasional rich dessert. But never a single spoonful of pablum or junk food.

Perhaps it was fortunate that the radio programs developed at a time when Biggs was not as involved in concert work as he would later become. He still taught, presided over the music program at his Brookline church, and took part in events such as the Bethlehem Bach festival and the summer concerts at Tanglewood. But his touring schedule was considerably curtailed, and he thus had the time to experiment and develop workable patterns of programing which were never repetitious or dull, as well as to build up a performing repertoire equal to the demand of a new program each week. This required both practice and research, and the latter deserves some comment here.

Biggs was not a musicologist, nor did he pretend to be. He was a practical musician with an eminently practical objective. Yet he had the instincts of a musicologist and an unerring sense for recognizing a good thing when he found it. In his search for interesting material he became a familiar figure in Harvard's Widener Library, the Boston Public Library, and other libraries in the area.

On the one hand he delighted in rediscovering and performing some forgotten but choice bit of early music; on the other he cornered composers whenever he could with requests for new pieces. Given the certainty of at least one radio performance, most of the Americans readily complied. The Europeans were less interested—perhaps because it was not possible for them to tune in on Sunday mornings and hear their works performed.

One inevitable result of the radio broadcasts was that composers began to deluge Biggs with manuscripts in the hope that he would give them a performance. Biggs always checked out these unsolicited donations, no matter how amateurish, and when he came upon something of merit, he did not hesitate to program it and to encourage the composer. The rest received tactful rejections, but nothing ever went unacknowledged.

Biggs sometimes went to extraordinary lengths to secure interesting music for the broadcasts. Somewhere Biggs had acquired an old pre-war Parisian recording of Concerto No. 3 for two organs by the Spanish Baroque composer

Antonio Soler. Efforts to locate a published score proved fruitless, so Biggs played the record over and over while Daniel Pinkham and Walter Piston each took down one of the parts of the duet by dictation, thus arriving at a workable performing score. As there was but one organ at the Museum and no immediate likelihood of securing another, Pinkham brought in his harpsichord, and the work received what was undoubtedly its first American performance as a duet for organ and harpsichord. This arrangement, however, was not authentic enough for Biggs, and early in 1950 (having at last located the scores) he programed another of Soler's Concertos—this time as a duet with himself. This was accomplished by prerecording one part and playing the second part with the recording live on the broadcast. Still later, by borrowing a Dutch chamber organ from Charles Fisher, Biggs and Pinkham were at last able to play Soler's pieces as they were intended.

New music and little-known old music contributed to the continuing interest in Biggs's programs, but so did the frequent inclusion of works involving other instruments. Thus the public heard, often for the first time, such gems as Handel's works for oboe or flute with continuo, the sinfonias to some of Bach's cantatas, Buxtehude's trio sonatas, Gabrieli's works for brass and organ, Mozart's "Epistle" Sonatas, some of the English organ concertos, and, of course, many modern compositions. The string, brass, and woodwind players, usually members of the Boston Symphony Orchestra, were always of the best quality, and Biggs was not the least reticent about securing suitable fees for them.

Other means of maintaining interest included programs built around the works of a single composer (often celebrating a birth or death anniversary) and programs with a seasonal emphasis. Christmas music of all periods got a good workout every December, the fare ranging from d'Aquin and Bach to Reger and Templeton; and for several years Biggs added a special Christmas Eve broadcast to his schedule. Around the Fourth of July there would be an American emphasis, and it was on one such program, in 1944, that Biggs introduced the works of William Selby, a Boston organist and music teacher of colonial days. Biggs had unearthed the manuscripts at the Massachusetts Historical Society, and he later edited Selby's *Lesson* and *Fuge or Voluntary* for publication.

A publicity release prepared by Biggs in 1947 reported that during the five years he had been on the air, he had played music by 126 composers of all periods, including 242 concerted works by 67 composers and 126 premiere performances of new works. In addition he had aired the complete organ works of J. S. Bach, W. F. Bach, Mendelssohn, Brahms, and Hindemith; all sixteen Handel organ concertos; all seventeen of Mozart's "Epistle" Sonatas; all of d'Aquin's *Noëls;* and such esoterica as Haydn's "flute clock" pieces and the sonatas of Frederick the Great. "So extensive, however, is the musical literature of the organ that so far only a small proportion has been performed." Biggs obviously intended to tackle the rest of it for as long as the network would let him continue to broadcast. But why perform organ music over the radio?

> The Bach Passacaglia heard in a Cathedral may be a greater musical experience than hearing the same music in a concert hall [but] music lovers no longer frequent Cathedrals as they once did centuries ago. [Therefore] for five years CBS has almost literally brought the Cathedral to your living room. . . . For the great organ literature, from Bach to the moderns, forms ideal radio listening. Ideal, because it is music of structure and strength, rather than emotion; and it does not depend on conditions of actual concert performance for its effect. The Romantics wrote "audience music," but Bach and the Classicists wrote for sheer perfection of artistic and musical content, and a listener may well find this music most stimulating and enjoyable when heard in the privacy of his own home.

Fortunately the program was securely established in the CBS routine by its fifth anniversary, for in 1946 Mrs. Coolidge had found it necessary to cut back somewhat on her personal benefactions. Through the Coolidge Foundation, however, she sponsored Biggs in an ambitious concert for organ and orchestra in New York in the spring of 1946 as part of the 50th anniversary of the American Guild of Organists. The concert drew enthusiastic reviews, and Biggs sent roses to Mrs. Coolidge, who allowed that she was "not in the least surprised" by the program's success. The following year she sponsored some public concerts at the Museum, including a performance by Biggs of Bach's *Art of Fugue* that drew an audience of nearly 800 to the small auditorium.

But Mrs. Coolidge was getting on in years, and most of her charitable work was being handled by the Coolidge Foundation. She was unable to subsidize some ambitious concerts that Biggs wanted to include in the American Guild of Organists' 1950 national convention. Nor could she fund a series of concerted programs that Biggs hoped to mount in celebration of the tenth anniversary of the radio broadcasts in 1952, although she continued to contribute to the expenses of the broadcasts through that year.

Although Biggs did not realize it at the time, the years of the weekly broadcasts were numbered. In 1950 CBS had slashed his budget for instrumentalists, making him wholly dependent on Mrs. Coolidge for such extras at a time when she was not always able to provide them. After her death in 1953, the programs consisted largely of solo organ music, with only an occasional single instrumentalist. And CBS's commitment to radio, particularly the nonsponsored programs, was dwindling as it turned its corporate attention increasingly to that fast-developing new medium, television.

Biggs and conductor Richard Burgin in the Germanic Museum, preparing for the premiere of Sowerby's *Classic Concerto,* to be broadcast over CBS, early 1940s. Photo by Fay Foto.

During the 1950s Biggs's recital and recording schedules reached grueling proportions, but the broadcasts went on, still with the Germanic Museum as the base of operations, and in 1957 a contract was signed for a new organ there. But occasional programs now originated from other places in the country where Biggs was concertizing, and guest organists—usually Biggs's friends and students from the Boston area—were heard more often. Bach's "Sheep May Safely Graze" was still the well-loved theme music that ended the program, but the tape recorder now allowed it, and often the whole program, to be prerecorded, easing the tension of the earlier live broadcasts, when "the announcer and engineer were right there in the gallery, the announcer leaning on the console with the script, and the engineer just by, watching the signal level."

By 1958 Biggs must have had an inkling that CBS was reshuffling its priorities relative to nonsponsored programs, but all correspondence gave the appearance of business as usual. The new organ was opened with great fanfare in September, and programs were planned for it well into 1959. The bad news arrived unexpectedly, and it caught Biggs in the middle of a concert series in Mexico City. He had already left for some earlier stops on his tour when Peggy opened a letter to him from James Fassett, dated November 7, 1958. In view of Fassett's long years of association with Biggs, it was probably a difficult letter to write:

> For some time I have seen the handwriting on the wall and now at last has come the final blow. As of the first of the year, the CBS network will vastly curtail the daily number of hours it will service its owned and affiliated stations, and all but the commercially sponsored programs and a few traditional public service broadcasts like the Philharmonic will cease to exist as network programs. Your weekly broadcasts, I regret to say, are among the many casualties, and the final broadcast will be that of Sunday, January 4th. . . . Needless to say, I feel the loss of your programs after so many years more acutely than any others which are now to be terminated.

After discussing some matters relating to a special December broadcast, he closed with, "It is very sad for me to write you this letter, but still I have the feeling that some day we will be working together again under brighter circumstances."

Peggy was horrified; the timing could not have been worse. "I had a great debate with myself," she wrote Biggs, "about holding off with this information until your four Mexico City programs were past, but it's dangerous to do this, since it's possible that some good break might come, and you would not be prepared for it." She knew that Biggs would fight, that he would immediately start casting around for alternatives, and so she sketched out a few ideas of her own. But she was not too hopeful and accurately saw the root of the problem: "I guess radio just isn't anything nowadays—except the FM stations and the Educational stations who ride on the coattails. It just seems that one's own records put one out of business."

Biggs was not going to let anything put him out of business if he could help it. He went into immediate action, reporting the results to Peggy in a letter written on November 28:

> I phoned Fassett today. He told me that he took my letter to him (the one I wrote from here, so I'm glad you sent *his* on, & didn't just keep it) into a meeting yesterday. But the result is, unfortunately, the same. He says they are not keeping any sustaining programs, except the N.Y. Phil[harmonic], his "Festivals," and the Cleveland Orchestra—which "doesn't cost them a cent."
>
> I said—that if we did ours with the greatest economy, the obstacle would be only the fee paid me. He said—yes, & unfortunately they wouldn't pay even *that!* Because the stations "could make more money arranging their own shows"—(that is, playing records!) than taking a network show! Silly, isn't it! Well, that's that. I may send a line to the manager of WEEI, to ask if they would like to consider continuing the show. But I will think about it first.

Biggs was stuck in Mexico, but in Cambridge Peggy kept on working, thinking up more ideas, wondering about the possibilities of FM and TV, and phoning Biggs's friends to urge them to write to CBS. She hardly needed to do the latter—letters from listeners began to pour in to CBS from all over the country as soon as the cancellation was announced. But all to no avail. Despite Biggs's efforts to present new ideas and alternatives to CBS as late as June 1959, a rather remarkable occurrence in the musical life of America had become history. Writing on Bach and the influence of radio in the December 24, 1984 issue of *Newsweek,* critic Alan Rich observed, "For better or for worse, Landowska, Biggs, and a few other hardy pioneers gave back to the world something of Bach's original sound."

From the encouraging words that attended the very first broadcasts in 1942 to the protestations aroused by their demise in 1958, Biggs's radio programs drew a steady stream of fan mail. After 1950, when his concert schedule began to peak and his record output increased, a growing proportion of fan letters came from concertgoers and discophiles. But at the outset, Biggs's largest and most supportive following was the radio audience.

One of the most faithful groups of listeners, and one toward which Biggs felt a patriotic obligation, consisted of people in the armed services. World War II had been going on for nearly two years when the broadcasts commenced, and from the beginning they were beamed overseas on Armed Forces Radio. For many young people, separated from their families for the first time, the programs were a fragile link with a saner and more peaceful world. In 1943 a Connecticut father wrote, "Before the war scattered my family we listened together every Sunday morning, and now that we are scattered far and wide I like to think that at 9:15 every Sunday we are all sitting somewhere listening to you, one in spirit and the love of what you bring us."

Some of the servicemen were former students of Biggs's, including Wesley Day, David Gifford, and Henry Kaufman. Kaufman, describing himself as a "pretty lonely soldier," was reminded by Biggs's broadcasts of the "pleasant, peaceful days at good old Longy, when this business of war seemed pretty distant." A British organist, serving with the R.A.F. in Canada, listened to Biggs in 1943 while "engaged, not too romantically, frying eggs and bacon over colossal hot stoves while your music drifts in like something from another world." Most armed forces listeners were not homesick organists, however, but simply music-starved music lovers. Some sent requests for music to be played, which Biggs complied with whenever possible; others requested photos and autographs, which he invariably sent. The further away people were stationed, the more eager they were not to lose touch. A sergeant in Australia pleaded with CBS to broadcast Biggs on short wave "for the benefit of

America's vanguard abroad." A Canadian Air Force man, on the West Coast, listened to the early broadcast under the covers "so as not to wake the rest of the boys in the barracks." A pharmacist's mate in New York deplored the fact that his buddies did not share his appreciation of Bach; and Lt. Mary Morrison, writing on behalf of a "group of faithful listeners on the night watches" at Seattle Naval Air Station, voiced the group's opinion that Biggs was "a peach of an organist."

Biggs's radio listeners transcended all age, economic, and geographic barriers. Young people often sent enthusiastic letters. In 1946 a fourteen-year-old wrote, "When I get a little older I want to be a GREAT ORGANIST LIKE YOU." In 1952 a fifteen-year-old Californian admitted that "you cause a little trouble in the Palmer household on Sundays. Your broadcast . . . comes to the west coast at 6:30 Sunday morning. This interrupts the family's sleep a little, but I couldn't miss your broadcasts." The elderly were just as appreciative, though perhaps for different reasons. In the same year a 71-year-old woman wrote, "Even I who have many friends see them as treasures that cannot be held, with any sense of security, near one indefinitely. So I am always hoping that one or another bit of beauty may remain dependable—as this Sunday morning broadcast of yours. Long may it come over my radio."

Some devotees went to considerable lengths to hear the broadcasts. People who moved to localities where the stations did not carry Biggs's program would badger the management until it did. A New Jersey man had a radio installed in his car for the specific purpose of listening to Biggs as he drove to church. Perhaps the most determined listener was a priest in Arizona. En route to his mission duties, he had been catching the program on an Albuquerque station on his car radio, but there were problems: "They always had the first five minutes chopped off. Then they chopped into the end, and finally the whole thing was engulfed in hill billy." Nothing daunted, the padre acquired a powerful home receiver, changed the times of his masses, and tuned in to Biggs on a station a thousand miles distant in the comfort of his livingroom.

Although it is only too true that one cannot please all of the people all of the time, Biggs certainly tried. Requests regularly came in for favorite Bach, Handel, or Mozart selections, which Biggs always endeavored to work in. But some, who remembered a different sort of repertoire, would occasionally ask for such pieces as *Kammenoi Ostrow,* Schubert's Serenade, Sibelius's *Finlandia,* or *The Lost Chord.* These requests were politely sidestepped, but those with lighter tastes were usually satisfied with some of Biggs's less weighty offerings, such as transcriptions from Handel's *Water Music,* Haydn's delightful flute clock pieces, Mozart's "glass armonica" music, or an arrangement of the Purcell/Clarke *Trumpet Tune.* The greatest differences of listener opinion usually centered around contemporary works. When Biggs played Sowerby's Passacaglia in 1952, a Massachusetts man expressed "Thanks, warm and sincere" for the performance, but a German lady in New Jersey definitely did not agree: "Pfui, pfui! Ach, this was too horrible a composition!"

Some listeners, who were used to electronic instruments and theatre organs, found the organ in the Germanic Museum a new experience. "Certainly a bit different from many organs one is accustomed to hear via radio," wrote a Canadian in 1943, "usually they are not a thing of beauty." In the same year a Massachusetts fan wrote, "When you first started the series I didn't care for the organ you play on, but the more I hear it the more I like it. There is a rich quality not heard in most instruments." A Connecticut listener of singularly determined open-mindedness offered this testimonial in 1949:

> Your Sunday morning broadcasts on that classic organ are having a very bad effect on me! Like dope! I used to be able to turn you off after listening for a minute or so. Gradually I stuck it out for two or three minutes—now, by Jove! I can't even take a bath while you're playing—I like to hear every note of the entire program.

Tuning in to Biggs's program became such a ritual that some listeners became upset when, for whatever reason, there was any change in the format. One Sunday morning the announcer, having forgotten to change his watch to Daylight Savings Time, failed to show up to introduce the live broadcast, and Peggy Biggs gamely stepped into the breach. This prompted an outraged protest from a militant male chauvinist "against the use of *any* female announcer on your program!" Sometimes, when Biggs was away on tour, local organists such as Mary Crowley, Daniel Pinkham, or Lawrence Moe would fill in. Good as they were, these substitutes were merely tolerated by the faithful. "Your relief organist did a fine job," wrote a Seattle parson, "but somehow I like to think of you as my friend playing for me."

Biggs's sign-off music was his transcription of Bach's "Sheep May Safely Graze," which always faded out somewhere around the middle as air time ran out. By 1951 so many requests had been received for the complete piece that Biggs decided it was time to do something about it. Thus a CBS publicity release for December 5, under the heading "A Full Meal for the Sheep," announced that,

> For the past ten years organist E. Power Biggs has been playing a fragment of Bach's "Sheep May Safely Graze" at the close of his Sunday morning CBS Radio program. Many listeners have written him, to say that they would like to hear the whole piece played right through. Accordingly, the sheep will graze safely all through their meal, as the lovely fragment of a cantata will be played in its entirety in Mr. Biggs' own arrangement for two flutes and organ on Sunday, Dec. 16. . . .

The general tenor of letters concerning Biggs's broadcasts was complimentary. The majority of complaints were leveled not at the music, the organ, or the players, but at the cavalier treatment sometimes given the program by local stations, which would occasionally curtail all or part of the broadcast to slip in locally sponsored programs or sometimes cancel the program altogether with no warning. In 1952 a midwesterner wrote:

> Sunday mornings are kept from being monotonous by the uncertainty as to whether we will be allowed to hear all, half, or none of the Biggs program. On these occasions when the station switches to "the friendly neighbors of Renfrew Valley and their olde tyme hymnes" I am in anything but a pious mood.

Some had the equipment to surmount these inconveniences—when Biggs was taken off a local station in 1943, a Seattle man switched to short wave and pulled him in from a Baltimore station.

In 1944 an Arkansas professor appealed to CBS on behalf of three local colleges and a sizable group of music lovers to encourage at least one midwestern station to carry Biggs's program. In 1949 CBS's rival, NBC, began airing the Bach Aria Group at 9:30 A.M. on Sundays, and a Bach lover found himself on the horns of a unique dilemma. He was sure that it could be resolved, however, if Biggs would program any Bach works at the beginning of his 9:15 program, thus avoiding conflicts of listener interest.

In some areas Biggs's program was cut to fifteen minutes in 1949, and listeners complained about pieces being chopped off in the middle. When a California station dropped it entirely, patients at the Orange County Hospital protested. In 1952, when a fifteen-minute cut was made by some eastern stations, the complaints again poured in. "What do you mean," raged an indignant New Yorker, "by cutting E. Power Biggs to 15 minutes? And putting in some lousy program of talk? I'm deeply disappointed." Within a few weeks Biggs's full half hour was restored.

While Biggs's audience obviously included many musicians, far more were like the psychologist who described herself as a "Bach-lover who plays no instrument and who is wholly dependent on the radio for music." Listeners who did not attend church were both surprised and delighted to discover that the organ had a secular side. On the other hand, a California churchgoer found Biggs's music "a great relief from the mediocre organ music we get in our churches here." And a New Hampshire clergyman testified that the radio program got him "into an excellent mood for conducting my church service."

Perhaps the most colorful of Biggs's radio fans was Hugh B. Birch, of Lower Lebarge, Yukon, Canada, who described himself as a "telegraph operator, lineman, weather observer, and just about a Jack-of-all-trades." He tended a relay and maintenance station for the Dominion Telegraph Company between Whitehorse and Dawson City. An independent spirit, he seems to have enjoyed the seven months of isolation his job required of him each winter. For companionship he had his "faithful little pal," an equally independent-looking tabby cat named Lady Peggy, who was "wiser than many humans and better company too." He also had a radio, on which he listened to all of CBS's musical programs via its Seattle station. In 1946 he wrote, "I particularly enjoyed this morning's broadcast—Reception full and strong, the beautiful tone of the organ just singing in, and I do not think I have ever heard such fine Trumpet music before." With the letter he enclosed snapshots of himself, sporting a magnificent grey beard, and Lady Peggy, perched atop his woodpile.

Biggs was an admirer of free spirits, and Birch became one of his favorite correspondents. Besides his radio, Birch also had a record player, and in 1947 Biggs sent him a gift of some records and autographed photos of himself and Arthur Fiedler.

> A steamboat stopped here early this morning to put off some supplies, mail, etc. Also one express parcel. Imagine my surprise, and great pleasure, when I saw the label on it. Your records had arrived, in perfect condition. You surely did a superb job packing them. A matter of five minutes, and I was playing your Variation, then the other three. I am really at a loss to find words to express my appreciation and thanks for such a wonderful gift, and the music itself, together with the artistry in its performance, is just heavenly.

That was July. No steamboats came up the frozen Yukon in December, but a small plane flew over and dropped three months' mail, Christmas presents, and a couple of bottles of "good cheer." In January 1948, Birch wrote,

> Although alone here, I had a grand Christmas. . . . The only thing to rather spoil Christmas was that my radio blew up a week before Christmas and I missed out on all the holiday music I love so well. . . . Needless to say I drew heavily on all my organ recordings.

Rising each Sunday at 5 A.M. Yukon Time, Hugh Birch remained one of Biggs's faithful listeners and correspondents until 1952, when modern technology caught up with his frozen Shangri-La. The Yukon River Telegraph Line, built in 1899, was closed down, and Birch was made manager of the Whitehorse station. Perhaps the worst thing about Whitehorse was that "radio reception conditions here are rotten—far too much high noise level from so many power plants and so on, never do hear your broadcast, or many other old favorites, any more, worse luck."

Radio fans were by no means the only ones to heap praise on Biggs's broadcasts. In 1952, the tenth year of the program, *Musical America* noted that for seven of the nine years in which they had conducted a reader poll of "serious music on the air," Biggs had received the Favorite Organist award. Perhaps the most unusual tribute to the salubrious effects of Biggs's Sunday morning broadcasts was penned by David McCord, whose whimsical poem, "More E. Power Biggs to You," appeared in the April 1948 issue of *The New Yorker*. Biggs was often interviewed by newspapers and magazines, and he himself wrote a number of articles concerning his radio career for musical periodicals. Certainly there is little doubt that his radio-engendered popularity materially aided his career as a recitalist and a recording artist.

9 | *Concert Hall Organs*

A basic question one must ask is: Is it necessary to have an organ in a concert hall? The answer is yes—absolutely yes. Because without an organ you don't have a *real* concert hall. You cannot perform the large orchestra-organ literature, you lose the possibility of many choral works, as well as the solo literature.

These words, spoken by Biggs in an address before the New York chapter of the American Guild of Organists on June 7, 1976 could have been uttered at almost any point in his career. Commitment to the organ as a concert instrument meant commitment to the cause of concert-hall organs—a cause that Biggs promoted throughout his entire professional life with the zeal of an evangelist.

In the course of the same talk, Biggs recalled the first true concert-hall organ on which he had had direct influence. In 1936 the Boston Symphony began giving summer concerts in the Berkshire Hills of western Massachusetts, and in 1938 it found a permanent summer residence at Tanglewood, near Lenox. Serge Koussevitzky, then the orchestra's conductor, had a deep interest in the education of young musicians, and in 1940 the activities at Tanglewood were expanded to include the Berkshire Music Center, where young musicians could study and perform under the guidance of Koussevitzky and the leading players in his orchestra. The focal point of the Berkshire Music Center is a building bearing the somewhat ungracious title of The Music Shed. That is what it is, however—a large wooden shed with a stage, acoustically designed to project sound, and open at one side to face a partially open-air audience. Senator Emerson Richards, in an article in the October 1940 issue of *The American Organist,* provided a colorful (but accurate) description of it:

Architecturally it appears to have been the offspring of a clandestine affair between the Oberammergau Festival Hall and Yankee Stadium. Structurally it consists of a vast fan-like roof of wood and steel; nothing more. The floor is the good Berkshire earth, and the side walls the chill night air of the encircling hills. Serried rows of metal chairs complete the discomfort. The normal capacity is seven thousand but another three thousand can be seated out under the stars, or more usually in the rain.

On the other hand, as G. Donald Harrison observed, it was "quite a remarkable place for sound."

Biggs recalled that during the 1939 Tanglewood season, the orchestra attempted the Saint-Saëns "Organ" Symphony with the aid of only an "electronic device"—the lowly and ubiquitous Hammond. ("Not then being with the orchestra, I did not play it," Biggs hastened to add.) Koussevitzky was patently displeased with the result. Immediately afterward he announced to the trustees that he was planning Bach's Mass in B minor for the following summer, "and for that I must have an organ." The trustees knew from long experience that if Koussevitzky wanted something, they would have to find some way of getting it. Shortly afterward, George Judd, the orchestra's manager, contacted Biggs with the request that he take Koussevitzky to the Germanic Museum to have a look at the organ there.

> This I did in my Model A Ford, recently acquired from a college student for $75.00. I *think* Dr. Koussevitzky quite enjoyed the ride, but I *know* he enjoyed the organ, for, after hearing a little music, he came up the stairs and said, "Fine—send it all up to Tanglewood." Well, it was explained to him that this was not the organ for him, but that a similar one could be readily designed for Tanglewood.

With little further ado, apparently, the trustees secured a grant from the Carnegie Foundation, and Biggs was soon collaborating on a specification with G. Donald Harrison of the Aeolian-Skinner Company. A contract was signed in March 1940 for the firm's Opus 1002, and construction was begun immediately, since completion had been promised in time for the coming summer's concerts. The organ was finished in record time and was first used on July 8. On the 16th and 31st it was featured in solo recitals played by Biggs, and on August 15 it was used to accompany the B minor Mass, as Koussevitzky had desired.

The organ was situated horizontally in open-fronted boxes over the orchestra stage; during the winter heavy shutters covered the enclosures to protect the organ from the weather. The influence of the Germanic Museum organ is evident in the stoplist and scaling of the organ, but there were important differences. The Museum organ, because of its location in a live, intimate room, could be voiced fairly gently and still be effective. Although the Music Shed organ also occupied an advantageous acoustical location, it had to be voiced more strongly and fundamentally in order to serve as a suitable foil to the orchestra and be heard by a large outdoor audience. For this reason, the Tanglewood organ spoke on 3 1/2 inches of wind pressure, an inch more than the Museum organ. The only other significant differences were the addition of four enclosed stops to the otherwise unexpressive Positiv division and the provision of a lone 32' low C pipe for use in Strauss's *Thus Spake Zarathustra*. As Biggs was later to observe to Charles Fisk, nearly all the big organ/orchestra pieces, including the Strauss and Saint-Saëns, are in the key of C.

Senator Richards, in his pithy account of the Tanglewood organ, offered some erudite observations that suggest that in some respects this knowledgable and well-traveled amateur may have been a few steps ahead of even Biggs and Harrison in his understanding of the classical organ. He decried the lack of a tremulant, not because of the requirements of Romantic music, but because he was aware that the organs of Bach's time had them. He would also have liked a stronger 16' reed stop, more mixtures, and a 2' Blockflote in the Pedal division. On the other hand, he also favored a few more enclosed stops, including a Celeste. It is possible that the organ's designers would also have welcomed such additions but were restricted by finances.

But Richards's criticisms were, on the whole, minor. Both the Museum organ and the Tanglewood instrument had impressed him favorably, and he felt that with the latter "another step had been taken in the revolution of organ design." He also observed that the non-organists were more likely than the organists to be in sympathy with the new trends:

> One of the most interesting, if somewhat ironical, results comes from the fact that [the organ] has not yet made nearly so great an impression upon organists as it has upon musicians not generally considered as interested in this vehicle of musical expression. This seemed to be particularly true of the music-critics. . . . It is likewise interesting to note the reaction of the men in the orchestra itself. These reactions ranged from expressions of approval and interest in the rendition of classic organ literature, to particular reminiscences concerning the similarity of the ensemble to that of well-known Continental organs with which they were familiar.

The builder's own evaluation of the Tanglewood instrument is revealing. In a letter to William King Covell in October 1940, Harrison wrote,

> All in all, I think the Tanglewood organ is one of the most successful instruments we have built, and it is surprising how large it sounds in that enormous partly-open-air auditorium. . . . I have yet to discover a person who had any criticism of this particular organ. In my opinion it is a far finer organ than the Germanic.

Commenting on an appreciative letter received from the rather conservative "Doc" Davison, organist and choirmaster of Harvard Chapel, Harrison noted with satisfaction, "it shows he must really have been impressed."

Biggs, of course, had plans for the organ. He was now the official Boston Symphony organist, and he and Peggy spent part of each summer at the pleasant little Appletree Cottage at Tanglewood, where no season passed without the organ being used with the orchestra or chorus. In 1946, alarmed at the cancellation of some planned major works for organ and orchestra, Biggs sent Aaron Copland (who had assumed some of the administrative duties) some ideas for revitalizing the role of the organ at Tanglewood: greater involvement of students who were organists, a series of Sunday evening organ recitals, and the inclusion of organ works in the traditional "Bach week" and "Mozart week" repertoire. As long as Biggs was involved with it, there would be organ music at Tanglewood. Unfortunately, this tradition has not been well upheld in the years since Biggs relinquished his post with the orchestra.

In early 1947 Biggs became involved, along with G. Wallace Woodworth of Harvard and Wallace Goodrich of New England Conservatory, in the planning of a more far-reaching project. The old Hutchings organ in Symphony Hall had been on borrowed time from a mechanical standpoint since before Biggs's connection with the orchestra, and it was growing increasingly unreliable. A note from Biggs to the organ tuners dating from around this period listed some of the problems a performer had to face: unreliable combination pistons, stops that would not operate on the crescendo pedal, stops that would not operate at all, and a certain note that would "not speak unless [the] cable is jiggled."

At first George Judd, the orchestra's manager, and Henry Cabot, one of the trustees, thrashed around rather unproductively on their own. Before soliciting the advice of Biggs and Harrison, they considered in turn the proposed donation of a second-hand residence organ and a rebuilding proposal from an obscure Chicago firm. In a letter dated January 15, 1947, Harrison reported to Judd with regard to the Hutchings organ:

> Much of the pipework is still in an excellent state of preservation, and can certainly be rehabilitated. On the other hand, a great deal of the mechanical equipment is obsolete, and must be entirely replaced. You have known for some time that a new console and combination action is necessary, and the blowing apparatus in the basement is also of an obsolete pattern.

He also made note of the extreme sluggishness of the key action and other problems facing the performer, concluding that since a thorough rebuilding would cost about 75 percent of the price of an entirely new organ, he would recommend acquiring a new organ. A relatively restrained three-manual scheme (with two "floating" divisions) was included with the letter.

Biggs endorsed Harrison's proposal wholeheartedly, adding some observations of his own on tonal matters:

> We know far more today about the musical requirements of an instrument in Symphony Hall than the Hutchings company could know in 1900. In certain

respects the voicing is wrong, and many of the present stops are thick and heavy in tone, and are not useful in either solo or orchestral playing. It is often impossible to find soft but bright stops to accompany the B minor Mass and other choral works, and Dr. Koussevitzky invariably finds much fault with the organ on these occasions, criticism that is never directed to the Tanglewood organ. At the other end of the tonal scheme, the organ does not have the climax necessary for works such as the Saint-Saëns Symphony or Zarathustra. We surely should revise the tonal scheme according to our needs, for though the action might be improved by new chests, the tonal scheme would not be satisfactory if left as is.

It should be noted that Harrison's proposed scheme already included the seemingly obligatory 32' low C for *Zarathustra!*

Biggs began to work out recommendations for a final specification with Woodworth and Goodrich. Koussevitzky muddied the waters a bit with an unexpected request for reduction in size. Biggs defended his originally proposed 32' Pedal reed stop and interposed the practical suggestion that the console should have three manuals instead of four, so that it would be easier for the organist to see over it. Goodrich, who had previously been Symphony organist for twelve years, favored a heavy foundation and thought that the old Hutchings was fairly adequate tonally as it stood. He was concerned that "our good friend Harrison, whom I admire tremendously, is rather prone to reduce the strength of the 8 ft. foundation stops." Both Biggs and Woodworth disagreed with Goodrich on this point, but on most other matters, including the adding of a classical Positiv division, the use of "tracker touch," and the avoidance of borrowed stops in the Pedal, the three advisors were basically in agreement. By the end of the summer they and Harrison were coming to grips with such details as whether the console should be on an elevator, whether the old case front should be altered, and what the pitch of the organ should be.

Finally, on September 27, 1948, the contract for Aeolian-Skinner's Opus 1134 was signed. The final stoplist was not too different from the first one proposed. A number of ranks from the old Hutchings were re-used, and Biggs got his 32' Pedal reed—a Contra Bombarde. During the year that the organ was in building, considerable interest was generated among the organ cognoscenti. Albert Schweitzer paid a visit to Boston and was taken to the workshop to see the instrument, where he autographed a piece of wood inside the console. No small part of the musical community's interest in the organ had to do with the fact that its completion was to coincide with the bicentenary, in 1950, of the death of J. S. Bach. It was also to be featured at the national convention of the American Guild of Organists in the same year.

Completion of the instrument actually occurred in the fall of 1949, and it was inaugurated in a special concert on November 14, the proceeds of which

Albert Schweitzer at the Germanic Museum, 1949

were donated to Schweitzer's African hospital. Charles Munch, a friend of Schweitzer's and a fellow Alsatian, was the conductor, and Biggs was the featured soloist. In addition to solo works, the program included Haydn's Organ Concerto in C major; Hindemith's Concerto for organ, brass, and woodwinds; and Poulenc's Concerto for organ, strings, and kettle drums.

The concert was a standing-room-only success, and critical acclaim was high. Paul Stevens of the *Boston Herald* reported that "The playing of the Hindemith composition brought enthusiastic audience response, but it paled by comparison with the truly great ovation Biggs received by demonstrating his virtuosity in three succeeding Bach compositions." Harold Rogers of the *Christian Science Monitor* thought the organ a bit loud, but praised the "tremendous power and brilliance" with which Biggs played a Bach Toccata. John William Riley of the *Boston Daily Globe* nominated the concert as the outstanding musical event of the season.

Thanks to the thoughtful planning of Biggs and Harrison, the Boston Symphony Hall organ was one of the most versatile concert hall organs in the country, and it was a model for subsequent instruments in other halls. In the

Charles Munch, Biggs, and G. Donald Harrison at Symphony Hall, Boston, 1950

Boston Symphony Orchestra program booklet, Biggs pointed out that all possible uses of the organ, including broadcasting and recording, were taken into account in the design process. The "classic" concept, the balanced chorus, and the full organ effect were mentioned, but so were the softer "Romantic" stops such as the Viola Pomposa. Biggs also noted that "no stops—for example the Hautbois or the Trumpet—aim to imitate their orchestral namesakes [for] it would be inappropriate and indeed folly to introduce imitative stops into any organ that shares a hall with an orchestra." Indeed, how could the organ take its place among the other instruments if it did not maintain its own identity? While all stops must have individual character, "they merge their individualities into the full ensemble, which is, after all, an organ's chief glory."

In 1976, more than a quarter century after the Symphony Hall organ was built, Biggs discussed concert hall organ design in general, and the Symphony Hall organ in particular, in a telephone conversation with the organ builder Charles Fisk, who noted down many of Biggs's comments. Although his tastes in many things had changed by that time, Biggs felt that there were some basic things about concert hall organs that remained constant and ought not be ignored. He still found the Symphony Hall specification serviceable if it were stripped of some of its "characterless stops," and he made special mention of the four-stop Bombarde division (reeds at 16', 8', and 4', with a six-rank mixture), calling it "extremely good" and very useful. As to consoles, the detached and reversed type was best, and the use of mirrors was bad—"good visibility of the conductor" was important. An enclosed division was necessary, also as many combination pistons as possible, because "conductors never understand you aren't flexible." A crescendo pedal and a sforzando piston were likewise considered essential. The Symphony Hall organ had all these things, and by the time of his conversation with Fisk, Biggs had had ample experience in their use.

Throughout the rest of his tenure as official Boston Symphony organist, Biggs tried to have at least one major work involving the organ included in every season. After the introduction of the new instrument to the organ world at the 1950 American Guild of Organists convention, the local chapter, with the assistance and cooperation of Biggs, sponsored a regular series of Symphony Hall organ recitals. It ran for several years and featured a number of notable players, including, of course, Biggs.

Biggs's involvement with concert hall organs—encouraging their procurement as well as advising on their design—by no means ended with the Symphony Hall instrument. Because Biggs played so many concerts with orchestras throughout the country, his advice was frequently asked, willingly given, and often taken. His zeal in this regard never slackened, and toward the end of his life he was outspokenly involved in the controversy surrounding an organ that had been donated to Carnegie Hall and refused.

10 | *Exclusive Artist for Columbia*

> My first experience of recording for Columbia began in a
> giant snow storm. A session at St. Paul's Chapel, 125th Street in
> New York, coincided with the great blizzard of 1948. The city
> came to a standstill. It was perfect for us. The music threaded its
> way via special cable under the side-walks of New York to the
> mid-town Columbia studios, where it was cut directly on to a
> platter.

The chapel mentioned in Biggs's reminiscent account (which appeared in 1976 in the *Bicentennial Tracker*) was on the campus of Columbia University. It contained a new 70-stop Aeolian-Skinner organ of five manual divisions with a large and virtually independent Pedal division. This organ embodied many of G. Donald Harrison's most advanced concepts of voicing and tonal design and was housed in a building of excellent acoustical properties. Thanks to the silence afforded by the traffic-stopping snowstorm, the conditions were nearly perfect for the making of Biggs's first recording on the Columbia label, a five-disc album comprising four large Bach works. "The only mishap occurred when a hardy individual, seeking shelter from the storm, entered the chapel, stamped the snow from his boots, and sneezed. It's still on the record, for there was no editing in those 78 rpm days."

The "78 rpm days" were nearly over, however, for record companies were already experimenting with the new "long-playing" microgroove records. The Bach album was issued in March 1948, and in December of the same year it was re-issued as a single 33 1/3 rpm disc, Biggs's first. Since many record buyers were still using their old equipment, Columbia released many recordings in both the old and the new form until 1950.

Biggs had a strong commitment to the medium of the phonograph record. The idea of his records whirling around on hundreds of "gramophones" (as he persisted in calling them) was every bit as pleasing to him as the thought of the thousands of radios that received his broadcasts every Sunday morning. And one could play a record whenever and as often as one wanted—altogether a delightful means of gaining converts to the cause of good organ music.

The road to Biggs's quarter-century career with Columbia had been educational and rewarding if not entirely smooth. Having parted company with Technichord over a legal disagreement concerning royalties, Biggs spent seven fruitful years with Victor, only to be told in December 1946 that the firm planned no organ recordings at all in 1947 and 1948. But Biggs was brimming with ideas for new recordings, and when he conveyed some of them to Goddard Lieberson of Columbia's Masterworks Division a few months later, he was rewarded with a contract. Lieberson may well have seen the advantage, in the light of recent technical developments, of having a good organist on deck.

Long-playing records were then in their birth throes. Each recording company was developing its own techniques of microgroove recording, and it was obvious that the new techniques would lead to higher musical fidelity and a wider dynamic spectrum. The organ, because of its great range of color and dynamics—not to mention its complex interaction with room acoustics—had always been difficult to capture faithfully with the old 78 rpm technology. Recordings of large organs in reverberant rooms were always disappointing, although smaller organs in more intimate surroundings, such as the one in the Germanic Museum, yielded better results. For this very reason the organ was an ideal medium for showing off the advantages of the new processes, and in the battle between RCA and Columbia as to whether the former's 45 rpm system or the latter's 33 1/3 rpm system would become the standard for the trade, every bit of ammunition was needed. One cannot help but wonder what part Biggs's early Columbia releases played in the final resolution of that conflict.

Columbia certainly felt that it had the inside track with its new "LPs." In the summer of 1948 Biggs's producer, Tyler (Paul) Turner, wrote, "If you haven't already heard any LP records, you are in for a surprise. Advertising aside, they are all that is said for them—quite a revolution." Shortly afterward, Edward Wallerstein, Columbia's chairman of the board, knowing of the interest Biggs had in the technical side of things, sent him a Columbia player attachment and some of the new microgroove records. They arrived in October, and Biggs wrote to Turner that "after a bit of expert work with a soldering iron" the player was in operation. As for the records, "They are simply wonderful. Congratulations again for being first in the field."

There were a lot of differences, both obvious and subtle, between the new LPs and the old 78s. The latter had to be miked fairly close for maximum clarity, resulting in an overly intimate sound, which differed from the way an audience in a hall would normally perceive the music, and in an almost total loss of room ambience. Biggs, who was as good a listener as he was a player, realized that the new recording techniques could capture the organ sound in a more normal way.

Because he knew his Bach recordings would be issued as LPs as well as 78s, and because St. Paul's Chapel had a fair amount of resonance, Biggs put some of his new theories on microphone placement into practice with his first Columbia release. While trade journals such as *The American Organist* heaped praise on these recordings for their enriched sound, certain other publications, notably, *Musical America,* did not. Turner, who shared Biggs's feelings on the subject, was annoyed. In September 1948 he wrote to Biggs:

> Apparently, the current vogue, among critics at least, is for a bald, brash, antiseptic type of sound which no one in his right mind would choose to hear if he were in a recital hall. Imagine listening to a trumpet which was blown straight in your ear, or sitting in the middle of an orchestra. . . . If your Musical America critic could not hear the detail in the first part of the St. Anne Prelude, it would seem to me that an ear specialist might be useful.

Biggs rolled up his sleeves and jotted down some ideas for a rebuttal on what he termed the question of "to resound or not to resound":

> For about a thousand years organs have inhabited cathedrals and other spacious auditoriums, and with a consequent independence the instrument refuses to be thrust into the present day "acoustically treated" studios. Resonance is the priceless ingredient which gives the organ and its music character and splendor. The measure in which this essential quality can be transferred to records is the measure of the records' excellence.
>
> Should resonance, the most essential characteristic of the organ, be omitted on records? As the current interest in listening to organ music via records gathers momentum, what should be the ideal for transferring this magnificent musical literature to discs, and thence to the listener through his gramophone? Should resonance be cut out, or should records aim to reproduce as truly as possible actual characteristics of performance?
>
> It's quite possible, and an easy way out for the recording engineers, to record a small organ in an acoustically dead room. This has a rather limited and dry effect, totally remote from the splendor of actual performance under better acoustic conditions, and it's indicative that this method has never found favor with English or European recording companies. The grandeur of organ music cannot be put on discs in this way. Such records may have the questionable advantage of not trying the limitations of the average small phonograph. Neither, for that matter, would recordings of Wagner played by a string quartet. But that wouldn't be Wagner, and pure Bach is not necessarily sterile Bach.
>
> Add too large a period of resonance to a piano or string quartet, in actual performance or in recording, and you ruin the musical effect. But take away this cushion of resonance from the organ, in actuality or on records, and you divest the instrument and music of its essential quality and grandeur. Fortunately, with modern recording techniques, and today's phonographs, there is no need to do this.

Aside from the two obvious ingredients, talent and ambition, Biggs had other qualities that contributed to his success as a major concert and recording artist who just happened to be an organist. One was a capacity for hard work; Biggs could and did drive himself (and often those around him) to the limits of endurance and ability. In addition he had an open and inquiring mind and a very astute sense of what might or might not work. He made the best possible use of whatever opportunities and materials came to hand. Faced with the limitations of the 78 rpm record, but convinced of the importance of recording organ music, he found the Germanic Museum organ and the relatively intimate (but by no means acoustically dead) room in which it stood ideal for recording, and the result, from a technical and musical standpoint, could not be faulted.

But Biggs was also aware that this situation was not totally ideal, and when Columbia's technical advances convinced him that the time was ripe, he was ready to move his recording activities to larger instruments and more reverberant rooms. His use of the Germanic Museum for recording ended when he left Victor Records, and until his first European tour in 1954, all of Biggs's Columbia LPs were, with one exception, made on the larger organs in St. Paul's Chapel and Boston's Symphony Hall. Tyler Turner, in jacket notes written for an album of French music recorded at St. Paul's Chapel shortly after the Bach recording, showed himself to be totally in accord with Biggs:

> Perspective, proportion, the plastic hand of open space, are as necessary to the proper sound of organ tone as they are appropriate to organ music. We are fortunate today that modern methods of recording have made it possible to reproduce not only the notes which the organist plays, but also the atmosphere in which he plays them.

Time has proven that the judgment of Biggs and Turner was sound. Criticism of their "reverberant" recordings quickly died down, to be replaced by criticism of those organists who continued to record on LP in too closely miked, unnaturally sterile situations.

The Symphony Hall organ was not ready for use until the fall of 1949, but even while it was still being built, Biggs was recommending it to Turner as a recording instrument. Two more recordings, a French Romantic album and a 10″ Bach/Mendelssohn disc, were made at St. Paul's Chapel, but in 1950 Biggs realized his plans to use the brand-new Boston instrument. Because it was impossible to transmit over phone lines from Boston to the recording studio in New York, these 1950 recordings brought about another technical "first" for Columbia—the use of magnetic tape for making a master recording. The tape medium was so new that even the engineers were not completely sure how it behaved. Following the Symphony Hall sessions, the chief recording engineer hand-carried the tapes back to New York on the train, worrying all the way that they might be spoiled or erased by magnetism from the electric motors in the railway coach.

Nineteen fifty was a busy recording year for Biggs. Five albums were made, of which all but a single side were taped at Symphony Hall. Although they included the first two volumes of the Bach's Royal Instrument series, not all were for solo organ; one featured the Poulenc Concerto, which had been performed at the inauguration of the Symphony Hall organ, recorded with the Columbia Symphony (really a pick-up group) under Richard Burgin. So technically advanced was this record that a purchaser, probably not blessed with the best playback equipment, complained to Columbia about a "blemish" near the beginning of the performance. In reality the "blemish" was a soft 32' low C on the organ, faithfully captured by Columbia's best equipment. In December the last of Biggs's 78 rpm releases appeared, a two-record album of Franck works.

Recording was not the only thing that kept Biggs busy in 1950. He had always been an active supporter of the American Guild of Organists; when the Massachusetts (now Boston) chapter hosted an ambitious national convention, Biggs, as program chairman, threw himself enthusiastically into the project. Not only did he and Peggy take on the monumental task of handling all the correspondence relative to the selection and engagement of players, conductors, and lecturers, but their duties spilled over into the realm of writing publicity, laying out the program booklet, and even concocting the delightfully corny verses plugging the convention in the trade publications.

Biggs's fine hand was everywhere apparent in the program. The list of recitalists read like a Who's Who of major American organists: Arthur Poister, Ernest White, George Faxon, Robert Noehren, Catherine Crozier, Robert Owen, Alexander McCurdy, Virgil Fox, and several rising young players. The noted German organist Fritz Heitmann was engaged for a recital at Methuen Music Hall; and the choral conductors included Fred Waring, Ifor Jones, Everett Titcomb, and Theodore Marier. Biggs's friends were also evident in various roles: his pupil Mary Crowley Vivian, Oliver Daniel of Columbia Records, G. Donald Harrison, and English horn player Louis Speyer. Biggs's old producer from RCA Victor days, the witty Charles O'Connell, gave the banquet address. Biggs's own artistic contribution was a performance of Sowerby's Concerto in C major with the Boston Pops Orchestra under the direction of Arthur Fiedler.

Only the finest organs in Boston and Cambridge (mostly Aeolian-Skinners) were used for concerts; and, contrary to the practice at some conventions, electronic instruments were not officially used, even for the humblest of functions. Aeolian-Skinner installed a small two-manual unenclosed instrument (later purchased by New England Conservatory) in the ballroom of the

Biggs and Arthur Fiedler at the 1950 A.G.O. convention

Copley Plaza Hotel for concerts and workshops; and three other builders (Wicks, Estey, and Möller) were persuaded to send small sample "stock" organs to display and demonstrate. After the convention Biggs wrote to all four builders, thanking them for helping to prove that pipe organs need not be large to be effective and that "authenticity of organ tone is an essential to the presentation of great organ music." The four organs, all located in the large ballroom, also provided some not-so-great organ music in one of the un-programed lighter moments of the convention, when Biggs and three co-horts commandeered them for a four-organ rendition of "I'm Looking Over a Four Leaf Clover." Biggs is also suspected of having had a hand in a Gil-bert and Sullivan style skit entitled "The Organist Who Never, Never Lost a Chord."

In their planning of the convention, Biggs, Peggy, and their two major co-workers, Ruth Barrett Phelps and Joseph Whiteford, made the most of the new Symphony Hall organ and the fact that 1950 was the 200th anniversary of the death of J. S. Bach. They also set a standard of quality and organization that had a far-reaching influence on subsequent national conventions. The Boston event was a huge success and turned enough of a profit to establish a chapter scholarship fund.

But 1950, a year not untypical for Biggs in this period, had more activity in store. Recital engagements were scattered all over the year and were in-ternational in scope. During the spring he took part in the Toronto Bach Festival; and in August the Biggses took a trip to England, where Biggs performed the Sowerby Concerto in C in a "Proms" concert at Royal Albert Hall, gave an all-Bach recital in Westminster Abbey, and was presented with an honorary fellowship by the Royal College of Music. The couple also paid a visit to Biggs's old mentor, J. Stuart Archer, bringing him what in those postwar days of shortages and high prices was a precious and much-appreciated gift—fresh eggs.

In the closing months of the year Biggs presented a well-received series of three concerts at Symphony Hall. The second one was an all-Bach program patterned in part after the concert given by Felix Mendelssohn in Leipzig in 1840, which inspired Robert Schumann's oft-quoted appellation, "Bach's Royal Instrument." Two records in a series bearing this title were issued in 1950; a third, plus an album of concerted works entitled *Music of Jubilee*, appeared the following year. The Bach recordings received high critical acclaim, perhaps summed up by Delos Smith in the *New York World-Telegram* for April 29, 1950: "Biggs not only has a musician's sense and feeling for his instrument; he has sense and feeling for Bach. His organ is the magnificent new one in Symphony Hall, and the recording is expansive and clear."

T. Scott Buhrmann, the crusty editor of *The American Organist*, admitted in 1951 that he liked Biggs's earlier Piston, Poulenc, and Reubke recordings "too well to place anything else above them," but he enjoyed the colorful interplay between organ and instruments in *Music of Jubilee*, asking, "What more logical conclusion can we draw than that this is the way Bach liked his music to sound?" The new microgroove medium also came in for praise:

"Anyone remember the good old days when the recording companies couldn't record organ satisfactorily? They're doing it to perfection now."

Music of Jubilee was, indeed, an inspired recording; Biggs was to ring the changes on the theme of Bach's concerted music in three subsequent albums (1953, 1964, and 1976), as well as on his radio broadcasts and in recital. A reviewer in *The Gramophone*, a British publication, waxed positively poetic over the release in the April 1952 issue:

> The title is excellent: here is something to lift the spirit above the day's woes, now heavy indeed: and Oh, irony supreme, the record comes from the U.S.A. Well, I have had some of life's best pleasures there: and death should not affright him whose latest joy is Bach. No more exhilarating and caressing concert could well be given.

The writer went on to commend the "rich instrument, not over-powerful" (the Symphony Hall organ), the arrangement of the program, the "diversities of scoring and stimulus," and the instrumentation. "Here is light for the darkness to come."

With the success of their first LPs, both Biggs and his producer at Columbia were aware that they had a good thing. *A Bach Festival,* issued in 1953, was based on the same concept that had made *Music of Jubilee* such a success. In 1953 and 1954 Columbia made a brief foray into the 45 rpm field, reissuing a few excerpts from Biggs's previous 33 1/3 recordings, but the shorter discs did not prove popular with the devotees of classical music, and the experiment was soon dropped.

Between 1950 and 1953 Biggs did all his recording, both solo and concerted, at Symphony Hall, where Columbia had installed a semi-permanent recording setup. In January 1952 Biggs received a challenge from his friend Edward Flint, a trustee of Methuen Memorial Music Hall, who wrote:

> I shall not be content until you do some recording on the Methuen organ. It is just not right that with all the organ recordings now on the market, the Methuen instrument should not be represented; and who could bring it to the attention of the "record" public better than you?

Biggs was well acquainted with the organ. He had taught at the summer Organ Institute run by Arthur Howes and had given recitals on the instrument both before and after its rebuilding in 1947 by Aeolian-Skinner. He acted on Flint's suggestion by proposing a two-disc set containing music of Reubke, Liszt, and Dupré.

By June Biggs had engaged a local engineer to make some tapes, which impressed both Biggs and Turner. Biggs would have liked to have put those very tapes on wax but was prevented by problems with Columbia's union engineers. As a result it was nearly a year before Columbia could be persuaded to send personnel to Methuen to do the job. From this session came a single disc of Reubke and Liszt works, which remains one of the best recordings made on this famous organ. Biggs had lived with this music since his student days and had already recorded the Reubke *Sonata on the 94th Psalm* for Victor. The Methuen recording differs in some interesting ways from the earlier one, which was played in Harvard's Memorial Church and was quite good in its own way. The new version had both polish and vivacity, and it added to Biggs's growing store of rave record reviews. Flint was delighted and warmly thanked David Oppenheim, Columbia's music director: "For ninety years this organ has been a headache to its various owners; and if tomorrow it should go up in smoke I should feel less badly than I would have a fortnight ago."

The recording may have relieved some of the trustees' headaches, but its release caused one in other quarters. Throughout his career Biggs wrote most of his own his own jacket notes and even assisted in the design of the covers. For the cover of the Methuen record he had found an elegant photograph of the organ before its most recent rebuilding, and in the notes he had given the stoplist and a brief history of the instrument. The original builder, Walcker, was mentioned, but there was no reference to the 1947 rebuilding or to Aeolian-Skinner, which had executed the work. Columbia very shortly heard from Aeolian-Skinner's lawyer. While the matter was something of a tempest in a teapot, it left some bad feelings and cost both Biggs and Columbia in legal fees. In the end it was simply agreed that credit would be given to Aeolian-Skinner on the jacket the next time the Methuen organ was recorded by Columbia. There seem to have been plans for another Methuen release to follow on the heels of the Liszt/Reubke record, but either not enough of the unreleased material came up to Biggs's standards or Columbia was unwilling to send engineers to Methuen again, for it never materialized. Biggs did keep his word, however, and the next time he made a recording on the Methuen organ credit was duly given in the jacket notes to G. Donald Harrison. But that was in 1976—twenty years after Harrison's death and several years after Aeolian-Skinner had closed its doors for good.

Three subsequent Symphony Hall recordings were released after the Methuen album, in 1956 and 1957, but there is evidence that they had been taped at an earlier date and kept "in the icebox" for later release. Biggs was never to record on the Symphony Hall organ again. He later remarked to Charles Fisk that there was "only just so much mileage in an organ," meaning recording mileage. He had gotten all that he could out of the Germanic Museum and St. Paul's Chapel organs and was perhaps feeling the same way about the Symphony Hall instrument, which had gone quite a few recording miles in its first five years of life. In some jacket notes written in 1982 for

Biggs in Methuen Memorial Hall, early 1950s

Titanic Records, Fisk expanded on Biggs's comment: "For each of the organs [Biggs] recorded, whether new or antique, had its day, was caught in the penumbra of his inextinguishable limelight, danced for him *his* dance, then fell back into the shadows as he moved on." And in the mid-1950s Biggs was indeed moving on. An important phase of his career was ending, shortly to be superseded by another quite different, but of equal or greater import for the musical world.

11 | A Portable Organ and a Glass Armonica

It may be a little organ, but I have big plans for it!
—E. Power Biggs to Herman Schlicker, 1952

Few people had a better opportunity than Biggs to feel the pulse of the American organ-building world. His popularity as a recitalist peaked during the 1950s, and of the hundreds of recitals he gave nationwide during this period, many were dedications and openings of new instruments. Keen observer that he was, and possessed of more than the average organist's interest in what made an organ tick tonally and mechanically, he was quick to note the trends exemplified by some of this newer work and always generous in his praise of good tone and design.

During the 1930s and 1940s the Aeolian-Skinner Company, under the leadership of G. Donald Harrison, was the bellwether of the industry, and from its soot-stained brick factory in Dorchester came some of the most distinguished and innovative organs of that era. But the 1950s saw the emergence of other firms whose work Biggs began watching with interest. Although Walter Holtkamp of Cleveland had made some rather bold innovations in the 1930s and 1940s—Rückpositivs, insistence on unchambered placement, and the use of slider windchests—his work remained largely unrecognized by the eastern moguls until the early 1950s, when he began to gain a following among avant-garde organists such as Melville Smith, Arthur Poister, Robert Noehren, and H. Frank Bozyan. Their support led to Holtkamp's securing prestigious contracts at Syracuse University, Yale University, Oberlin College, and Massachusetts Institute of Technology, which in turn gained him a following among the younger organists.

Likewise stepping out of the shadows was Herman Schlicker of Buffalo. Trained in Alsace and Denmark, he emigrated to the United States as a young man in 1925 and set up his own workshop in Buffalo in 1932. But again it was not until the 1950s that Schlicker became nationally visible and began to collect his own coterie of partisans, particularly in Lutheran circles, where certain influential organists were embracing the "neo-baroque" concepts of the German *Orgelbewegung*. Biggs had concertized on some of the newest instruments by Holtkamp and Schlicker and noted with approval the tonal direction these firms were taking. When Biggs's advice concerning organ builders was solicited in the early 1950s, he usually recommended only three: Aeolian-Skinner, Holtkamp, and Schlicker.

Meanwhile, relations between Biggs and Harrison had cooled somewhat. In late 1952 Biggs had requested some tonal alterations in the Germanic Museum organ. In particular he was dissatisfied with the Principal in the Great and suggested that it be replaced by something he termed an "English Salicional." Just what he had in mind is not certain; perhaps this was the name of a stop he had admired in another Harrison organ. What he got was a standard Viola da Gamba, and he did not care for that any more than for the old Principal. At the same time he also ordered a 16' bass extension for the Quintaten, the installation of which seems to have been delayed. Early in 1953 Harrison sent Biggs a bill for the work, and Biggs complained: "I'd be glad to pay for anything that represents progress for the organ, but its shortcomings won't be cured in this way. I should think that the company would have the artistic interest to improve the instrument, and it's too bad if this isn't so." He also complained about the mechanical condition of the new Symphony Hall organ: "we can hardly depend on it when scheduling broadcasts or a recording session. On practically every occasion we have had difficulties."

Biggs's letter had an edge of exasperation to it; Harrison's reply had a somewhat wounded tone: "Some of the things you say may be justified. However, other things hurt me not a little." Harrison agreed that if Biggs did not like the replacement for the Principal they should get together and decide on something else: "I certainly agree that you must have exactly what you want in this regard." As for the Symphony Hall organ, Harrison allowed that while there had indeed been troubles, 90 percent of them concerned the console cables, which the builders were planning to replace with a newer type. He also made a point of criticizing "the way the console is banged up and pushed around" by the stagehands, since the elevator that both Biggs and Harrison had hoped for had never materialized.

The rift between Biggs and Harrison continued to widen, however, and in the summer of 1953 Biggs arranged to have the maintenance of the Symphony Hall, Tanglewood, and Museum organs turned over to Roy E. H. Carlson, whose subsequent work, particularly in tuning, seems to have met with Biggs's approval. Harrison, for his part, probably did not fail to notice that Biggs was recommending other builders. By fall the gossip was on the organ fraternity grapevine, and Biggs received a fatherly reprimand from Walter Holtkamp:

> Jimmy, me boy,—there is too much talk going around about the parting of the ways of one E.P.B. and G.D.H. I don't like it. You both have too much meaning for each other and together, you have too much meaning for the American organ scene to so upset your public. If I may, I would suggest an arms around the shoulder picture in Father Gruenstein's paper. You are clever. You can contrive it.

Holtkamp's conciliatory snapshot unfortunately never materialized, in *The Diapason* or elsewhere, and the incident of the Methuen jacket notes in 1954 only widened the breach. What little interaction there was between the two after this time was not particularly cordial. In June 1956 Harrison was felled by a heart attack while finishing the organ in St. Thomas's Church in New York. Into his place as tonal director of Aeolian-Skinner stepped the leading shareholder, Joseph Whiteford. Biggs, among others, felt he was ill equipped to inherit Harrison's mantle—an opinion shortly to be confirmed by the beginning of the firm's decline. But even before Harrison's death Aeolian-Skinner's name had ceased to appear in Biggs's recommendations to organ purchasers.

For a concert organist, practice is both a necessity and a problem. Biggs had access to two good Aeolian-Skinner instruments, in the Germanic Museum and in the Harvard Congregational Church, but use of the first was restricted by the Museum's hours, and the church was farther away. At home, he relied heavily on piano practice, having acquired a good Steinway for that purpose, and worked out his pedaling on an electrified Estey reed organ.

In the spring of 1952 Biggs dedicated a large Schlicker organ in St. Paul's Church in Buffalo, with which he was considerably impressed. At the same time he visited Schlicker's factory and noted with interest a small and compact practice organ being built for a local university. The more he thought about it, the more interested he became. In May he wrote Schlicker, "Be sure to let me know when the little two manual with pedal practice organ is finished! We want to come right out to Buffalo to see and hear this."

The instrument in question was a "unit" organ, in which certain ranks of pipes are made to do duty for more than one stop or pitch, and of course it had electric action. But its stoplist and voicing followed neo-baroque lines, it was unenclosed, and its visual design, while compact and functional, was not unattractive. Biggs, with typical caution, wanted to see how the prototype would work out, but it is evident that he had decided that he wanted something similar for himself. By the fall of 1952 he had seen and been impressed by Schlicker's first attempt and had placed his order. Biggs's instrument was to be a little larger than the one for the University of Buffalo, but the major difference was that Biggs wanted his made so it could be easily dismantled and reassembled. With his usual ingenuity, Biggs had decided that besides serving as a practice organ at home, it could do double duty as a portable concert instrument, thus extending his range to places where there was no permanently installed pipe organ.

Biggs was conversant with the technical and tonal aspects of organs, and as the work progressed, his suggestions found their way to Schlicker's desk with a fair amount of regularity. The pitch was to be higher than A=440, to enable the organ to be used with Symphony orchestras, most of which tended to play sharp (even in 1952 the Boston Symphony Orchestra was playing at A=444). Also on Biggs's list was tracker touch—"just a very slight resistance, of course, to approximate the sense of playing a larger instrument." By December he was addressing the details of the pipework. Schlicker wondered whether the organ should be scaled for a small room or a concert hall. Biggs suggested that it be

> designed for concert use (both solo and with instruments) in small auditoriums, and for broadcasting and recording. Its use as a practice instrument in a small room is secondary, and one can always practice on just a few stops. However, quality rather than quantity is the idea, and I picture the instrument as having a certain beautiful softness of effect, rather than volume.

He hoped that the reed stop (Ranket) could be available on both manual and pedal at more than one pitch, and that the Gedeckt could be extended down from 16′ pitch so that a 16′ flue would also be available on the Pedal.

By early spring of 1953 Biggs was urging Schlicker to move ahead with the design work of the organ, which in the meantime had acquired an additional reed stop and, at Schlicker's suggestion, 16′ extensions on the Great as well as the Pedal. By summer the pipes were being voiced, Biggs had made an inspection trip, and concerts involving the organ were being planned for the following spring. Still later the Bourdon unit, now fully detachable for instances (such as continuo playing) where the Pedal might not be needed, had been stretched from 44 to 56 notes to allow for a 4′ extension. By December the organ had been christened "The Cambridge Portative" and was being measured for a specially constructed trailer to be hauled by Biggs's Studebaker. In the same month it was played with its "twin" at the University of Buffalo in a concert that was also broadcast over CBS radio.

Biggs lost no time in publicizing his new acquisition. Trade journals were notified, an article appeared in the *Christian Science Monitor,* and a photograph of the portative accompanied Biggs's recently written article for the *Encyclopedia Brittanica.* Biggs was enthusiastic about the new instrument's potential; writing to Schlicker in February 1954, he predicted a bright future for the design: "I think it's very evident that you could sell the Portatives like hot cakes if you made a brochure and sent it to all colleges and schools of music in the country." Shortly after this the Cambridge Portative was packed into its trailer and taken to Washington, D.C., where it was heard on March 5 in a concert of chamber music for organ and strings at the Coolidge Auditorium. Biggs's program notes sum up the rationale of the organ's design:

> Standing in the open the organ gains in "presence"—both aural and visual. Seventy-six of the pedal pipes, grouped together into two units, serve as a reflecting shell for the instrument. The instrument may be disassembled and transported anywhere for concerts, thus affording a new flexibility and musical usefulness for the organ.

The "76" pedal pipes may have been a misprint; there were actually only 56. In describing the organ, the *Washington Evening Star* reviewer added a folksy touch that probably tickled Biggs's well-developed funny bone: "The large pipes [are] enclosed in a reflecting shell in the rear and the pretty small ones out front [are] like curios in a whatnot."

The same reviewer, in a more serious vein, revealed not only a fair knowledge of what was going on in the organ world but also a sensitivity to what Biggs was trying to convey musically. He liked the new organ's crispness and clarity, the "marvelous almost touchable quality" of its sounds, and the "brilliance and intimacy" of Biggs's performance of the Mozart "Epistle" Sonatas. "The organist," he wrote, "seemed a part of the proceedings, not like a player in a large church who presses the keys and after a lapse of time listens to a reflection of the music he has made." But the reviewer was disappointed with the one work (Piston's 1944 Partita, originally commissioned by Elizabeth Sprague Coolidge) that was played on the Auditorium's old Skinner organ: "The hollow and muffled sound of the organ seemed to be coming from the green room, rather like the ghost of Hamlet's father on strike." Since Biggs never cared for that particular organ, he probably could not disagree with the critic, especially since the comparison helped to put the Portative in an even more favorable light. Apparently the Auditorium's administrators were themselves finding the Skinner organ something of a liability, for a year later they sold it to a Catholic church in Georgetown.

Shortly after the Washington concert, Biggs embarked on a three-month European tour, one of the souvenirs of which was a more portable portative, a little one-stop Steinmeyer instrument of limited musical use, but ornamental, and handy for some of Biggs's occasional illustrated lectures. In August 1954 Biggs took the Cambridge Portative to Canada for a well-reviewed concert. The instrument spent the rest of the year as a practice organ, occupying half of the large double parlor in the Biggs's home; but in 1955 it went on the road again and was played in June by Biggs at a regional convention of the

Biggs with the Cambridge
Portative, 1954

Biggs with a model of a
hydraulis on the
"Omnibus" show, 1956

American Guild of Organists in Reading, Pennsylvania. On this and many subsequent occasions the Portative was to prove the validity of its original concept by providing a suitable organ in halls where the only alternative would have been an electronic instrument. It also gave Biggs additional ammunition when it came to answering inquiries from small churches that did not think they could afford a real organ, for the instrument cost little more than a suitably sized electronic substitute.

Biggs was in a position to know the going price of the Portative because, as his correspondence with Schlicker proves, he paid it in full. Rumors were being circulated to the contrary, however, and Biggs became highly indignant upon hearing insinuations that his endorsement of Schlicker was due to the Portative's having been a gift. The source of the rumor appears to have been Aeolian-Skinner partisans, and Biggs thought it a matter for his lawyers. He wrote to them in May 1955, stating firmly that he had "always paid full professional price for all instruments, including our present Schlicker, also the Aeolian-Skinner in the Germanic Museum, and contributed a thousand dollars ... towards the Aeolian-Skinner organ in Symphony Hall." The episode blew over quickly, but it did nothing to improve relations between Biggs and Aeolian-Skinner, which, intentionally or not, had irritated Biggs further by the unauthorized use of his picture in an advertising brochure. Actually it was an old picture, depicting Biggs, Harrison, and Albert Schweitzer at the factory in more congenial days. Had the former good feelings still existed, Biggs probably would not have objected to its use.

In December 1955 Biggs made his first television appearance with the Portative. He braved the wintry weather to tow it to Montreal, where he appeared with the CBC orchestra on CBC-TV's "Concert Hour." In February 1956 he was in New York for a solo telecast of his own on the popular "Omnibus" program, sponsored by the Ford Foundation. In that half-hour special, Biggs, with all the stage presence and aplomb of a seasoned TV personality, reviewed the whole history of the organ and its music in laymen's terms. Sharing the stage with him were the Cambridge Portative, on which he demonstrated the various families of organ tone, and a variety of props, including an assortment of organ pipes, a syrinx, the little Steinmeyer portative, and a half-scale model of a hydraulis borrowed from the Boston Museum of Fine Arts. The script was written by Biggs himself, who also supplied some of the graphics along with taped excerpts from his recordings of European organs.

Biggs and Schlicker collaborated on two other projects during the 1950s. Both had their creative and adventurous elements; and while one of them, with some qualifications, might have been called a success, the other was almost a total disaster.

The first of these projects involved the rebuilding, in 1957, of a late nineteenth-century tracker-action organ housed in a handsome eighteenth-century case in Boston's famous Old North Church. A gift for musical purposes had been made to the church by Amelia Peabody, and Charles Russell Peck, then vicar of the church, approached Biggs for advice. Since the amount of the gift was insufficient to purchase a new organ, Biggs recommended that the old one be thoroughly rebuilt by Schlicker. Schlicker's firm at that time was one of the few in the country that had some familiarity with new tracker-action organs, but it had only limited experience in rebuilding old ones. It was agreed that a new and enlarged Pedal division was essential, and although the original mechanical action of the manuals was retained, the new Pedal had electric action. The Tenor-C Swell windchest was extended to full compass, but no wholesale rebuilding of either of the two manual chests was attempted, thus some serious faults in the form of ill-fitting sliders and cracked table-boards remained. Several tonal changes were made, but attempts at revoicing some of the nineteenth-century pipework in the neo-baroque style were less than successful. A rather crude electro-pneumatic combination action and a unified Quintadena rank on a separate electric-action chest, playable on all divisions, added to the confused eclecticism of the result.

Despite its faults, the Old North project was a noteworthy breakthrough in a period when the standard treatment of similar organs was still routine electrification or worse. Biggs dedicated the completed organ on June 9, 1958, and he later featured the instrument on a broadcast. This exposure, plus good publicity in the trade journals and newspapers, gave needed encouragement to both organists and builders who were leaning in the direction of a more sympathetic treatment of old American organs. Biggs chose to ignore the hybrid nature of the rebuilt Old North instrument when he stated his views on organ action in an article in the *Christian Science Monitor* for June 29: "The tracker action makes an organ a musical instrument. Electricity makes it a mechanical instrument."

The other project in which Biggs and Schlicker were involved was in many ways a quixotic one. It grew out of Biggs's interests in Americana and musical technology, plus the coincidence, in 1956, of the 200th anniversary of Mozart's birth and the 250th anniversary of Benjamin Franklin's birth. Biggs put the two together and came up with the Glass Armonica, a musical instrument invented by Franklin and written for by Mozart.

The idea of extracting music from glasses was not original with Franklin. No one knows who first discovered that rubbing a wet finger around the rim of a wineglass will produce a pleasing musical sound, or that a series of glasses can be "tuned" to produce a musical scale by varying the amount of liquid in them. By the eighteenth century specially made and tuned sets of graduated glasses had been fitted in wooden cases so that they could be played by a single performer. And such performers began to materialize, to the delight of novelty-seeking audiences. One of the most notorious of these virtuosi was the Irishman Richard Pockrich, whom Franklin apparently heard perform in England.

The manner in which this sort of glass instrument had to be played placed limitations on the speed and complexity of the music performed. On his return to America, Franklin conceived an improvement on the instrument whose sounds had so charmed him. The glasses were replaced by glass bowls of graduated size, nested inside each other and mounted on a spindle turned by a treadle. This construction allowed the compass of the instrument to be increased by as much as three octaves. Since the edges of the bowls were closer together and it was they, rather than the fingers, that went around, performance of more sophisticated music was possible, and serious composers were attracted to the improved instrument.

By the end of the eighteenth century Franklin's invention had become more popular in England and on the Continent than in his native country, and it was only a matter of time before attempts were made to provide it with a keyboard. In Europe, at least, this seems to have met with some success. A blind girl, Marianne Kirchgessner, emerged as a virtuoso on the keyboard version, which now went by Franklin's Italianate sobriquet of "Armonica." Marianne's playing attracted the attention of Mozart, who wrote a solo and a quintet for her, plus a third work that was never completed. Beethoven, Naumann, Martini, and others contributed to the growing repertoire, but, as Biggs observed in some program notes written in 1956, "the gathering thunders of nineteenth century romanticism gradually blotted out the soft and subtle sounds of the glasses," and the instrument faded into obscurity. At the height of its popularity there were a fair number of armonicas around, with and without keyboards, but glass is a fragile substance, and the mortality rate was high. One armonica was accidentally dropped following a successful concert; another was knocked over by an unhappy sow; yet another was shattered by a falling painting. The few survivors now rest silently in museums.

With the Mozart and Franklin anniversaries approaching, Biggs thought it a good time to break that silence. His voluminous correspondence and library research began early in 1955, and one of his first discoveries was that while Franklin's own keyboardless Armonica still existed in a Philadelphia residence, not one keyboard version or fragment thereof survived anywhere. This, of course, was the instrument Biggs was most interested in, since only with a keyboard could some of the more complex music of Mozart be played. When hopes of finding a restorable antique faded, Biggs persuaded the American Academy of Arts and Sciences to sponsor the construction of one, and the

Academy in turn interested the Franklin Savings Bank in financing the project. One of the Academy's members, Harlow Shapley of the Harvard Observatory, caught Biggs's enthusiasm and became a willing accomplice to his research and fund-raising activities.

With funding secured, Herman Schlicker was engaged to devise and build the playing mechanism, and the Corning Glass Company was to make the hand-blown glass bowls. The future of Biggs as armonica virtuoso looked rosy, and he began collecting scores of works that had been written for or played on eighteenth-century armonicas. As word got around, there were offers of concerts, and Columbia showed mild interest in a recording.

Work got under way in the spring of 1955, with the deadline for completion a year away. By November the glasses were finished, and Biggs and Schlicker went to the Corning plant the following month to assist in their tuning. By January the glasses were being fitted to the mechanism in Schlicker's shop, and the problems began showing up. Corning's glasses seem to have been partly at fault. When Schlicker visited the original Franklin instrument in Philadelphia he found that the old glasses were thinner, especially in the treble, and thus easier to make speak. Corning's glasses were also somewhat irregular in shape. In addition, the rubber mounting turned out to be too soft and had to be replaced with wood; and it was discovered that the smaller glasses had to be rotated faster than the larger ones. Finding a suitable covering for the mechanical "fingers" that played the glasses from the keyboard also proved problematic. Wet pigskin and dry rubber gave the best (though slightly differing) effects, but neither was as good as human fingers. And of course there was that nemesis of all musical glasses, breakage. Biggs was still optimistic but, as he confided to John Burchard, president of the Academy, he was also "touching wood, holding on tight, and keeping my fingers crossed."

A concert featuring the new armonica and (fortunately, as it turned out) other instruments was scheduled for April 11, 1956 at the Kresge Auditorium of the Massachusetts Institute of Technology. By March 24 there was a note of urgency, even desperation, in Biggs's correspondence with Schlicker. Biggs had planned to come to Buffalo on the 28th "to record a few sounds" for a broadcast, but "as far as a fair chance for me to learn how to play the instrument—we're way past it!" The Academy wanted the instrument on hand by April 3 in order to unveil it to the press. If they could not have it by then, "the concert will have to take place without it, and our work will have come to nothing, for the anniversary occasion will have passed."

The instrument arrived in time, and the concert went on, a program of works by Franklin and Mozart, performed by Biggs, six members of the Boston Symphony Orchestra, and the popular tenor, Roland Hayes. Biggs wisely brought the Cambridge Portative, on which he played not only Mozart's Fantasia in F and four of the "Epistle" Sonatas, but also the armoni-

Biggs trying his hand at glass blowing in the Corning glass factory, 1956. Photo courtesy Corning Glass Works.

ca part of Mozart's Adagio and Rondo for Armonica, flute, oboe, viola, and cello. Although Biggs gave a preliminary demonstration of the principle of "glass music" on eight tuned glasses, the armonica itself was used only for three "Divertimenti"—a Minuet from an armonica tutor, an Irish folksong that had been a favorite of Captain Pockrich, and Mozart's short Adagio for Glass Armonica. The tone of the new armonica was wobbly and erratic and was frequently accompanied by gratuitous squeaks and scrapes. As one of the students later observed, it "wasn't quite a flop, but almost!"

The discouraging performance at the concert may have had something to do with the Franklin Savings Bank's sudden loss of interest in the project, leaving the Academy and Biggs to hunt up a donor to make up the deficit caused by Schlicker's extra costs in trying to perfect the mechanism. Biggs and

Shapley were discouraged, but not quite ready to give up. Just enough publicity had been given the experiment to generate requests from orchestras, chamber music groups, radio, and television for concerts involving the armonica. "Unfortunately", wrote Biggs to Ralph Burhoe, another Academy official, "in every case the answer has had to be no, because the one test of success is whether the Mozart Adagio and Rondo can be played on the Glass Armonica!" He still had hopes that it might be perfected, though, for, "It's certain that if the Glass Armonica were successful it would fill a unique niche, and have continuing interest and use over a number of years."

In the summer of 1956, Biggs received a request from his old friend Harold Spivacke of the Library of Congress for the use of the armonica in a December program linked to the Mozart/Franklin anniversaries. Biggs doubted that the instrument would be any improved by then and candidly outlined the problems: the glasses themselves were too thick and not perfectly circular, and more research was needed on the "finger" material. Between $3,000 and $4,000 had already been expended on the instrument, and while the Academy hoped to coerce Corning into making a new set of glasses at no cost, Corning decided that it wanted nothing more to do with the project. The harpsichord makers Hubbard and Dowd suggested making a striking mechanism to operate the stationary glasses, but since the musical result would have been more that of a glassichord or celesta, this idea was quickly abandoned.

In a last desperate attempt to salvage the project, the armonica was turned over to a "think tank" of MIT engineering students. Concentrating first on sound production, the students found that their fingers, dipped in vinegar, still produced the best effect. Other substances and means of exciting the glasses, from violin bows to electronics, were tried without success. Nothing very conclusive emerged, and most of the students felt that the contraption was better as Franklin had left it, without the keyboard. One was optimistic enough to suggest that "With unlimited funds, it would serve the memory of Franklin well to establish a research project to investigate the use of different bowl and exciting materials and build an accurately engineered Armonica." But the "unlimited funds" were nowhere to be seen. In 1958, at Biggs's suggestion, Shapley approached Henry Ford II regarding the possibility that the glass-blower at Greenfield Village might be able to produce better bowls than Corning had, but nothing came of that either.

In 1965, answering an inquiry from Leonard Labaree, editor of the Franklin papers, Biggs gave a short and rather dispassionate account of the armonica venture. While the word "failure" was not in his vocabulary, Biggs did have to admit that "our experiment was quite inconclusive," and, with regard to his performance of Mozart's Adagio, K. 356, "one cannot claim that the tone did any sort of justice to the music." His vision of what might have been was still intact, though, and at the end of his letter he wrote, a bit wistfully,

> Mozart's *Adagio and Rondo*, K. 617, which we had hoped to give with such a flourish, was played on the flute stops of the organ. The sound of a delicate flute stop, incidentally, rather resembles that of a glass armonica. Though it lacks, of course, the effect of coming from nowhere, and the slow dying away into silence, which is a quite magical effect with the glasses.

12 | *Europe*

> Every instrument you approach is different. A pianist can be reasonably satisfied that most pianos will be about the same. An organist has to climb up to his instrument; he's got to make friends with it.

Biggs made these comments in May 1954, in an interview with a London correspondent for *Time* magazine. He was on the first leg of a backbreaking three-month concert and recording tour that was to take him through a dozen countries, from Portugal to Iceland, and give him the opportunity to make many new friends—both organs and people.

The trip was at first intended solely as a concert tour. But David Oppenheim of Columbia Records had a "brilliant idea," as Biggs was later to recall. He suggested that the Biggses take with them "a small tape recorder, and let it run while you play." They thought that a lovely idea, visualizing a tidy little "miracle-box, about the size of a portable typewriter." While such machines are now a reality, they were not in 1954, and the Columbia engineers soon demolished this pleasant fantasy with "some recording facts of life." As a result, Biggs and Peggy found themselves embarking with 500 pounds of excess baggage in the form of tape recorders, generators, cables, and microphones. It was a lot of extra work, and it was definitely a gamble, for no American had done such a thing before. More than a gamble, it was an adventure, and Biggs had a decided taste for adventures.

The last notes of the Easter Sunday broadcast had barely died away when Biggs and Peggy were on their way to the airport bound for Lisbon, where Biggs gave a late-night recital at the National Conservatory. He then had a few days to make friends with some 200-year-old Iberian organs—"very playable, though often in need of a good tuning," as he later observed in a *Diapason* article about the trip. He was charmed by the gentle foundation stops and the fiery horizontal reeds.

From Lisbon they went to London, where Biggs gave a recital on an "old friend"—the Westminster Abbey organ—and was introduced to some new ones, a pair of small but pleasing antiques by Willis and Snetzler, recently

112

Biggs at Westminster Abbey, 1954

restored by the London builder Noel Mander. In London and in several other places Biggs programed the Sowerby Symphony in G. The London critics were not enthusiastic over its dissonances, but at least they did not mistake the piece for jazz, as a Norwegian reviewer did. Biggs also gave concerts at Leeds and in Birmingham City Hall, where his old teacher, G. D. Cunningham ("of whom I am proud to have been a pupil"), had for many years been municipal organist.

The next stop was Holland, in tulip season. The beauty of the countryside was not wasted on the two travelers, as they journeyed to The Hague for a concerted program. But it was the monumental old organs of Amsterdam, Leyden, and Gouda that made the most profound impression on Biggs: "What a tremendous revelation these Dutch organs are! Here surely in the organs of Holland . . . is the great tradition of organ building in its clearest form." Biggs was moved by the thought that the steep steps he climbed to reach the organ gallery of Amsterdam's Oude Kerk were the very steps trod by Jan Pieterszoon Sweelinck. "How magnificent are the sonorities of Sweelinck's music as heard in his own church! One seems never to have heard the music before."

In Holland Biggs met for the first time the organ builder Dirk A. Flentrop, whom he saw as an inheritor of the tradition he was rapidly learning to admire. This meeting would have far-reaching consequences for Biggs and his audiences, and indeed for Flentrop himself. Both old and new Dutch organs possessed qualities Biggs had not encountered before, in either England or America. The articulate, unforced voicing of the pipes made an indelible impression on him, as did the sensitivity of the mechanical key actions and the reverberation of the massive old masonry churches. The trip was truly turning out to be a voyage of discovery, and Biggs soaked up every new sight and sound like a sponge. He also made certain to document as much as he could for future reference—the sights with his camera, the sounds with his tape recorder.

Across the border in northern Germany, Biggs gave a recital on the great Schnitger organ in the church of St. Jakobi in Hamburg. The instrument, which had recently been taken out of its wartime storage place, was temporarily set up in a side aisle of the church while restoration of the organ gallery was being completed. Biggs then visited two more of Arp Schnitger's masterpieces, in Steinkirchen and in Neuenfelde, where Schnitger is buried and where his house still stands. Biggs did not fail to observe that here at least was one town that honored its organists and organ-builders, even to the point of naming streets for them.

Schnitger country led to Buxtehude country—Lübeck and Lüneburg. In the latter city Biggs played an organ that Bach, presumably, "had a whack at" when a student there in 1700. From there the route led to Berlin, where Biggs gave a concert in the Martin Luther Memorial Church in memory of the recently deceased Fritz Heitmann, whom Biggs had come to know and respect during his visit to Boston in 1950. On the plane from Berlin to Frankfort Biggs caught a glimpse (from a mile up) of the red-roofed village of Eisenach, Bach's birthplace. Heidelberg was next, then Nuremberg, where Biggs proved that he still remembered the servicemen of his radio audience: after completing a recital on the large modern organ in the Cathedral, he played another at the Army base—on a chaplain's folding reed organ.

Then it was off to Scandinavia, with concerts in Denmark on organs ranging from the 1610 Compenius organ in Frederiksborg Castle (Biggs's first encounter with the old meantone tuning) to modern Frobenius and Marcussen instruments. In Trondheim, Norway, Biggs concertized in the world's north-ernmost cathedral, St. Olaf's. The scenery was breathtaking, and "the weather was warm and the sun shone brilliantly until practically midnight." At the request of the Norwegian Society of Organists, to whom he brought greetings from the American Guild of Organists, Biggs played an all-American program at the Cathedral of Nidaros.

Sweden followed, with concerts on both modern instruments and on an organ by the Swedish baroque builder Hans Heinrich Cahman, a disciple of Schnitger. Then it was England again, where Biggs performed on Harrison & Harrison's new neo-baroque instrument in Royal Festival Hall. While he felt that the organ was a step in the right direction for the British, its sound came off second best to the gentler and more cohesive sounds of the old Dutch and German organs, which were still very fresh in his memory. Biggs wondered if it were not better, if one wished an organ built to certain concepts, "to deal with a builder brought up and trained in this tradition."

The last stop on the journey was Iceland. Its Viking history, rugged scenery, and friendly, appreciative people, made a lasting impression on Biggs and Peggy. At the invitation of composer and organist Pall Isolffson, Biggs gave two concerts in the "smallest cathedral in the world," in Reykjavik, and recorded a program of American music to be broadcast over Icelandic Radio on the Fourth of July.

In three months Biggs had given thirty concerts in fourteen countries. That would have been activity enough for most people, but Biggs and Peggy still found time for sightseeing, recording, searching out new European music, and collecting souvenirs. And they made friends: organists, composers, organ builders, music lovers—even a Dutch driver named John Sebastian Bach.

Biggs's tour had been largely arranged through the International Educational Exchange Service of the Department of State, and Biggs probably did little better than break even on concert fees. The excess baggage charges for the recording equipment, taxi fares, battery rental, and gratuities to churches and sextons added up to a whopping $2,739.95, according to Biggs's meticulous accounting, but this expense was absorbed by Columbia Records.

The recording equipment had been specially designed by Columbia's engineers for field recording, but communications from Biggs at various points in his progress reveal that not all of the "bugs" were out of it. It did not always perform as it was supposed to, and there was a constant problem in getting sufficient fresh 12-volt batteries to provide even power for the motors. At the trip's end, many boxes of precious recorded tapes were held by the United

States Customs Service for an aggravatingly long time while Columbia un-snarled the red tape. Biggs returned in July, but it was not until the end of the summer that Biggs and Columbia could be certain that they did, indeed, have material for an album.

And what a maverick album it was! Biggs's previous Columbia releases had all been essentially virtuoso performances, consisting largely of big works with which Biggs had a long familiarity, played on American organs of a type with which he was thoroughly at ease. The programs had been carefully prepared and meticulously recorded under ideal conditions, and, while the best organs were invariably used, the player and the music were the intended center of attention. *The Art of the Organ* (David Oppenheim's title suggestion) is very much a field recording. The quality of both the playing and the recording is noticeably uneven. Despite much diddling with the tapes in the Columbia studios by Biggs and the engineers, some parts are simply not as good as others, and much footage proved unusable. With little time to practice on organs, which, however much he may have liked them, presented Biggs with unfamiliar and sometimes awkward console arrangements, some of the play-ing emerges strangely wooden and labored. Registrations, too, are not always ideal. But Biggs wanted to show off as much of these organs as he could—what other reason could there be for using a lumbering (if impressive) 32' Pedal reed stop in a Pachelbel partita?

Biggs the virtuoso does appear in the performances of familiar works on modern organs in Trondheim and in London, but the attraction of this album is not so much the playing as the sonorities of the instruments themselves. That indeed was the purpose of the recording, for Biggs was not so much intent on showing off his own considerable abilities as he was in impressing his listeners (as he had himself been impressed) with the unique sounds of the best Eu-ropean organs, both new and old.

Nearly two decades later, in his Smithsonian tape of 1973, Biggs recalled the strong impression that the 1954 tour made on him:

> Playing the great historic organs of Europe had, for me, the impact of a revelation. For the first time, I became aware of the enormous reservoir, the sum total, of the art of the organ in its building and tonal aspects from five or six centuries. The sound of these instruments was so enormously different and supe-rior to what we were accustomed to, and the instruments, despite their age and different playing dimensions of the console and pedalboard, were so much more responsive. Many things thus suddenly came into focus—the importance of track-er action, of articulate voicing, of the organ case, of the windchest, and so on and so on; and particularly the complete interaction of playing action and pipe sound. One suddenly realized the truth and enormous vitality of all that Schweitzer had written about many years before. Everyone reads his books and pamphlets about the organs, but the truth of what he says doesn't percolate until you hear and preferably play these older organs.

Many ideas were generated by that exploratory trip, most of which had to do with future recordings, such as *A Mozart Organ Tour,* which Biggs accomplished the following year. And there was also the barest germ of an idea that the Aeolian-Skinner organ in the Germanic Museum should be retired to make way for something more representative of the organs that had stretched Biggs's ears during those frenetic months abroad.

While *The Art of the Organ* was the most important album to come out of the 1954 tour, there was sufficient material on Biggs's tapes for two additional discs. One, issued at the same time as *The Art of the Organ,* was aimed at the hi-fi buffs: Bach's Toccata in D minor played on fourteen different organs (the fourteenth with the fugue attached). The other, released in 1956, featured Bach's Eight "Little" Preludes and Fugues played on eight historic organs, a record that deserved more attention than it received at the time.

What did the critics think of these recordings? Were their ears stretched too? Apparently so. A review in the *New York Times* for April 17, 1955 commended Biggs's programing of works by composers having geographical and chronological ties to the organs played, and observed that "The older organs . . . take the laurels from the new ones when it comes to beauty of tone." In November the same reviewer covered *A Hi-Fi Adventure* (the Bach Toccata disc) and was again captivated by the beauty and variety of the organs. A review in the May 1955 issue of *High Fidelity* also caught the point that Biggs wanted to get across, "that baroque music is heard in its true colors and glory only on the kind of instruments for which it was written." And the critic conceded that these instruments were "superb."

One of the most thoughtful reviews appeared in *The American Organist* for May 1955. *The Art of the Organ* was judged "one of the outstanding issues of the year," and although the reviewer took exception to some of the modern organs in the album (singling out the Royal Festival Hall instrument as "decidedly disappointing"), he was enchanted with the older organs and what they revealed:

> Heard on the type of instrument their music was conceived for, Sweelinck, Pachelbel, Buxtehude seem in their best work more vivid in expressive coloration, more ship-shape in tonal architecture than ever before. It is as if three centuries of grime had suddenly been removed from a roomful of paintings that had always commanded respect but that now communicate the full force of their vibrant spirits.
>
> In the presence of such a transformation, many new thoughts leap to mind: An entire body of musical literature may be rehabilitated through recordings of such instruments. It is possible we have underestimated Biggs and other American organists in their previous efforts to play baroque music on instruments incapable of producing the sounds 17th-century composers had in mind.

Such reviews must surely have encouraged Biggs to plan future recording trips, and fortunately his enthusiasm for these projects was shared by his producers at Columbia.

Save for the European tour, 1954 was just another typically busy year for Biggs. The radio broadcasts went on (Biggs arrived back from Iceland just in time to do his traditional "Americana" program on the Fourth of July); and he had a heavy domestic recital schedule, including a West Coast tour that involved him in master classes at Pomona College in California and a recital at the Mormon Tabernacle in Salt Lake City.

When Biggs's fingers were not busy on the organ keys, they were rattling the keys of his old typewriter. Early in the year he had completed a large commissioned article on the organ for the *Encyclopedia Britannica,* which he researched carefully and rewrote innumerable times. A near-final draft was at last submitted to various friends for critical scrutiny. The organ builder Walter Holtkamp liked it, but gently reproved Biggs for what he felt was a bit too much propagandizing, generating yet another revision. After the European tour, more writing was in order, not only for the extensive jacket insert that accompanied *The Art of the Organ* but also for various periodicals. Here Biggs could (and did) propagandize to his heart's content.

Even before his return from the 1954 tour, Biggs was incubating plans for international jaunts in 1955. The first of these was a concert tour of Iceland, partly motivated by new friendships there and partly by patriotism, for Biggs was intensely loyal to his adopted country, the United States. For economic reasons Iceland was being wooed by the Soviets, who, among other things, had initiated a cultural exchange and had sent musicians of the calibre of Aram Khatchaturian to give concerts there. The United States had an Army base in Iceland but seems not to have concerned itself with cultural offerings until Biggs suggested the idea. Thus, with State Department backing, Biggs revisited Iceland in the spring of 1955, this time accompanied by seven members of the Boston Symphony Orchestra.

Iceland had no organ builders, but it did have a number of organs, mostly good modern instruments of Scandinavian manufacture. In one handsome contemporary edifice, however, in Iceland's second largest city of Akureyri, Biggs discovered that the authorities had succumbed to the blandishments of American advertising and had purchased an electronic instrument. Biggs was distressed, for he felt that such a splendid building deserved better. On his return to the United States, on his own initiative, he attempted to stir up interest—first in a Scandinavian-American organization, then in the Ford Foundation—for a gift of an American pipe organ to the Akureyri church, but unfortunately to no avail.

Biggs's second 1955 trip, in August, followed what he dubbed "the Mozart trail." His interest in Mozart was of long standing. Over the years

Biggs, Peggy, and Pall Isolffson, Iceland, 1955

On the Mozart trail, 1955

Biggs had often programed Mozart works in recitals and broadcasts, had recorded a few shorter pieces in 1947 and 1950, and had even attempted to revive the glass armonica, for which Mozart wrote. But 1956 was the Mozart bicentennial year, which gave high priority to the recording of Mozart's complete organ works. Biggs's major focus was Salzburg Cathedral, where Mozart had been organist at the age of 21 and had even carved his initials (backwards!) into the organ case. The Cathedral organ still contained many stops from the 1705 Egedacher instrument Mozart had known, and the building had splendid acoustics. The setting was ideal in every way for recording Mozart's seventeen "Epistle" Sonatas for organ and chamber orchestra (called "Festival" Sonatas on the record jacket, possibly because Biggs did not care for the "churchy" connotations of the original title).

But Mozart wrote other works for organ (if one includes the mechanical self-playing organs popular in his day), and he played other organs. Fortunately for Biggs, he left a detailed record of them in his letters, for Mozart might have been called the original "organ tourist." While Mozart's total written output for the organ is small enough to fit on three long-playing discs with room to spare even with a few transcriptions thrown in, Mozart enjoyed improvising on the organs he encountered in his journeys as a *Wunderkind* pianist, and a number of these organs were still extant. What better excuse for putting more historic organs on records than to follow quite literally the trail Mozart himself had blazed across Austria and Germany?

Peggy Biggs once remarked that during these early recording trips "we spent quite a few nights in churches" and wondered if she would even recognize some of them in the daytime. Night was undoubtedly the best time for recording, especially in cities, where normal daytime street noises, amplified by the resonance of large masonry buildings, created an intolerably high level of background noise on sensitive tapes. The major effort of the Mozart project, accounting for three of the six record sides, was the seventeen "Epistle" Sonatas. They were recorded in Salzburg Cathedral with the Camerata Academica under the noted Mozart conductor Bernhard Paumgartner. "Cathedral authorities and the Salzburg police obligingly rerouted all traffic from the Cathedral Square so that we could have complete quiet," wrote Biggs in *The A. G. O. Quarterly* for October 1956, "and the drama of the great Cathedral at night during these evening performances is something long to remember." Also memorable was the "splendid reverberation" of the Cathedral and other old buildings, which added "a mantle of magnificence to the wonderfully articulate organs."

After finishing in Salzburg, the Biggses, with Bavarian organ builder Georg Steinmeyer as their guide, began checking out some other places where Mozart is known to have played the organ. Some, such as the great cathedrals of Ulm and Passau, had modern instruments. But in other places—Kirchheimbolanden, Mörlenbach, Fügen, Lambach, and the Church of St. Cajetan in Salzburg—they discovered fine old instruments "still just about as Mozart played them." To these were added historic organs in Ebersmünster, Innsbruck, Absam, Monchsdeggingen, and Ludwigsburg—places Mozart is known to have visited and where he *might* have played the organ. But the supply of Mozart organ music ran out before the supply of Mozart organs, so part of the sixth side of the three-disc album consists of what Biggs called "snapshots in sound" of some of the organs and bells Mozart (and Biggs) heard in their travels.

Biggs learned some important lessons from his 1954 European venture, and was not slow in putting them into practice. He quickly realized that no good purpose was served by spreading himself too thin or by tiring himself out. The Mozart trip and all subsequent ones concentrated on well-defined musical and geographical areas, and, with one exception, were of shorter duration. For a while Biggs continued to bring his own equipment for some of the field recording, but as time went one he relied more and more on local engineers and their equipment for major projects. In the mid-1960s, when Hellmuth Kolbe of Zurich became CBS's staff recording engineer in Europe, Biggs was entirely relieved of this extracurricular responsibility.

The changes in Biggs's approach are clearly evident in the Mozart recording. Biggs the virtuoso is back in full measure, most notably in the Fantasia, K. 608, and the Adagio, Allegro, and Adagio, K. 594, for organ solo. The "Epistle" Sonatas could not have been better technically or musically if they had been recorded in Columbia's own studios. The album was highly praised by the critics and was considered by many to be the definitive recording of Mozart's organ works.

In 1956 another specialized tour captured the sounds of the Spanish and Portuguese organs that had so impressed Biggs at the outset of his 1954 trip. The resulting record was one more in what would become a long list of "firsts," for outside of a handful of determined organ tourists, few Americans had ever heard the sounds of these remarkable instruments.

As on nearly all his recording tours, Biggs worked in a few concert appearances, one of these being at the Deutsches Museum in Munich. There he also found time to record Rheinberger's Organ Sonata No. 7 on the large Steinmeyer organ. Biggs had lived with this work for a long time; one of its movements had been his audition piece when he applied for entrance into the Royal Academy of Music. Since the Rheinberger work took up only one side of a disc, Columbia filled the flip side with Hindemith's Concerto for Organ and Chamber Orchestra, taped four years earlier with the Columbia Chamber Orchestra under Richard Burgin. Except for the release in 1957 of another "icebox" tape of Biggs playing the Saint-Saëns "Organ" Symphony with the Philadelphia Orchestra, it would be three years before Biggs would again be heard playing an American organ in a recorded performance.

The European recordings continued to surprise and delight audiophiles and critics alike. *The Diapason* for June 1957 praised both *Organ Music of Spain and Portugal* and *A Mozart Organ Tour,* noting in the case of the former that music that seems uninteresting on modern organs "takes on new meaning" when heard on the Iberian instruments. With regard to the Mozart release, the reviewer took exception to the "sluggish-sounding" organ in Passau Cathedral, but was otherwise impressed with the album: "the results approach perfection itself!" Biggs's well-illustrated and informative jacket booklets also received their share of praise. The Hindemith/Rheinberger package, however, was considered something of a mixed blessing in the March 1958 *Diapason:* Hindemith was "pure joy", while Rheinberger, with allowance for a "fine interpretation on an instrument ideally suited," was "pompous and dull." Biggs's advocacy of Rheinberger was not so easily dampened; some years later Biggs made a recording that admirably vindicated his faith in this composer's music.

Next to their first tour, in 1954, the recording trip made by Biggs and Peggy in 1957 was the most ambitious, even though all its objectives were not achieved. Lasting from May through August, it was the longest tour Biggs ever made, but the pace was more comfortable than in 1954. Traveling was considerably facilitated by the use of Biggs's new Volkswagen Microbus, loaded with new two-track equipment, for Biggs was now recording in both monaural and stereo. Save for a few "sound snapshots" there was not much field recording scheduled for this trip, and in both Holland and England technicians from the Philips firm stood ready, by prior arrangement with Columbia, to assist in any way necessary.

The first stop was Zwolle, in The Netherlands. On previous visits Biggs had admired the "inexhaustible resources" and "tone of unique splendor" of the recently restored 1720 Schnitger organ there. With the cooperation of Dirk Flentrop and the genial organist, J. J. van der Waarde, he recorded three major Bach Preludes and Fugues on this instrument. A handsome old map of the city graced the cover of the resulting album, entitled simply *Bach at Zwolle.*

The troubles that were to plague the entire trip began in Zwolle. The new recording equipment refused to function properly: Thyratron tubes burned out at an "alarming rate," and much tape footage was spoiled by unexplained noises and incomplete erasure. Unable to locate the trouble himself and getting behind schedule, Biggs took the machines to the Philips technicians in Baarn. Then there were difficulties with microphones, and a buzzing speaker had to be replaced. But with perseverance Biggs was finally able to get what he later

The Schnitger organ at Zwolle, 1957

described to his producers as "some exciting Bach tapes." In addition to Bach at Zwolle, Biggs also recorded d'Aquin at Gouda, but either there was not enough usable tape or Biggs was dissatisfied with the result, for the latter was never released, and Biggs later re-recorded the d'Aquin *Noëls* on the new organ at the Germanic Museum.

The Biggses arrived in Germany in late June, and there they encountered problems of a different sort. Concerts had been booked in both East and West Berlin, as well as in Leipzig, Halle, and Freiberg in East Germany; and arrangements had even been made with an East German recording company to make some tapes in Leipzig and Freiberg. At the last moment, with Biggs already in Berlin and the East German concerts publicized, the whole project became hopelessly bogged down in bureaucratic red tape. Biggs was denied his East German visa, and all but two West Berlin programs had to be cancelled. Biggs was frustrated and angry. On July 8 he wrote to Debbie Ishlon of Columbia Records, "Instead of making a record on this trip to Germany I've broken one! And that's the record of never having missed an announced concert or broadcast. Now I've missed three. 'Editorial comment' would be easy, but I'll refrain from it." Friends in East Germany wrote to express their disappointment, and Biggs graciously wrote apologies to the organists of the churches that were to have sponsored him. Biggs had no intention of giving up his ambition to play and record in Bach's own church, but it was not until 1970 that he actually achieved it.

In mid-July Biggs and Peggy retraced their steps through Holland en route to England. The major project there was to record the sixteen Organ Concertos of G. F. Handel with members of the London Philharmonic under Sir Adrian Boult. A Mendelssohn recording at St. Paul's Cathedral in London was also scheduled.

Biggs had expended no small amount of effort in getting the Handel project set up. He felt it important to use an authentic "Handel" organ for this recording, one built during the composer's lifetime, and, if possible, one he is known to have played. Research by mail and investigations on previous trips turned up what seemed to be the ideal instrument. A well-documented two-manual chamber organ built around 1749 for Handel's librettist Charles Jennens, to a specification recommended by Handel himself, was found to exist intact in the Parish Church of St. James in Great Packington, on the estate of the Earl of Aylesford. The Earl's son, Lord Guernsey, was cooperative, and the setting was ideal—an acoustically favorable masonry church in the quietest location imaginable. But even in the planning stage there were a few obstacles to overcome. Columbia at first balked at the cost of hiring the London musicians, and the church building lacked electricity. But Columbia's reticence was soon overcome, Lord Guernsey persuaded the Electric Board to lay an underground power line to the church (paid for by Columbia), and it appeared for a while that the Handel project would have smooth sailing.

Biggs soon found that this was not to be. He rarely neglected the smallest detail in his planning process, but he had overlooked a rather significant one here. He knew from a previous visit that the organ was not tuned to concert pitch, but he had the impression that it was about a half-step sharp. That did

Biggs, Peggy, and engineers in Great Packington, 1957

not concern him unduly, for he knew that orchestral musicians were in the habit of playing a little sharp, and that their instruments could be tuned a bit sharper if necessary. But the organ was not sharp; it was in fact nearly a half-step *flat,* and that posed serious problems indeed. Biggs first considered transposing the organ part, a difficult but not impossible exercise, but Handel had written his organ parts to the extreme limits of the keyboard, and in transposing Biggs would run out of keys. The orchestral players tried to flatten their instruments, but the strings would not stay in tune, and the woodwinds could not flatten sufficiently to tune with the organ.

Clearly something drastic would have to be done to keep the whole project from being scrapped. In desperation Biggs consulted with the organ builder Noel Mander in London, and between them they came up with a solution. Although he was in the midst of preparations for an impending meeting of the International Congress of Organists in London, Mander came to Great Packington with one of his men, removed the pipes from the organ, and took them to his workshop in London. There they were cleaned, repaired, regulated, shortened slightly to sharpen them, and fitted with tuning slides so that the original flat pitch might later be restored. From Biggs's standpoint the operation was a success. The organ was in excellent tune and regulation, and its sound was all the brighter for the pipes having been cleaned. An electric blower was also installed, much to the relief of Peggy and the engineers, who had up to this point been taking turns at the instrument's two bellows handles ("handles Handel handled," quipped Biggs). The recordings went on with no further hitches, and the resulting album is still in print and still regarded by many as one of the finest and most authentic of all Handel Concerto recordings.

The ensuing Mendelssohn recording session at St. Paul's went smoothly, but Biggs's worries were not yet over. Word about the tuning alterations at Great Packington had gone out along the grapevine, and when Biggs returned home in late August he was confronted by letters from some fairly influential people deploring the "vandalism" he had committed in altering the pitch of a historic organ. The critics were all members of England's "early music" circle, and in fairness it must be said that at the time this group was well ahead of the organ world in its concepts of restoration and conservation. Biggs answered the letters as diplomatically as he could, explaining that the organ could be returned to its original pitch any time Lord Guernsey or the rector of the church authorized it. As added insurance against further repercussions, he aired the matter himself in an article in *The Diapason* for December 1959. But the "teapot tempest" proved more difficult to quell than Biggs had anticipated. A few years later it cropped up again in a Dutch publication, and Biggs had to prevail upon his friends in The Netherlands to defend his good name. Fortunately for Biggs the matter seems never to have troubled those in actual charge of the organ, and he was welcomed back warmly when he returned to make further Handel recordings in 1970 and 1971.

One other record album resulted from these European tours of the 1950s. Entitled simply *The Organ*, it was issued in the fall of 1958 and was both a sequel to *The Art of the Organ* and a progress report on the development of Biggs's views on organ tone and design over the previous four years. These thoughts first began to take shape in an article in the March 1956 issue of *The Diapason*. Here Biggs expressed the opinion that "our modern organ building must be measured by the degree in which it approaches the best of the classic models. Rarely do our modern instruments measure up, and almost certainly never do they excel the best examples of the old."

But Biggs knew it was not enough just to talk and write about organ tone. A sound, like a picture, could be worth so much more than mere words. In this rather lavishly packaged album, Biggs combined words, pictures, and sounds not only to sketch out the musical and technical history of the organ but also to hammer home his concept of the ideal organ, a concept that had ripened considerably in four short but eventful years. On the record (dubbed the "talking dog record" by Biggs and the Columbia staff), Biggs's voice, backed up by numerous taped examples, propounds the credo of a new movement in organ building, already begun in Europe and in its infant stages in America: No organ chambers, no "classic cabooses" on orchestral organs, no baroque stoplists rendered in Romantically voiced pipes; no unification, remote-controlled electric action, inarticulate speech or dead acoustics. No compromise whatever of the time-honored principles of organ design and construction. Heard at a quarter century's remove, Biggs's voice is the voice of a prophet—one who, fortunately, lived to see his prophecies come to pass.

But prophetic voices are not always heeded or agreed with in their day. By 1958 Biggs was not the only organist who had been to Europe, but he was surely the most visible. In the period Melville Smith and Arthur Howes were conducting tours that introduced many American organists to historic European organs. Other organists were touring on their own, and some of the younger ones were obtaining Fulbright scholarships to study at European conservatories. Nearly all of these travelers came to share Biggs's views in whole or in part. But many who stayed home did not, and during the 1950s the trade journals were enlivened by articles and letters pro and con such things as tracker action, articulate pipe speech ("to chiff or not to chiff," as one editor expressed it), *Werkprinzip* designs, organ cases, and live acoustics. The "pros" had an eloquent champion in Biggs, the only major recitalist who cheerfully and enthusiastically went out on a limb for his, and their, views. The "talking dog record" was a persuasive milestone in the controversy. "Biggs stumps for the restoration of the classic style organ and demonstrates most dramatically the advantages of such an instrument over most modern church or theatrical monsters," wrote critic Paul Affelder in the *Newark Sunday News* for October 5, 1958.

Biggs stumped not only for the classic organ but for the album itself. Articles and interviews in such prominent magazines as *Newsweek, Time,* and *The New Yorker,* gave Biggs the opportunity to bring his message to the world at large. "Does Biggs expect to convert others to the classical organ?" asked *Newsweek's* interviewer. "One sound is worth a thousand words," replied Biggs.

13 | A New Organ for the Museum

The new Flentrop tracker-action organ, installed in 1958 in the Busch-Reisinger Museum of Harvard University . . . is symbolic of changes that are rapidly taking place in the building and playing of organs in the United States.

In November 1963, when these words of Biggs's were published in the British periodical *The Organ*, it was already clear to the organ world that Biggs's prophecies of the 1950s were neither idle fancy nor wishful thinking. Encased tracker-action organs of classic or neo-baroque tonal bias were being imported from Europe at an increasing rate, and the first modern American-made three-manual organ with mechanical key action was being installed by Charles Fisk in Boston's King's Chapel, where Daniel Pinkham was organist. In part because of the efforts of the Organ Historical Society (of which Biggs was an early and supportive member), old American organs were being rebuilt or restored in a more sympathetic manner.

By 1963, also, the new Germanic Museum organ had been thoroughly broken in. At Biggs's request Flentrop had provided a new bench top, and Fisk had replaced the Pedal sharps with ones more like the standard American type; with Flentrop's advice, he had also corrected a problem in the Borstwerk wind supply.

And the organ had been heard: first (if briefly) by the radio audience, then in recitals and on records. Many of the recitals were given by Biggs, of course, but during the first few years of the instrument's existence, concerts were also given by Biggs's Cambridge neighbor Melville Smith and other local organists, as well as by such European visitors as Finn Viderø, Piet Kee, Gustav Leonhardt, and Anton Heiller. The organ also had proved its worth with instrumentalists and with choral groups such as the Harvard Glee Club. "It is excellent with voices," observed Biggs, "and it is obvious that it would be perfect for church services."

Biggs had been dissatisfied with the old Museum organ ever since his ill-fated attempts to have Harrison make some improvements to it in the early 1950s. His first serious thoughts about replacing the instrument seem to have occurred in 1953; and Schlicker, whose Cambridge Portative had proved so satisfactory, was his logical choice for a builder. But the 1954 tour changed all that. Biggs found the old Continental organs, particularly those of northern Europe, infinitely superior to anything he had experienced in England or America. Of the new organs he encountered, those built by the Dutch most closely resembled the old models in their unforced voicing and comfortable, responsive playing actions. And of the modern Dutch builders, it was Flentrop of Zaandam whose work made the most favorable impression on Biggs. Dirk and Marian Flentrop had been hospitable and helpful to the Biggses. They were genuinely interested in what Biggs was doing, and went well beyond the bounds of simple courtesy in support of his efforts. Flentrop and Biggs were soon addressing each other by the nicknames of "Biggsie" and "Dick."

In 1956 the American Guild of Organists held a national convention in New York, and while it was still in the planning stage, a visiting organist from the host chapter suggested to Flentrop that he send a small organ to exhibit. When Flentrop asked Biggs's advice on the matter, Biggs urged him strongly to do it, and then arranged for Flentrop himself to lecture on "Trends in European Organ-Building." Biggs too was on the convention program, utilizing the Cambridge Portative in a program of concerted works at Hunter College Auditorium.

In 1957 Flentrop gave Biggs invaluable assistance during the recording session at Zwolle, and when Biggs was putting together the extensive jacket booklet for *The Organ,* Flentrop contributed a thoughtful and articulate article to it, based partly on his well-received convention address.

By the fall of 1956 the possibility of a new organ at the Museum was very much on Biggs's mind. His friendship with Flentrop, as well as his liking for Flentrop's work, had convinced Biggs that he had found the man who could create it. In a letter to Flentrop dated September 22, Biggs first discussed some details of a future recording project and then came to the real point of the communication:

> You may remember the Busch-Reisinger Museum at Harvard University, where our CBS broadcasts originate? And you may remember the excellent room acoustics, the present organ, and particularly the space available in the gallery.
> Would you like to consider the idea of building a new organ for the Museum? It seems to me that there could not be a better spot anywhere over here in which to set forth your philosophy!
> The present organ belongs to us. We were compelled to purchase it from

Aeolian-Skinner some years ago. Thus we would ourselves purchase the new organ, and sell the present one to help with the cost.

An organ of a design similar to the little organ in Lübeck would look very well in the Museum gallery. But a design would be quite up to you.

Cost might dictate two manuals, but three would be much better if possible. Incidentally, cost does of course enter into our considerations. Yet we do not want any favors, and expect the price to be whatever you would normally quote.

With the perfect placement and live acoustics, volume is not important, but articulation and texture and beauty of sound is everything.

Biggs went on to suggest a center gallery location with a Rückpositiv division on the railing and sufficient space around for a small orchestra. A very quiet blower would be needed to eliminate background noise on broadcasts and recordings, and, as for action, "Naturally it would be tracker!" Pistons might be nice but were not essential, and "it would be advisable to have the pedal board to AGO dimensions." Biggs expressed concern in the letter about past verbal commitments to Herman Schlicker and wondered if he could still be involved in some way, but this idea seemed unworkable. Financial arrangements were discussed, and the letter concluded with the hope that Flentrop would be interested in the project, since "it does seem that a little revolution might begin over here in the Museum hall."

Flentrop responded barely a week later, saying "It seems a wonderful idea to me!!" and began making tentative designs, which served to heighten Biggs's enthusiasm for the project. An attractive visual design would unquestionably enhance the instrument, but Biggs's foremost concern was how the organ would sound. In December he wrote to Flentrop,

> If your organ can have a persuasive, outgiving mellow quality, and a rich but never "hard" ensemble (yet very articulate in speech beginnings) I think it will just bowl people over! They will say THIS IS IT! It will be nothing less than an earthquake, for which America is ready *right now!*

Biggs shared Flentrop's preliminary drawings with Charles Kuhn, the director of the Museum, whose interest in the new organ was keen. A contract was signed, and Roy Carlson and others were alerted to the impending availability of the Aeolian-Skinner organ, although it was nearly a year before anything transpired in this regard. Early in 1958 it was finally sold to Boston University for $11,500, and shortly thereafter it was installed in the auditorium of the School of Fine and Applied Arts. In October 1957 a one-manual, six-stop Flentrop organ was sent to the Museum on loan, and for a brief time it shared the gallery with the Aeolian-Skinner instrument. When the latter was removed in the spring of 1958, the small Flentrop, occasionally in combination with orchestral instruments, was heard on the radio broadcasts until the new organ arrived in the fall.

Flentrop's first speculative drawings for the new organ depicted a some-what flamboyant contemporary case, but the design gradually evolved into a reserved and dignified traditional scheme. Its basic shape was not unlike that of the small Gothic organ Biggs had admired in the Church of St. Jakobi in Lübeck, and it was executed in sleek mahogany. The tonal plan was also traditional: *Hoofdwerk, Borstwerk, Rugpositief* and *Pedaal,* containing the classical principal choruses, flutes, and reeds of the Baroque period. Biggs got his American-style pedalboard but decided to forego the costly combination pistons in favor of a straight mechanical drawstop action, and of course the manual and pedal key action was mechanical as well. The voicing was gentle but articulate, as Biggs wished it, and the wind pressures were low—from 1 $7/16''$ to 2 $1/16''$.

The organ was shipped from Flentrop's works late in July 1958, and a month later Flentrop's men arrived in Cambridge to begin installation. Dirk Flentrop himself came later to supervise the final tonal finishing, and he stayed for the opening festivities on September 22.

It was a gala occasion. A large invited crowd of organists, organ builders, critics, friends, museum officials, and Harvard faculty milled around the Great Hall and adjacent galleries, nibbling hors d'oeuvres and sipping drinks from an improvised bar tended by harried undergraduates from the student employ-ment pool. The assemblage was then hailed into the Great Hall, and after some words of welcome and introduction Biggs put the new organ through its paces in a brief recital of works by Sweelinck, Franck, Vaughan Williams, and Bach. The concert was followed by the traditional European ceremony in which Flentrop poured wine from a principal pipe into glasses passed by Peggy Biggs to all who had managed to jam themselves into the organ gallery. The taped-up mouth of the pipe leaked, the wine tasted of pipe size, and almost as much went onto the floor as into the glasses. But the mood was ebullient and nobody minded that the ceremony lacked the solemnity it doubtless had in ancient times. "Even the organ was smiling," reported the *Harvard Crimson.*

A few days later Biggs was preparing his first broadcasts with the new organ and knuckling down to a serious practice schedule. "I am gradually learning to play it," he wrote Flentrop in October, "and am discovering new things about it every day." Some of Biggs's discoveries had a marked effect on his own approach to the instrument. In the mid-1950s Biggs had begun to affect an excessively detached playing style, especially when playing electric-action organs (although it spilled over into his recording of the tracker-action organ in Zwolle). By 1958 it had reached the point where a reviewer in *The American Organist* saw fit to criticize the "yippiness" of Biggs's playing, which included a noticeable slapping of the pedals. Biggs was not the only American organist to adopt this overly detached style. It was a reaction common to many

Biggs, Dirk Flentrop, Charles Kuhn, and Peggy, celebrating the opening of the new Germanic Museum organ by serving wine from an organ pipe, 1958

organists whose consciousness had recently been raised relative to articulation, but who found themselves still having to play instruments that were slow of speech and lacked any articulation of their own. Once Biggs got used to the lighter, more responsive action and the clean, articulate speech of the Flentrop organ, he realized that such overcompensation was no longer necessary, and his style began to smooth out noticeably, as his recordings on the Flentrop testify.

Preparations for the new organ did not significantly curtail Biggs's typically busy schedule in 1958. Beginning with a spring recording tour in Europe and an appearance with the Oratorio Society of New York on his return in May, his schedule accelerated as summer approached. In June Biggs gave a major concert at an American Guild of Organists convention (a concerted program using a small Reuter organ similar to the Cambridge Portative), dedicated the rebuilt organ in Boston's Old North Church, and played a Handel organ concerto with the Boston Pops Orchestra under Arthur Fiedler in Symphony

Biggs at the Flentrop organ in the Busch-Reisinger organ, early 1960s

Hall. July was spent teaching and giving concerts at Syracuse University and at the Organ Institute in Methuen.

His pace did not slacken after the inauguration of the Flentrop organ in the fall. In addition to a program with the Boston Symphony Orchestra and various solo recitals, Biggs gave a special program for the Busch-Reisinger Museum Association in December, and the first of what was to become a traditional series of post-Christmas concerts on the large new Möller organ in

St. George's Church in New York. A year that had been so filled with high points ended on a dismal note, however, with the abrupt and unanticipated termination of the CBS Sunday morning broadcasts.

The cancellation was a serious blow to Biggs's plans for the new organ. The broadcasts had been an integral part of the instrument's *raison d'être*. But Biggs, as always, was flexible, and it did not take him long to retrench. If the increasing use of commercial recordings was driving live music from the air waves, then the new organ would be used for recording. During 1959 Biggs sketched out and began work on a whole new series of recordings involving the Flentrop organ. The first one, a lively collection of pieces for brass and organ by Gabrieli and Frescobaldi, recorded with the Boston Brass Ensemble under Richard Burgin, was released in February 1960. The second, an album of *Noëls* by d'Aquin, came out in September of the same year, just in time to get on everyone's Christmas gift lists.

The first recordings of the new organ were well received by the critics, as was the organ itself. *The Diapason* for May 1960 deplored the loss of the organ to the radio audience and called the organ and brass album "top drawer." Along with the Handel Concerto album done in England it was rated as a "must" for hi-fi addicts, who were warned to be startled by the realistic stereo effects of the Gabrieli Canzonas. Ross Parmenter in the *New York Times* for December 18 regarded the d'Aquin record as "particularly delightful" and praised the organ's "clear, reedy, baroque type of sound." An especially perceptive review of the Gabrieli and Frescobaldi release appeared in the *A. G. O. Quarterly* for October 1960:

> E. Power Biggs's records are not just aspects of a fine but fixed philosophy, but represent rather the philosophical growth of one of the most perspicacious minds in the organ field. This issue seems to match, though smaller in scope, the significance of Mr. Biggs's giant Handel and Mozart releases, for it presents—and this is a sure fact—America's first true classic organ in a lively performance of two Renaissance composers who opened the doors of the Baroque.

Other recordings on the new organ quickly followed. Back in the early radio days Biggs had discovered the sprightly concertos for two organs by the eighteenth-century Spanish organist-priest Antonio Soler. These light-hearted works were intended for performance by himself and his pupil Prince Gabriel de Borbón on the dual organs of El Escorial. Biggs had previously performed some of them with organ and harpsichord, and, aided by a tape recorder, with himself on both parts. It was not until of the Flentrop organ had been installed that Biggs finally contrived to play all six concertos as written, for two organs. The second instrument was an eighteenth-century chamber organ by the Dutch builder Hess, loaned by Charles Fisher of Framingham and played by Daniel Pinkham.

Recording the Soler Concertos with Daniel Pinkham, 1960

The Soler works were given a preview concert at the Museum, then recorded for an album released in 1961. In the summer of the same year, there appeared the first of a series of Bach recordings under the general title of *Bach Organ Favorites*. It was followed, in 1962, by the release of an album containing six of Sweelinck's Variations on Popular Songs, in commemoration of the 400th anniversary of the composer's birth, plus another organ and brass issue. All these recordings emphasized the versatility of the organ, all gave Biggs the opportunity to propagandize subtly in the jacket notes, and all got good reviews.

Versatile as this organ was, after a few years' experience with it, Biggs hatched an idea which would make it more so, and the so-called convertible stops were added in 1964. A 2' principal was made to be interchangeable with the 2' flute in the Hoofdwerk, and the 8' Rankett, standing in the front of the Borstwerk, was provided with an alternate in the form of a divided stop consisting of a 2' Schalmei from middle C down (which could be coupled to the Pedal for solo playing) and an 8' Dulzian in the treble range. The extra pipes were stored in boxes on the tuner's walkboard, and they could be exchanged easily by the tuner. Biggs thought this a rather clever twist, and when he told Walter Holtkamp about it, the organ builder jokingly told him to keep quiet about it, otherwise "every organist will want a batch of convertibles."

The Flentrop organ was heard not only on the radio and on records, but on television and, in December 1960 it was featured in a documentary film made for the United States Information Service. Biggs obviously enjoyed this particular project and wrote to Flentrop, "I think you'll like it. They photographed the organ from every angle, in color. And we have shots of the trackers going up and down, to the music of Sweelinck's Balletto. And of course of the audience, and of the Museum."

Because of such widespread exposure, the Flentrop organ attracted far more attention than other imported tracker-action instruments, including a sizable and equally worthy Rudolph von Beckerath organ in an out-of-the-way Lutheran church in Cleveland, which was recorded a few times for an obscure label by Robert Noehren. The Museum organ, located in a major eastern university and recorded on the Columbia label, was in the best possible position to garner converts not only to its style of action and voicing but also to its builder. There is little doubt that this instrument was a factor in the steady increase of American contracts for Flentrop after 1958. Fenner Douglass, in his preface to John Fesperman's Flentrop in America, expressed his belief that Biggs's records made on the new Museum organ "not only educated the American public on the subject of classical music, but . . . made Flentrop the most familiar organ builder from the Old World."

14 | *Americana*

> In its way the rediscovery, or reawareness, of these early American organs is every bit as exciting as similar enterprise in Europe. Many excellent organs were once built here, and heard by such notables as Thomas Jefferson, George Washington, and Benjamin Franklin. This seems to indicate that to build tracker organs again today is not to undermine the Constitution.

Biggs, for all his broad British accent, was fond of his adopted country and, by his own admission, something of an American history buff. His interest in American music extended forward to new compositions, but it also reached back to include the discovery, publication, and performance of older American works. An interest in Americana (plus a certain amount of admiration for the multifaceted Benjamin Franklin) was at least partially responsible for the abortive attempt to resurrect the glass armonica as a performance medium in 1956.

Having discovered the historic organs of Europe, Biggs began to wonder if there might also be historic organs of musical interest in the United States. From his own experience the only ones that came readily to mind were the rebuilt Boston Music Hall organ in Methuen, the late nineteenth-century organ Schlicker had rebuilt in the Old North Church of Boston, and the Brattle organ, a small and ancient English chamber organ that had long been unplayable, but whose pipes Biggs had once borrowed and played (from a voicing jack in the Aeolian-Skinner factory) for a broadcast in the 1940s.

The American Guild of Organists national convention in New York in June 1956, the occasion on which Dirk Flentrop was introduced to American organists, was almost certainly the first such event (but by no means the last) at which a modern tracker-action organ was played. During that eventful week an impromptu meeting was held in the choir room of St. Bartholomew's Church by a group of convention-goers who had for several years been in correspondence with each other on the subject of old American organs. The consensus of this gathering was that a more organized attempt should be made to document such instruments, to save them from destruction or alteration, and to educate the public as to their worth. Thus was born the Organ

Historical Society. From the handful at that meeting the membership continued to grow, and within a few years the group's mimeographed newsletter had become a printed quarterly called *The Tracker*.

Through the accidental circumstance of sharing a table at the Friday night convention banquet with some of its organizers, Biggs became one of the first members to be recruited by the fledgling society. Somewhere between the main course and the side-splitting antics of Anna Russell that accompanied the dessert, Biggs broached a question that had apparently been on his mind for a while: Were there historic organs in America worthy of being recorded? The unanimous reply of the Organ Historical Society delegation was that there indeed were.

Although this information furnished Biggs with another useful recording idea, his time-consuming 1957 European tour and the arrival of the Flentrop organ in 1958 meant the deferment of any real action on it until late in that year. In the meantime, the growing Organ Historical Society grapevine was being tapped for suggestions of suitable organs, and in early 1959, while Biggs worked on another Museum recording, Peggy and the writer scoured libraries for early American music and began writing letters to owners of some of the organs under consideration.

A recording trip, much like the original European "field trip," was scheduled for the spring. But because of various delays it was not until July 1959 that the tape recorders, microphones, cables, playback equipment, and other assorted paraphernalia were loaded into the Biggs Microbus, that battered veteran of two European jaunts and occasional encounters with Boston traffic. In the bus too went Biggs and Peggy, with Columbia engineer Buddy Graham and the writer following in the Graham sports car.

Like the first European tour, this trip was in good part an expedition into the unknown, filled with both discoveries and disappointments. An initial swing around New England and upstate New York found the Brattle Organ still unrestored and a potentially interesting three-manual Ferris instrument of the 1840s in too precarious a state to use. Other organs, while usable, were in acoustically poor churches or had noisy blowers. But a delightful 1827 George Hook chamber organ in Salem, Massachusetts; a George Jardine "finger and barrel" organ in Pierrepont Manor, New York; and a well-maintained Hutchings and Plaisted organ in Woodstock, Vermont, made up for the disappointments. Biggs's stirring if slightly rattly rendition of the Ives Variations on "America" on the Woodstock organ is still the only recording of the work on a "period" instrument.

The recording party next headed for Pennsylvania, in hopes of finding a usable instrument by the late eighteenth-century Moravian builder David Tannenberg. While several of his instruments were known to exist, most of them turned out to be in no condition to be recorded. But fortune smiled in York, where Tannenberg's last instrument, built in 1804, had only recently been moved to the reverberant auditorium of the local Historical Society and put in good playing condition. The recording conditions were excellent, and as a bonus the Society's director, Frederick J. Stair, was able to provide some useful background material and graphics for the jacket notes.

There is little question that the Tannenberg organ was Biggs's favorite of all the organs encountered on the tour. In the September 1960 issue of *The Diapason* Biggs wrote, "By any standards, American or European, this must be rated a most distinguished instrument. Its tonal excellence is apparent the moment you hear it, and its playability the instant you set hands to the keyboard." He went on to praise the instrument's "wonderful blend of ensemble, marvelous flutes, the absolute 'togetherness' of the speech," as well as the light key action and the "organ case that delights the eye and would be an ornament to any church. . . . Here, in short, is an organ built in America a century and a half ago that in its variety of musical possibilities, achieved through the simplest of means, carries a vital lesson and indeed poses a challenge for us today."

Stair also told Biggs of a small organ in the Reading Historical Society, built by Tannenberg's contemporary John Jacob Dieffenbach in the memorable year of 1776. In poor condition and rather desperately out of tune, it was nonetheless capable of a bravely wheezy rendition of William Billings's hymn tune "Chester."

From Pennsylvania the tour headed south. A church in Virginia with a promising Henry Erben organ had to be passed up because it lay in the flight path of an exceedingly busy airport, but another Erben organ of 1845 in the old Huguenot Church of Charleston, South Carolina, proved an appropriate vehicle for music by Charleston composer Benjamin Yarnold. In the mid-summer heat, with open windows the only air-conditioning, Biggs worked in his undershirt while Peggy prepared refreshing snacks to be eaten (and shared with the resident cats) in the palm-shaded churchyard during breaks.

Later, back in Boston, Biggs recorded music by William Selby at the Old North Church, more for the historical setting than for any historical significance of the organ.

The music on the recording was an interesting mixed bag. Biggs wanted to confine his repertory to the eighteenth and early nineteenth centuries (the exception being the Ives work), but save for Selby's few pieces, very little authentic American music from that period survives. Fortunately, there was quite a reservoir of secular keyboard music available, intended for any kind of domestic keyboard instrument—spinet, fortepiano, or chamber organ. The "perky freshness" of these little pieces appealed to Biggs, who decided that it was "perfectly legal, and rather good fun" to include them, along with his own organ arrangement of James Hewitt's entertaining piano piece *The Battle of Trenton*. What to play on the Tannenberg organ that would have a suitable pedigree posed a bit of a problem, for the vast quantity of music that has come down to us from Tannenberg's Moravian sect contains no keyboard works. It does contain many pieces for instrumental ensemble, however; and some music by Tannenberg's contemporary David Moritz Michael, originally written for wind sextet, proved quite adaptable to transcription.

Biggs's jacket notes were in the same vein as his article in *The Diapason*, and he did not hesitate to inject a strong note of advocacy for old American organs:

> Churches which are fortunate enough to have an old organ, in whatever condition, should look seriously into the possibility of appraising and renovating the instrument, not only for history's sake but because chances are that if it came from a reputable early builder its musical qualities, if conscientiously restored, would far surpass what is generally available today.

Such statements did much to advance the cause of the Organ Historical Society, which eventually made Biggs an honorary member. The many organs seen on the tour, whether recordable or not, impressed Biggs sufficiently to make him henceforth a staunch defender of old American organs and a strong supporter of the Organ Historical Society's work. In the fall of 1959 he invited its members to the Busch-Reisinger Museum for a private demonstration of the Flentrop organ, and he later gave recitals at two of their national conventions without fee. Probably even its most diligent researchers will never really know how many fine old organs earned a reprieve from destruction because some music-loving church member chanced upon Biggs's recording of early American organs.

Reviews of the recording varied with the viewpoint of the reviewer. David Hall, in *Hi-Fi Stereo,* categorized the program as "charming American oddities" but praised it nonetheless and liked the sound of the organs. "Biggs plays this mélange of Americana with genuine spirit—especially the more outlandish episodes of the *America* variations—and has been excellently recorded throughout." The last comment is a testimonial to the perseverence of Buddy Graham under conditions that were often far from ideal. James Boeringer, in the *A. G. O. Quarterly* for October 1961, was somewhat less charmed by the music ("the instruments were of far greater significance than the music") but praised Biggs for his "foray into a field virtually unexplored." Fifteen years later, in recognition of the American bicentennial, Biggs made another foray into that field—one that made the "spirited" 1960 release appear staid and scholarly by comparison.

Biggs remained on the American continent during 1959 and 1960. He managed to reach just about every part of the United States, from the Deep South to the Pacific Northwest; and in November 1959 he gave a series of four recitals, each attended by four to eight thousand people, on the new five-manual Tamburini organ in the Auditorio Nacional of Mexico City. According to the *Mexico City News,* he played "works heard hitherto only in leading European and United States music centers." The music performed may have been new to Mexican ears, but in actuality the program consisted largely of old Biggs favorites by Campra, Clarke, Bach, Balbastre, Widor, Dupré, and others. Some of these selections, plus the Mexican national anthem, were recorded by the Mexican arm of Columbia records for south-of-the-border distribution. A reviewer in a Mexican hi-fi magazine praised the stereophonic effects of the resulting disc and Biggs's handling of the monster Italian instrument, with which Biggs was not particularly impressed. It was on all counts a successful trip and generated promises of future engagements.

Hardly a year went by in which Biggs did not participate in some way in one of the biennial regional or national conventions of the American Guild of Organists. In 1959 he was a featured recitalist at a regional convention in Indianapolis, and in 1960 he performed some of the "American oddities" at a national convention in Detroit. The next national convention was held in Atlanta, where Biggs played a new Flentrop organ. At a regional convention hosted by his own Boston chapter in 1961, he gave a lecture on historic European and American organs, illustrated with tape recordings, and Peggy served on the hospitality committee.

Peggy was an accomplished hostess, but her abilities far exceeded this easy role. While she accompanied and assisted Biggs on most of his recording tours, she usually stayed home to "mind the store" when he was on concert tours—managing business affairs; handling correspondence, phone calls, and visitors; and maintaining a lively correspondence with the peripatetic Biggs in which business, neighborhood news, comments on the recitals, "in" jokes, cartoons, and love notes were freely mingled. Biggs had long since parted company with professional managers, and much of the business end of things, from arranging recitals to sending out promotional material, was handled solely by Peggy until the 1960s, when Johanna Giwosky, one of Biggs's students, stepped in to help with the mounting volume of work.

Biggs continued to write persuasive and influential articles, not only for the trade journals but for such publications as the prestigious hardcover magazine *Horizon,* which featured a lavishly illustrated Biggs article in March 1960. The years 1960 and 1961 were filled with the inevitable coast-to-coast recital engagements, as well as recording sessions at the Museum, for, as Biggs wrote to Flentrop, "the *real* influence of the organ is through records." After some earnest attempts to get foundation funding for a National Public Radio series, Biggs decided that broadcasting was a lost cause. His recording activity was increasing in the early 1960s, and in addition to some of the previously mentioned releases, he also recorded the three Hindemith organ sonatas and an album of Baroque music entitled *Heroic Music for Organ, Brass and Percussion* on the Flentrop organ.

Biggs, who did not want to become pigeonholed as a "one-school" player, recognized that he would sometimes require a large middle-of-the-road modern American organ for Romantic music. In 1961 he made a recording of favorites by Franck, Widor, Alain, Dupré, and Gigout on the large new Möller organ in St. George's Church in New York. It was the first of several occasions when Biggs would record on this organ, for the situation at St. George's had much to commend it. The church was easily accessible for the engineers from Columbia's New York headquarters, it had excellent acoustics, and the organ's rather spread-out arrangement made it ideal for emphasizing stereophonic and, later, quadraphonic effects.

A review of the French Romantic issue in the *American Record Guide* for August 1962 indicates how effectively Biggs exploited this property:

> The *Scherzo* of Gigout is a self-contained stereo showcase in miniature. Such a batting about! . . . This instrument, with the majority of its pipes exposed, envelops you in a triangular whirl of sound. Here, as perhaps nowhere else, the church acts as the sounding board of a vast organ chamber.

Although the reviewer mildly deplored the fact that Biggs did not use the swellshades and found so many virtuosic showpieces on one disc almost too-rich a diet, he regarded the album as a "truly glamorous" production. Certainly it proved to Biggs's public that he was not neglecting the Romantic repertoire in his enthusiasm for early music or curiosities, nor had he lost his ability for artistically handling a type of organ that was still far more likely to be encountered on the concert circuit than either old American or modern Dutch instruments with tracker action.

15 | *Europe Revisited*

> But it's really necessary to come to Europe again, for
> everything must be done in stereo, and of course there are
> certain magnificent sounds, as for example at Zwolle, that we
> can never expect to get at the Museum. One just needs the huge
> space of the church.

Biggs's last European recording trip had been in 1957, and in January 1961 he wrote to Flentrop indicating that plans for another such tour were taking shape, although "It is no longer as easy as it was (not that it was ever really easy!) for the equipment needed is twice as much and more difficult to control. Also there are the customs problems to be solved, with which you so kindly helped us the last time."

What Biggs seems to have had in mind was a repeat or update of *The Art of the Organ,* but recorded with the newer equipment. John McClure, his current Columbia producer, thought that the least troublesome way to accomplish this would be in collaboration with the Philips firm's offices in Baarn, Holland, and Hamburg, Germany. As negotiations progressed, the plan for the album metamorphosed into a survey of Arp Schnitger's organs. Since they were all located in a rather narrow area of northern Holland and Germany, there would be considerably less travel than on the two earlier trips.

> One must look hard on the map to discover some of the smaller Schnitger
> towns. A visit to these rather remote places prompts many reflections. For here is
> the work of a man who made a better mouse trap. And true to Emerson's quip, the
> world has beaten a path to his door.

Biggs had recorded some of Schnitger's masterpieces on previous tours, but this time, in the words of his 1964 *Diapason* account, he meant to beat a path to the legendary builder's door in earnest.

The decision to employ the Philips engineers, while more costly than anticipated, proved wise, for Alex Saron of the Dutch office and Helmut Storjohann of the German branch took upon themselves a good part of the burden of making arrangements that would normally have fallen on Biggs and Peggy. There were, of course, the inevitable complications, not the least of which was the rising cost of using the church buildings. "The people at Alkmaar and Zwolle were very nice," wrote Biggs to Saron in June 1961, "and the figures quoted are about right for these larger churches. But the figure given you at Uithuizen, both for the church and for the organ tuner, is *quite* a hold-up." It was, in fact, "more than we have ever paid, even at such places as Salzburg Cathedral, for three nights and 3 LPs!"

Some problems were of a more comic nature, as when the engineers set up all their equipment in the wrong church. And after Biggs had received permission to record some Mozart works on the great Müller organ at Haarlem, he discovered that the church's automatic carillon played faithfully and loudly every quarter hour (but could be silenced for a price). Saron also reported, no doubt to Biggs's amusement, that the Haarlem people "were puzzled to hear you would need three nights, since organists who have recorded there previously, have always made an LP in one night."

But on the whole, the operation went more smoothly than usual, both in Holland and in Germany. Biggs was introduced to the eminent Schnitger authority Gustav Fock, who was enthusiastic about Biggs's project and provided valuable assistance, not the least of which involved sorting out the genuine Schnitger organs from the spurious ones. In Cappel Biggs found a recording artist's dream, a church "in the middle of nowhere" with one of the best preserved of all Schnitger organs and "the priceless virtue of perfect quietness." Steinkirchen was not quite so noiseless, for the town was in the middle of a shooting festival when Biggs arrived to record.

Only one little sticky situation threatened the full realization of the project. Just as Biggs was about to leave for Europe, word came from Philips that the organist of the St. Jakobi Church in Hamburg, home of one of the largest Schnitger organs (and where Biggs had given a recital in 1954), had "written a nasty letter . . . saying that he has a contract with the church giving him exclusive right to make recordings of the church's Arp Schnitger organ, and he has no intention of giving up any of his rights." The Hamburg organ was important to the completeness of the documentary, and Biggs fumed. Never before had he been refused the use of an organ for recording. The Philips people wheedled and intrigued, but to no avail. In September, after his return, Biggs wrote to Storjohann that "we were able to visit every Schnitger organ, with the exception of Hamburg." And he was still slightly sore: "A historic organ such as that does not belong to the organist, but to the musical world at large!" While he expressed hope that he might still be able to record the Hamburg organ on a later trip, that never happened—yet the instrument does appear on the completed record. The mystery is solved when one observes that the piece played on it is Bach's Toccata in D minor, the same work Biggs recorded on fourteen European organs back in 1954.

Biggs was building up quite a backlog of tapes for Columbia. The Haarlem recording was not released until 1966, although the Schnitger album, entitled *The Golden Age of the Organ* and accompanied by an illustrated jacket booklet containing an article by Fock, appeared early in 1964. Thirteen Schnitger organs are heard on that recording, playing mostly music by Bach and Pepping, the latter included to prove that old organs were not necessarily restricted to the playing of old music. It got good notices. Michael Steinberg of the *Boston Globe* called it "something that no one seriously interested in Baroque music will want to miss." The *New York Times* praised the "clarity, brightness, and roundness of tone" of the organs and seemed to note a subtle change in Biggs's playing: "Mr. Biggs takes advantage of his opportunities as guide and demonstrator; the role inspires some of his best playing, and it seems less impersonal than usual."

Recording in East Germany was still on Biggs's agenda, but while it first appeared that the Philips people might be able to arrange it, plans again fell through, and his dream of recording the fabled Silbermann organs and playing in Bach's own church was once more deferred. But if Bach country was off limits, there were plenty of other composers whose home territories were easily accessible. While on the Schnitger trail, Biggs took time out to visit Lüneburg, on the North Sea. There, in the cavernous Johanniskirche, he recorded a disc's worth of Buxtehude works on the large and recently renovated organ, which contained many pipes that were already old in Buxtehude's day. "This is really quite successful," wrote Biggs to McClure early in 1963. "The music is quite the best of Buxtehude, and the rough organ tone seems to suit it well." This tape also languished a while in Columbia's vaults, not being released until 1967.

One of Biggs's friends and correspondents in the musicological world was H. C. Robbins Landon, the distinguished Haydn scholar. In 1961 he was living in Italy, editing Haydn's complete works. Biggs wrote to him in the spring of that year, inquiring about some of Haydn's organ concertos, and received a most encouraging response. Landon had just finished editing two of these concertos, and he had recently discovered a third. Further, he knew of not one but four authentic "Haydn" organs in Eisenstadt, where Haydn had spent much of his life, "so you can pay Columbia's money and take your choice!" Biggs responded, "I mentioned the matter at Columbia records, and their reaction was immediate. Sure! When?" Biggs's reaction was likewise immediate; he asked Landon to send him the organ parts of the concertos, so that he could begin learning them.

Of the four eighteenth-century organs in Eisenstadt, two were quite small, and of the other two, both by Georg Mallon of Vienna, one was badly in need of restoration. But the other, in the Stadtpfarrkirche (where in 1951 Landon had discovered a hitherto unknown Haydn manuscript in a rain-soaked stack of music in a corner of the choir loft), was a true "find." The church's acoustics were ideal for concerted music, and the sparkling little two-manual organ of 1770, which had actually been played by Haydn, had been restored in 1942 and was in excellent condition. The church authorities were cooperative, Landon was eager to help (and was promptly signed on to do the jacket notes), and Columbia was able to engage a very good chamber orchestra under the direction of Zoltan Rosznyai.

The Haydn concertos were recorded in 1962, and the album, a pleasantly listenable "sleeper" that deserved more attention than it got in America, was released in 1964. But the Eisenstadt situation was so ideal for recording (and, from Columbia's standpoint, so favorable financially) that what had begun as the simple project of recording Haydn's music on an authentic Haydn organ soon grew into a recording marathon.

For a number of years Biggs had been realizing figured basses and making arrangements for organ and orchestra of movements from Bach's cantatas, and some had been recorded as early as 1951. Lately he had been working up some of them, perhaps on the off chance that his most recent bid to breach the Iron Curtain would be successful. In addition, his friend Daniel Pinkham had been commissioned to make some arrangements of familiar Christmas carols ("with all kinds of tonal tinsel") to be recorded at the Museum. With all this material more or less in readiness, it made sense to Columbia to switch the recording location to Eisenstadt, where Biggs, the orchestra, and the equipment would already be installed. In addition, Biggs thought that it was time for a stereo version of the seventeen Mozart "Festival" Sonatas," and since they were never far from his fingers, a complete new set was thrown in for good measure. Considering the amount of literature covered in this 1962 session, the quality of all of the resultant recordings is high. Biggs was in top form, having taken a short vacation in Bermuda before this session. There, besides relaxing, he could practice undisturbed in a small Anglican church, giving the parishioners a benefit concert in return for the favor.

On his return to the United States in the fall, Biggs had several years' worth of releases on tape from the Eisenstadt sessions and the Schnitger trip—and a monumental editing task ahead of him, which he dovetailed into his concert schedule with his usual efficiency. Columbia was eager to get the Christmas record in the stores by October 1963, so it was processed first. The Bach, Haydn, and Schnitger albums appeared the following year.

Unlike most other recording artists, Biggs did nearly all of his own editing, both on his own equipment at home and with the engineers at the Columbia studios in New York. His standards were rigid as he sorted out numerous "takes" on the tapes, and he was not above splicing parts of takes together if he felt that a better product would result. Unless one has actually seen the reams of correspondence and notes this editing generated, it is difficult to convey what a tedious and time-consuming process it was. Yet Biggs never gave the impression that it was onerous; he seems in fact to have rolled up his sleeves for the task quite cheerfully. The following excerpts from Biggs's letters to producer McClure during 1962 and 1963 may give some small hint of what was involved:

> Everything we worked on, we got. And as you'll see, there's plenty for the record. . . . But several things that we did hurriedly, or hopefully, we just didn't get. For example, the Oboe is wonderful in Ich Stehe [mit ein Fuss in Grabe, by Bach], but the strings play wrong notes, and there is no coverage. A different basic tempo in each take rules out certain other items. Altogether, a very illuminating session.

> Most of the details we were able to edit out. But in many of the Nowells "one more take" would have made all the difference. The first is just an exploration of the notes. The second is tentative, and only after that do tempi, levels, and other items settle down.

> [Music of] Jubilee is going to be all right—much better than on the tape you have. For I've found a way to redo the last chorus of the Christmas Oratorio, and now we have a much better and more convincing sequence of pieces.

> Enclosed are a few comments I ventured to list about the relation of the different instruments to each other in tone level.

> I hadn't considered [the Bach chorale prelude] before, because my copy is so distorted in the bass, and the irregular action of the organ shows up in one or two places. But I doped it out on the tape copy . . . and you may feel it's worth editing and popping in.

> There seems to be a hum on my tape copy, but I hope this is not in the original. Or it may be covered by the music. If you say the word, I'll be glad to run down and edit the item.

> This is just a preliminary splicing, so that you can get the idea of things. And there are still a few spots that will be improved. All suggestions will be welcome, and I hope you will like the different order of menu.

> I've literally been listening, copying, splicing and editing for two weeks and more! But I'm getting near the end of all the European stuff.

> Better not go into the editing room . . . there's a great pile of work there.

Reviews of the entire batch of European recordings were favorable. The British liked the Haydn album particularly. *The Gramophone* for June 1965 called it "unsuspected treasure." *Records and Recording* for the same month noted that Biggs played the organ parts "with impeccable taste and unfailing vivacity on a gem of an organ," but that the orchestra played "with rather less sense of period than the soloist." The May *E. M. G. Monthly Letter* rated the Haydn release with their "best of the month." *Music of Jubilee* (the album of Bach cantata excerpts) also fared well, as did the Christmas issue, Biggs's first real venture into the more popular market.

The mountain of editing did not prevent Biggs from hatching another ambitious "Five Year Plan" in 1963. Most ambitious of all was a proposed Historic Organs of Europe series, each album to focus on the organs and music of a different country. Additional Bach Favorites albums recorded at the Museum were to be the main thrust of domestic recording. Other albums featuring single composers were under consideration, but not all of them materialized. Having discovered an authentic "Bruckner" organ in the monastery of St. Florian in Austria, Biggs sounded out Landon on sources of that composer's music: "Already I have a number of pieces (none of them particularly good, incidentally) but I'd like to find more." Apparently he never did, for the project was eventually shelved. Meanwhile, Biggs had earned a few years' respite from European recording tours, and, as it turned out, there was plenty of work to occupy him at home.

16 | *Organ and Orchestra*

Old Biggs he tickled the ivories
And William directed the tune;
Icelanders all were delighted to hear
The strains of "Eileen Aroon,"
For oboe and drums, sackbut and saw,
A bottle of beer and a spoon,
And Biggs was playing a packing case,
Oh yes he was playing a packing case,
In the merry old month of June.

Biggs left the country only once in 1963, and that was for a short tour of Iceland, which he had not visited for several years. His itinerary included some solo recitals, and at least one concert with an orchestra in Reykjavik, directed by William Strickland. That appearance inspired the above "Epode to Biggs," written by another visitor to Iceland, Thomas MacAnna of the Abbey Theatre, Dublin. Unfortunately the program has not survived, so we do not know whether Biggs actually played an Irish folk tune; judging from the instrumentation cited, MacAnna employed more than a little poetic license, and Biggs's "packing case" was probably a positive organ of some sort.

It is probably safe to say that no other twentieth-century organist performed or recorded as much with orchestras, instrumental ensembles, and solo instruments as did Biggs. His zeal for promoting the organ as an ensemble instrument led to his obtaining concert engagements in places even more remote than Iceland, his encouragement of the writing of new works, and his activism on behalf of pipe organs in concert halls.

Although his concertizing went on almost continuously, Biggs had to devote large chunks of time to recording, editing, and jacket note preparation between 1959, when the first batch of recordings on the new Flentrop were made, and the end of the second European tour in 1962. While Biggs did occasional ensemble work during this period, there was little time to learn or even practice the kind of literature that major orchestral collaborations demanded. In 1960, for example, he played with the Little Symphony of Seattle, the Buffalo Philharmonic, and the Shreveport Symphony Orchestra, but, with

149

the exception of the Poulenc Concerto, the repertoire consisted only of shorter works by Handel, Bach, Mozart, and Corelli, all of which, including the Poulenc, he had played many times before. In 1960 he also gave a solo recital to inaugurate the new Aeolian-Skinner organ in Philadelphia's Academy of Music, an instrument with which he was not particularly impressed: "There were ciphers, and endless mechanical trouble," he wrote to a friend shortly afterward. "No real ensemble, though some of the individual stops are nice."

But the new Philadelphia organ was a portent of things to come, for the early 1960s saw the building of other new concert hall organs, and Biggs was usually the conductor's first choice when it came to organ-and-orchestra programs. With a good backlog of unreleased tapes at Columbia, Biggs was ready to work on new repertoire and take to the concert hall stage again.

The early part of 1962 was taken up with a European tour and a number of solo concerts, including the opening of a large Tamburini organ in San Juan, Puerto Rico, which drew an audience of three thousand and some rather flowery reviews. But much of the summer was spent preparing for a formidable round of orchestral appearances in the fall. The first, in late September, was the long-awaited opening of Philharmonic Hall at Lincoln Center for the Performing Arts. It was supposed to be the splashiest and most glamorous occasion of the whole New York musical season, and in most respects it was—but not for Biggs.

Biggs had been booked well in advance to play the new four-manual Aeolian-Skinner organ, but neither the organ builders nor the Lincoln Center management had anticipated major acoustical problems or interference from Manhattan's feisty trade unions. The unions wrecked the installation schedule right at the outset by prohibiting the organ builders from using their own (non-union) employees for any carpentry or electrical work, and it is said that the plumbers' union even tried to muscle in with regard to the organ pipes. Since none of the union men had had any experience with organs, they had to be supervised by the builders, who ultimately had to redo much of the work. In addition, construction work related to last-minute acoustical changes made it impossible to carry on tonal finishing, or even, because of risk of damage, to plant the pipes in the organ. Joseph Whiteford of Aeolian-Skinner summed up some of the problems in a letter to Biggs dated August 28, 1962:

> I wanted to write you a note to say how very sorry I am about the situation at the Philharmonic Hall. I know we had all counted on great things at the right time. We did everything humanly possible to avoid the situations that have arisen. The organ was actually built last year and we delivered it in June, but subsequent acoustical changes in the Hall have created so much dust that it has been impossible for us to put pipes in and thus to do the finishing and tuning.
>
> The Union situation aggravated the problem considerably because the men

simply didn't know what they were doing, as you can imagine, and practically everything had to be done over again. But even if we had been installing it, there simply wouldn't have been enough time. Last week, just one month away from the opening, the entire interior of the auditorium is filled with scaffolding and there are two inches of dirt all over everything. You can imagine what a mess it is.

The formal organ opening was delayed until December 15, but the second inaugural program for the hall, to take place in September, had already been publicized as including Richard Strauss's *Festival Prelude* for organ and orchestra, and Biggs had signed a contract to play it. Then the Allen Organ Company offered to loan the hall a two-manual electronic instrument, and Biggs was placed in a no-win situation. He had always refused to play electronic imitations, but he had also never broken a contract, and in the end he consented to play the Allen. Unfortunately, Allen made several attempts during the next few years to capitalize on the incident in its publicity; finally, in 1967, Biggs was forced to threaten the firm with legal action.

The Strauss work, a not particularly inspired *pièce d'occasion,* opened the program, and it was probably not the most fortuitous choice for the spot. Whether it was the not-yet-adjusted acoustics, the substitute instrument, the antiphonal brass blaring from behind the audience, the composition itself, or an unfortunate combination of all these elements, it was the one work on the program that neither impressed nor pleased the critics. Louis Biancolli dismissed it as a "strident inundation," and most of the other reviewers glossed over it as hastily as possible to go on to praise subsequent parts on the program. But Miles Kastendieck plainly did not like the performance and said so:

> Quite the contrary must be said of the blatant horror stirred up at the start of the concert by Strauss's festival prelude for large orchestra and organ. From the raucous blasts of the electronic organ to the din of the supplementary brasses stationed in the second terrace, this was an ordeal.

How much of an ordeal it was for Biggs can only be guessed. To make matters worse, he had contracted to record the piece for Columbia.

After such a dismal beginning for the season, things could only get better. Early in October Biggs returned to Philadelphia's Academy of Music for a demanding program, which included the familiar Saint-Saëns Organ Symphony and Poulenc Concerto; Samuel Barber's *Toccata Festiva* for organ and orchestra, commissioned for the opening of the Academy's new organ two years earlier; and an organ solo, Bach's Fantasia and Fugue in G minor. Here the critics were kinder and the audience appreciative, calling Biggs back with their applause several times at the conclusion. Columbia had previously taped the Barber, Poulenc, and Saint-Saëns works, combining the first two with the

New York Strauss performance to assemble a single rather speedily released disc.

In November Biggs was at the Peristyle in Toledo, playing the Poulenc and a Handel concerto with the Toledo Orchestra, along with organ solos by Bach and Ives. The Bach work was the same one played in Philadelphia, where both critics had praised it; but Boris Nelson of the *Toledo Blade,* who liked the "nicely proportioned" playing of the Poulenc work, thought the Bach offering "the poorest part of the program." In December Biggs was in Pittsburgh, where he and 25 members of the Pittsburgh Symphony were crowded into the organ loft of St. Paul's Cathedral to perform two Handel concertos and the Poulenc Concerto with the new tracker-action von Beckerath organ. All 1,800 seats in the cathedral were filled, and the reviews were highly laudatory. December also brought Biggs back to Lincoln Center where, along with Catherine Crozier and Virgil Fox, he participated in the opening recital on the finally-completed Aeolian-Skinner organ. Among other works he played Virgil Thomson's *Pange Lingua,* which had been commissioned for the occasion.

Even more orchestra concerts were booked for 1963. Regular solo appearances found Biggs playing a wide range of instruments from the large Aeolian-Skinner in Boston's Symphony Hall to his favorite one-manual Tannenberg in York, Pennsylvania; and symphonic appearances were scattered throughout the year. In February Biggs was credited by the papers as being the drawing-card that brought out 1,500 Maine music-lovers in a snowstorm to a Portland Symphony Orchestra concert. The program included Handel's Concerto No. 10 and the familiar Concerto by Poulenc, who had died about a week before.

By spring Biggs was in Ann Arbor, Michigan, doing Poulenc and Saint-Saëns at Hill Auditorium with the Philadelphia Orchestra as part of the annual May Festival. Biggs was enjoying a rewarding relationship with this orchestra. The previous September Eugene Ormandy had revived a work that Biggs had not performed for some time, Sowerby's Concerto in C major for organ and orchestra. On that occasion, Max Schauensee of the *Philadelphia Bulletin,* who liked the work, wrote, "Mr. Biggs was ever the virtuoso at the console, meeting the dramatic challenge of Sowerby's concerto head-on." Ormandy and Biggs took the Sowerby work and Barber's *Toccata Festiva* to New York's Philharmonic Hall in October 1963. The tough New York critics were kinder this time around. Alan Rich praised Biggs's footwork, and even Kastendieck, although rather lukewarm about the concert in general, thought the organ and orchestra pieces the best part of it. It was the audience that was unkind this time; some of the concertgoers rudely walked out on the Sowerby, prompting a scathing commentary by *New York Times* critic Harold Schonberg on the narrowminded attitude of New York audiences toward contemporary music.

In front of Philharmonic
(now Avery Fisher) Hall,
New York, 1961

Biggs and Eugene Ormandy at a rehearsal of the Philadelphia Orchestra, 1962

November found Biggs playing Barber and Handel with the Detroit Symphony in Ford Auditorium, and Handel and Sowerby with the Wichita Symphony.

In February 1963 the veteran organist Channing Lefebvre, having been asked to do some concerts in Manila, sought Biggs's advice on pieces he might play with an orchestra there. Biggs's commentary on some of the works with which he was most familiar is illuminating:

> The Hindemith isn't terribly hard, just awkward. It's about 14 minutes in length. Woodwinds, brass, 'celli but no violins or violas. Trouble is, the middle movement is rather dull, though the first and last are fun.
>
> Music of Jubilee, and Bach Festival, are just a grouping of Bach chorales and cantata movements, Jesu Joy, Sheep may safely graze, and so on. Some are played exactly as Bach indicated, and others are arranged. Particularly effective, perhaps, is My Spirit be Joyful, for two Trumpets and Organ.
>
> The only thing like the Saint-Saëns is the Strauss Festliches Praeludium. . . . It's a work that packs a huge wallop, and which lets the organ be heard solo, in much the same way as the Saint-Saëns.
>
> There are, as you know, the Handel Concertos. Which did you do last year? Then there is the Barber Toccata, but I really don't feel it's worth the work. I did it because I had to.
>
> There is a very charming Partita for English Horn and Organ by Jan Koetsier. . . . And there is an original suite for solo Violin and Organ, Opus 166, by Josef Rheinberger. . . . It's a very elegant work.
>
> Then, there's the piece that Mozart wrote for Glass Armonica, with Flute, Oboe, Viola, and 'Cello. This can be very effectively played on the organ.
>
> And, of course, there are the Frescobaldi and Gabrieli pieces for Brass and Organ. But you know about them.
>
> Finally, if you hear the record "Heroic Music" and would like any of these things, I can probably send you photostats of whatever you like.

Appearances with orchestras and smaller ensembles continued through 1964. In March Biggs was in Florida, performing Poulenc and Handel with orchestras in Tampa and St. Petersburg. In April, he included soloists from the Boston Symphony Orchestra in a Symphony Hall program; and in August he performed music of Handel, Haydn, Mozart, and Telemann with the Royal Festival Orchestra of Ontario.

In October, Biggs returned, in more congenial weather, to the Kotzschmar Memorial Organ in Portland's City Hall, performing Saint-Saëns and Handel with the Portland Symphony Orchestra. In the same month he played the Sowerby Concerto in Grand Rapids, and the composer, a native of that city, was present for the occasion. A week later, while in Milwaukee for a solo recital, Biggs was told of efforts by the local chapter of the American Guild of Organists to install a pipe organ in the Music Hall. He immediately went to bat for their cause. "Milwaukee's Music Hall must have a real organ, one with character," he told a newspaper reporter. "That you must have and not settle for a substitute." In 1969, through the generosity of the Miller family (of brewery fame) Milwaukee did at last acquire a "real organ" for its Music Hall—and of course Biggs was engaged to play it.

Biggs went abroad again in 1965. He stepped up his domestic recording activity, but the flurry of orchestral appearances was winding down. In February he took the Sowerby work to Detroit's Ford Auditorium (where it again met with a lukewarm reception), and in March he played Saint-Saëns, Poulenc, and Handel with the Florida Symphony Orchestra in Orlando.

The number of new and rebuilt tracker-action organs in America had been increasing steadily during the early 1960s, and Biggs was a natural choice when a major concert was given on any of them. Some of his 1965 engagements included recitals on a von Beckerath organ in Florida's Stetson University, a restored nineteenth-century Johnson organ in Sacramento, and an instrument by the German builder Bosch in the Ethical Society of St. Louis. But the engagement that doubtless gave him the greatest satisfaction was the dedication of the splendid new four-manual Flentrop organ in St. Mark's Cathedral, Seattle. Biggs had been in correspondence concerning it for several years with both Flentrop and the Cathedral's organist, Peter Hallock, and was probably responsible for having initially recommended Flentrop. The organ, in an ideal gallery location in the reverberant, high-ceilinged concrete building, was the largest instrument Flentrop had yet exported to the United States and the first new tracker-action organ of any consequence on the West Coast. It was, and remains, a positive musical force in the Pacific Northwest.

In December 1966 Biggs revived Aaron Copland's Symphony for Organ and Orchestra with Leonard Bernstein and the New York Philharmonic Orchestra, and finally wrung a compliment out of the New York press when Robert Jacobson of the *Post* wrote:

> The role of the organ, as intended by Copland, is as an integral part of the orchestra, rather than as a solo instrument; and last night's performance benefited from the highly authoritative performance by E. Power Biggs. Mr. Bernstein gave the Symphony a super-charged reading which received an enthusiastic reception from the audience who also saluted the beaming Mr. Copland, seated in the first terrace.

Biggs turned 60 in March 1966. He had been troubled with arthritis for nearly a decade, but he showed few signs of slowing down. He took good care of his health, and conscientiously followed all of Dr. Carey Peters's orders save one. Over and over again the physician patiently suggested that Biggs take things a bit easier. "I wish you could arrange to take some time off," he wrote in 1962. "The constant pressure and always being on the production line certainly is a stressful situation. . . ." Dr. Peters further suggested that Biggs take a bona fide vacation of a week or two twice a year, and Biggs did yield a little on this account, taking occasional spring breaks in Bermuda or Curaçao. But one wonders if Peters ever found out that Biggs also managed to arrange for practice in these places, giving complimentary recitals in return. At any rate, Peters's admonitions to slow down continued with every annual checkup, although the physician must eventually have realized that this just was not Biggs's style. Inaction probably caused him more stress than activity, which he seemed to thrive on.

That Biggs's credo of hard work and confidence in one's own abilities still held meaning for him is revealed in his answer to a letter received in December 1966 from a sixteen-year-old admirer in California. The youngster confessed that he had not known there was more to music than just the Rolling Stones until he had heard a recording of Biggs playing Bach's Toccata and Fugue in D minor on the radio. He wanted to know how Biggs had gotten started, and if—as his parents and others had told him—it took a lot of money to become successful. Biggs, who had come to America unknown and almost penniless in the middle of the Great Depression, must surely have chuckled at this question. He replied to the boy,

> Thanks so much for your letter and your comments. I think the only way to succeed in music or in any other field is to work at it just as hard as you can. And you may have confidence that you can do this just as well as anyone else.
>
> Don't feel that "you have to have money to be noticed." You'll earn that as you go along. In any case, if you love music just stick to it.

17 | *The Pedal Harpsichord*

If you don't want to get bitten by the harpsichord bug,
don't go near such an instrument—for if you do, you will!

The bite that Biggs warned his colleagues against in the January 1977 issue of *Music* was sustained by him more than fifteen years earlier. During the American Guild of Organists convention in Detroit in the summer of 1960, a number of participants responded to an invitation to visit the workshop of the noted harpsichord maker John Challis. Among the instruments to be seen there was an impressively sleek two-manual and pedal model, which drew the organists as flies to honey.

The harpsichord revival, in which Challis had been one of the pioneers, was just beginning to gather momentum. Most organists were already familiar with the increasingly ubiquitous little single-manual "kit" instruments and stock-model German imports. But this pedal harpsichord, standing large as life in Challis's Detroit atelier, was something else—something previously only read about in music history texts. It was in fact the first such instrument to be made by Challis or any other American maker, and it was frankly experimental in nature. Most of the organists left Challis's workshop nurturing heady dreams of one day seeing such an instrument carried into their living-rooms; Biggs had some bolder ideas.

Ideas, to Biggs, were something to be carefully filed for future reference, then acted upon when the time was ripe. In April 1962 he wrote to John McClure of Columbia Masterworks:

> I have the possibly slightly goofy idea of acquiring a pedal harpsichord. Challis in Detroit has a pedal harpsichord, with independent strings, which is set under the usual instrument. I played it a year or two ago, and the sonority is wonderful.
>
> The problem is, of course, to obtain the harpsichord, which involves a waiting list.
>
> In effect, I'd hope to sell the Schlicker [the Cambridge Portative] and thus transform it into this pedal-harpsichord—which might be better for practice, and which just possibly might open up some very interesting sonorities for other uses.

McClure questioned the wisdom of getting one of Challis's metal-framed instruments when the tendency among the younger makers was toward wooden frames and a less aggressive sound. Biggs, however, stuck with his choice of Challis. He liked the brash, varied sound, and he was probably thinking in terms of large concert halls, where such a sound was required. And the metal frame could be an advantage in an instrument that might have to be moved around quite a bit. Very shortly after writing to McClure, Biggs was off to Detroit to make a firm commitment with Challis.

Challis seemed a bit taken aback by this commission. In an interview in *Harpsichord* in 1969, he recalled that visit: "he [Biggs] came back and told me that he couldn't take my pedal harpsichord off his mind. And he asked me if I would make him one. Suddenly, I got scared!" But once he had agreed to do it, plans rapidly progressed. "Together we worked out the stop arrangement so that it would be most convenient to him." Biggs would stop by from time to time to check on progress. Challis had completed the pedal part of the instrument and was about to begin on the manual part when he was struck down by the first attack of a chronic disease that would claim his life a decade later. He was unable to do any work for six months, delaying the completion of Biggs's harpsichord until the summer of 1964.

The pedal harpsichord was crated and shipped off to Cambridge, and as soon as it was unpacked—on the Fourth of July, as it happened—Biggs rang up Challis and astonished him by playing part of Charles Ives's Variations on "America" over the telephone. Shortly afterward, he wrote jubilantly to Flentrop,

> When you're here, you may be tickled to try a Challis Pedal-Harpsichord, which has just been completed, after three years of waiting—just like a Flentrop organ! I'm hoping to sell the Schlicker, and thus graduate completely from electric action.

Biggs freely admitted that he did not know much about pedal harpsichords, but he thought his new acquisition "quite wonderful" and had no qualms about asking advice concerning its use. It was a whole new world to be explored, and he did so with characteristic openness and enthusiasm. In August he wrote to Leonard Burkat, vice president of Columbia, asking if he had any suggestions of repertoire to try on the new instrument, "for, frankly, I have never seen a Pedal Harpsichord before, and nor had Challis." Biggs's first impulse was to experiment with Bach. Trio Sonatas, as expected, worked just fine, but the instrument also sounded well in "more unexpected pieces, such as the Bach Toccata in D minor, the Prelude and Fugue in A minor, and other works with a good deal of bustle. In other words, the instrument doesn't turn out the way one might think, but turns out wonderfully well in unexpected ways." Burkat shared Biggs's enthusiasm, suggested Bach's *Art of Fugue* and pre-Bach pieces (and "impractical ideas like Robert Schumann's pieces for pedal piano") and encouraged Biggs to keep on exploring.

Before long Biggs was as hard at work on his new instrument as a heavy concert schedule would allow (taking time out to record at the Museum *Bach Organ Favorites, Vol. 2*, based on a famous recital by Mendelssohn at Leipzig in 1840). Biggs quizzed Challis on performance practice; Challis responded with some general suggestions and recommended reading Robert Donington's book *The Interpretation of Early Music*. Biggs promptly acquired it and, judging from the dog-eared pages in the "Keyboard" chapter, read it more than once. In May 1965 the pedal harpsichord made its debut in a program of six Bach works given at the Busch-Reisinger Museum.

Like some of Biggs's other Museum concerts, this one was a trial run before a recording, and a few days later the pedal harpsichord was shipped to the Columbia studio in New York for a June recording session. John Challis flew in from Detroit to tune and regulate the instrument. Despite continued poor health and the added blow of seeing his workshop property summarily taken by eminent domain by the Michigan Highway Department, Challis continued to be helpful and enthusiastic.

Biggs, equally enthusiastic over the possibilities opened up by the new instrument, was putting to use some of the ideas on performance he had learned from Challis and from the sources he had been studying. And something else. Whether it was the rhythmic emphasis of the instrument, the difference in its response, or just the mood Biggs was in, his performances on this all-Bach recording, particularly of the Fantasy and Fugue in G minor and Prelude and Fugue in G major, are some of the liveliest he ever made of these works. Swinging, happy, driving, they stay always on the proper side of good taste, as do Biggs's original cadenzas to some of the works. On the record jacket Biggs simply stated that he took "the opportunity to exploit totally the declamatory and improvisational aspect" of the music.

The record was released in 1966, and it seems to have taken the critics by surprise. *The Diapason* called it "the most controversial record of the month" and predicted "scandalized outcries" over Biggs's "free, rhapsodic style," cadenzas, and embellishments. But, "no one will be able to call this record dull or uninteresting; it may just accomplish for the harpsichord a bit of the kind of general introduction this artist has accomplished for the organ." *The American Organist* spent some time comparing Biggs's latest *Bach Organ Favorites* album with an Anthony Newman Bach release, but seemed at a loss to find anything with which to compare the harpsichord platter. "For the most part it comes off pleasantly enough, though I doubt the pedal harpsichord will ever replace the organ," the reviewer concluded weakly. Outside the organ world the reviewers took Biggs's harpsichord debut a bit more in stride. The only real criticism was of the engineering—some thought the microphone placement too close. *Records and Recording* for July 1966 provided a particularly long and perceptive writeup, in which the reviewer observed:

> E. Power Biggs' long experience with these works on the organ enables him to present them in this medium with a grandeur and spaciousness which harpsichord specialists might view with some suspicion. Personally, I found his interpretations quite thrilling. . . . No one would be so stupid as to claim that these performances in any way supersede ones of equal quality on the organ, but I can promise the inquisitive collector that new light is thrown upon the works by the pedal harpsichord.

Indeed, it is entirely possible that the pedal harpsichord threw new light on the music for Biggs himself.

Biggs's Bach interpretations may have raised a few critical eyebrows, but his next harpsichord album was definitely a hair-raiser. The idea for what he was later to call "an amusing spin-off" seems to have originated with John McClure or someone else at Columbia, but Biggs was game, and early in the summer of 1965 he wrote to McClure: "Since returning I have been meditating day and night on HOLIDAY FOR HARPSICHORD. It really can be quite a whiz-bang, I think."

This project represented the farthest Biggs had strayed from the traditional repertoire for either harpsichord or organ, for it turned out to be an unabashed and rollicking collection of music composed for neither instrument—a collection of popular classic "chestnuts," including Mozart's *Rondo alla Turca,* Schubert's *Marche Militaire,* and Saint-Saëns's *The Swan.* In short, transcriptions. Biggs, in his tongue-in-cheek jacket notes, maintained that he was only paying the pianists and conductors back for all the works they had looted from the organ repertoire over the years: "Turn about is fair play."

The album was released in the fall of 1966, and the hi-fi buffs loved it. So did some of Biggs's fellow organists, although there were some humorless souls among them who seemed to feel that Biggs had somehow betrayed them and who briefly vented their outrage in the letters to the editors of the trade magazines.

At least one harpsichordist, Larry Palmer, admitted to having entertained such musically heretical thoughts himself. In a 1979 *Diapason* article, he wrote, "I must admit that the thought for such a concert has often entered my mind, but Biggs had the instrument on which to do it, and the contract with

The pedal harpsichord, ca. 1966

Columbia. And what a pretty record it turned out to be!" John Challis was delighted with *Holiday for Harpsichord* and claimed his friends were too, "except for one stuffed shirt who even *admits* he likes it, but is very concerned about your image—and mine!" The record seems to have sold rather well.

But *Holiday* was only an interlude—and perhaps an experiment. Before it was released, Biggs was already working on another Bach album. This one, released in the fall of 1967, contained the six Trio Sonatas and two of Bach's Italian Concerto transcriptions, to which Biggs brought the same yeasty interpretation that had distinguished the first Bach album.

John Challis continued his encouragement and counsel. In August 1966 he wrote Biggs a long letter full of helpful advice, urging him on to greater freedom, more liberal use of agogic accent, and imaginative registrations:

> Why shouldn't the Trio Sonatas use all the tonally significant possibilities of the Pedal Harpsichord! They must never be conceived as technical exercises, but as flights of imagination in the hands of a great genius of elegant good taste.

Challis approved of the finished product. In October 1967 he wrote,

> Thank you very much for the recordings of the Trio Sonatas. . . . Of course I am prejudiced, but I think they have taken on a new life on the pedal harpsichord. I hope others find it so too. You may recall that I used to think they might not go too well on the p. h. and even you were not too sure at first. But you have shown that they do go and that superbly.

The critics agreed. One reviewer in Terre Haute, Indiana, found the Trio Sonata record "luminous"; another in Joplin, Missouri, called it "an adventure in an altogether different dimension of art."

But there were also some detractors who argued that, historically, the pedal harpsichord was never meant to be anything other than a practice instrument and was therefore out of place in a concert application. Biggs answered them in an article in *Music Journal* for February 1968.

> Such an idea is immediately dissipated by a few minutes of playing the instrument. . . . My chief interest, however, in the two years that I have had the Challis, has not been to raid the harpsichord literature, but rather to explore the possibilities of playing organ music in the novel sonorities of plucked strings rather than organ pipes. One can of course play organ music exactly as written on the pedal harpsichord, and the result is a challenging sound, combining as it does harpsichord sparkle and clarity with something of the bass richness and depth of the organ.

But for the next two years, the pedal harpsichord was indeed a practice instrument for Biggs. The Cambridge Portative had been sold to a party in

California, and Challis's instrument occupied its place in the sunny front parlor of the Biggs home. The two-record Bach Trio Sonata album was reissued as two separate discs in 1968, but it was not until the 1970s that Biggs recorded on the pedal harpsichord again—one "legitimate" album of Walther concertos, and (in Biggs's own words) two "illegitimate" ones of Scott Joplin rags.

18 | *Historic Organs and a Grammy*

> It is fascinating to play a composer's music on the organ he
> played. You feel that you have touched the lifeline of history. . . .
> Beethoven's orchestra, Bach's choir are all gone, but the same
> organs on which great musicians played are still available.

Biggs made these comments to an interviewer at Erskine College in South
Carolina, where he had inaugurated a new Holtkamp organ on September 29,
1966. Two days later he was off to Sion, Switzerland, to give a recital on one of
Europe's oldest extant organs.

Biggs had taken a few years' respite from European recording, his 1962
marathon there having provided Columbia with a good stockpile of releases.
Late in 1964 he received an invitation to play the opening concert at an organ
festival in Ravenna, Italy, to be held early in July 1965. He was already
discussing with John McClure his ideas for a Historic Organs of Europe series,
with each album devoted to the music and organs of a single country, in the
manner of his 1957 *Organ Music of Spain and Portugal*. Biggs had never
visited Italy, but the Ravenna engagement gave him the opportunity to look
into historic organs there. He wrote to the noted organist and musicologist
Luigi Tagliavini in Bologna, asking for suggestions of eight or ten historic
organs he might visit: "I'm not looking for recitals but merely for the privilege
of trying their tonal qualities." Not untypically, things began to snowball.
Before long Biggs had added Spain, Portugal, and Switzerland to his exploratory itinerary.

Reviews of the Ravenna concert, played on a large modern organ in the
Basilica of San Vitale, praised Biggs's musicianship and command of the
instrument. One paid Biggs a signal compliment by referring to him in the
headline as "voce dell'organo." While his program would not have been
unfamiliar in the United States, it probably contained much that was new to
the Italian audience, and, interestingly, it included no Italian works. "Encores
were demanded" reads a somewhat stilted translation of one of the reviews.

Biggs gave no other concerts abroad, but made a whirlwind investigative tour of potential recording sites in Italy, Spain, and Portugal. On his return to the United States at the end of July, he firmed up plans for a fall trip built around a Swiss recording session and a major engagement in London's Royal Festival Hall, followed by a lecture for the Royal College of Organists. Biggs had sent the Royal Festival Hall management one of his typical mixed-bag touring programs, only to have it censored. The committee intimated that certain works by Purcell, Soler, and Bach (movements from the *Anna Magdalena Book,* which Biggs was preparing to record at the Museum) were "below the Royal Festival Hall's usual standard." Also rejected was a Mozart work that had already been programed by another organist. Peggy forwarded their missive to Biggs, who was on a concert tour, with the marginal note, "I hope this strikes you as VERY FUNNY, for it is!" His reaction is not recorded, but he sent the Londoners a substitute all-Bach program that should have been heavy enough for anyone's taste. It too proved unacceptable, since it again duplicated some works already programed by other organists in the series. Finally he managed to come up with one that the committee liked. Biggs had good reason for wanting to include a few familiar and easy pieces in his recital, for he would be facing a critical London audience right after coming from the Swiss recording session, with little time to rest or practice.

When Biggs went on his first European recording tour in 1954, he had to contact the churches and arrange for tuning and other services himself, as well as make his own hotel and travel reservations and bring his own equipment. Later he had some help in making these arrangements and could hire equipment and engineers. By the mid-1960s, the Columbia empire had expanded, and permanent offices of CBS Records were located in most European countries. They served a number of functions, including the recording of European and American artists and the distribution of records. They were also a kind of ad hoc concert bureau for visiting Columbia artists, for since Columbia records were now distributed throughout Europe, local performances by these artists helped promote record sales. The European offices provided recording engineers and relieved Biggs of a lot of irksome paperwork, but they also required him to dovetail more concerts into his recording schedule.

The first record of the Historic Organs series was made in Switzerland, and it included the Gothic organ in the mountain village of Sion. At the time, it was commonly thought that this small instrument was built in 1390. More recent research now places it in the first half of the fifteenth century; it is still one of the world's oldest organs, even though some of its pipes are from the eighteenth century. Biggs admired the brave sound of its antique principals and used them to record some of the earliest organ literature known. Other organs in the album reflected the ethnic diversity of Swiss culture: an Italian instrument in Mendrisio, a German one in Sitzberg, and an organ in Arlesheim by the Alsatian builder Andreas Silbermann, to which Biggs took a particular liking.

The resulting record, the first of several such joint issues, was released simultaneously in the United States and Switzerland in 1967. Promotional concerts in Switzerland were in order, and in March 1966 Biggs returned to give a recital in the Cathedral of Zurich. He received considerable press, radio, and television coverage for both his concert and the forthcoming record.

Elated by the good publicity generated by Biggs in Switzerland, the various CBS Records branches in Europe scrambled to arrange more concerts for Biggs's next trip. The situation seems to have gotten out of hand, and in July Biggs found it necessary to write to Michelette Menthonnex of the Paris office, laying down a few ground rules:

> In many ways phonograph records are the very best ways of bringing organ music to people, for they bring the organ (maybe a very famous and historic one) along with the music. Thus, in general, even though a live concert has an immediacy that a record lacks, it's worth while giving a concert only if it can definitely publicise our records.

Biggs suggested choosing one or two important cities, which would provide maximum exposure in each country, and using the best organs whenever possible ("The organ in Lucerne is perfectly awful! Yet one has to take it, or else refuse the festival.") He also pointed out that it was necessary for him to arrive on the site a few days early to practice and choose registrations. But, "Of course any TV appearances, or Radio interviews . . . are excellent—maybe the best publicity of all." These remarks do not imply that Biggs preferred recording to concertizing at this particular point. He liked both and continued to carry a heavy concert schedule in the United States (where he could also command better fees). But time was at a real premium on the European tours. Because of commitments at home the trips could not be open-ended, and Biggs did not want to compromise the quality of his recordings. They were, after all, the major purpose of the tours, the concerts being only incidental.

Columbia was beginning to take a more active hand in Biggs's programing. In the past Biggs would present the powers-that-be with one of his "Five Year Plans"; they would rubber-stamp it and then leave him pretty much to his own devices. In due time most of Biggs's ideas would be converted into recordings, which Columbia would then release at suitable intervals. Biggs continued to propose his own record ideas, most of which were still sooner or later realized, but around 1965 Columbia began to involve Biggs in some of its own schemes, among them the Christmas records and *Holiday for Harpsichord*.

All were agreed, however, that the Historic Organs series was an excellent idea, and Biggs was encouraged to carry his plans forward as expeditiously as possible. He had to defer his Spanish trip until the spring of 1967, however, for the important organs at Toledo were still being restored, and Biggs felt that they were an absolute "must" for a recording. Another English album was also taking shape in Biggs's mind, and he still had ideas about recording in East Germany, having persuaded the CBS Frankfurt office to reopen investigations there.

The year 1967 opened busily and remained so. Biggs performed and recorded Copland's Symphony with the New York Philharmonic during the first week of January, appeared with the Boston Symphony in February, and played his usual round of late-winter concerts. In the spring he headed for Spain, where he was the first to record the just-restored "Emperor's organ" at Toledo, as well as historic instruments in Segovia, Salamanca, and Madrid—about all that could be found in usable condition, but fortunately all good examples. Hellmuth Kolbe hauled his recording equipment from Switzerland, the Spanish organ builder Ramón de Amezua provided helpful assistance, and the recording sessions were relatively problem-free. As a result of the trip Biggs, in his self-appointed role of "good-will ambassador," agreed to help solicit American funds toward the restoration of the small organ in Salamanca Cathedral. Unfortunately, despite appeals to large corporations, he was able to secure only $500 from a private benefactor.

On his return to the United States, Biggs played a concert with the Boston Symphony Orchestra as part of its summer series at Tanglewood and recorded *Bach Organ Favorites, Vol. 3* at the Busch-Reisinger Museum. Columbia wanted another Christmas record, and the harried Biggs agreed to do it only if Columbia obtained the musical arrangements themselves and took care of the rest of the details. Potential recording sites ranged from Zurich to Cambridge, but for the sake of convenience, since a chorus and a brass group were involved, it ended up being recorded in St. Michael's Church in New York, where the live acoustics and the von Beckerath organ contributed to a pleasing result. Biggs still preferred to make solo recordings on the Flentrop organ in the Museum, and continued to do so, but in September 1967, just before leaving for Italy, he very quietly did something that few people knew of at the time—he donated the organ to Harvard University.

A spectacular Gabrieli recording project in Venice still lay ahead. It had the proverbial "cast of thousands," and sometimes it was hard to tell who was in charge. It was truly an international effort, although, as it turned out, nearly all the performers were American. The British musicologist Denis Stevens was engaged to research and orchestrate the scores; Americans Gregg Smith and

George Bragg were to handle the choral resources; Swiss engineer Hellmuth Kolbe was to record; and John McClure, with the help of Sylvio Cerutti Rosatti of CBS Italiana, coordinated and arranged the many details. Special clearance was needed just to use Gabrieli's own church, since the hierarchy had previously banned "mechanical reproductions." Biggs was responsible for the organ accompaniments and for obtaining an organ, since San Marco in Venice did not have a usable instrument.

By midsummer a good deal of confusion had set in, and Biggs made a stab at straightening it out. In a memo to all principals, which began "S O S, maybe," he tried to get some consensus on the program. He listed the scores sent by Stevens, and what the various other parties had suggested and might even be rehearsing. "We certainly can't do everything! But we have to get together once and for all, so that we're all preparing the same music!!!" At the same time he approached the Austrian organ builder Josef von Glatter-Götz of Rieger Orgelbau concerning the possible loan of an organ. Fortunately, there was a nearly completed two-manual "stock" instrument at his factory that he was willing to voice along Italian lines. Getting a temporary import permit was something else again, but that was by no means the only problem to be faced. McClure later summed up the whole Gabrieli experience in the words of Virgil: "Futuram non cognoscere melior est"—or, in McClure's own rather loose translation, "It is better not to know what is lurking around the next bend."

The recording sessions were scheduled for September, but at the end of August there were still a distressing number of loose ends, and for every problem solved, two more seemed to materialize. The search for a conductor and instrumentalists finally and fortuitously settled on Vittorio Negri, the Edward Tarr Brass Ensemble from Germany, and a local string group, the Gabrieli Consort La Fenice. Deciding where in the huge building to station the various musical forces for optimum recorded effect was another knotty problem. Cerutti (who is always referred to by his middle name) was having trouble with the Basilica authorities and begged the Swiss to come down and back him up. McClure and Biggs, who two years earlier had innocently thought it would be a dandy idea to record Giovanni Gabrieli's music in the composer's own church, were beginning to realize that the enterprise had somehow turned into the most colossal project Columbia had ever attempted to stage overseas.

The schedule was tight. Not only did Biggs have other commitments, but so did Bragg's 43-voice Texas Boys Choir, the Gregg Smith Singers, and the Ithaca College students Smith had recruited to beef up the adult portion of the chorus. As the participants began to arrive, so did more complications. The Basilica authorities had to be humored and bargained with on almost every point. They could not see why Columbia wanted to place the musicians in the two widely separated choir galleries, when all previous concert performers had stood in the nave. Columbia, however, had two very good reasons for the divided placement: historical authenticity and stereo. They finally got it because of the tourists. The authorities did not want the equipment cluttering up the nave by day, so everything, including the organ, ultimately went up into the galleries.

Then there was the matter of transportation. One cannot truck 4,000 pounds of recording equipment into a city where everything moves by water, but one of Cerutti's friends came to the rescue here. The organ was anxiously awaited, but days went by and it did not appear. Word came that there were problems with customs, and Biggs sent a panicky telegram to Glatter-Götz: "UNDERSTAND THERE ARE PROBLEMS CONCERNING TEMPORARY IMPORT ORGAN INTO ITALY BUT PLEASE MOVE HEAVEN AND EARTH TO ACCOMPLISH THIS. WE ABSOLUTELY NEED YOUR INSTRUMENT OTHERWISE WHOLE PROJECT MAY BECOME FIASCO."

Although a straight drive from the Rieger workship to Venice took only about seven hours, the organ was fourteen days in getting there, since the only way the customs problems could be overcome was to bring it in over the Swiss border. It arrived just 48 hours before recording was to start and was hurriedly assembled in the gallery by workmen from the nearby Ruffati factory. Tuning, like recording, could be done only at night. During the day the Basilica was thronged with tourists, and frequent masses were said. Meanwhile, risers were being set up in the galleries for the singers, and 3,500 feet of cable was laid from the church to a control center in a nearby building. The day before the recording began, Kolbe, his assistant, and a half-dozen Venetians were still struggling to get all this equipment installed, along with a dozen microphones and an intercom system.

Then Smith and his singers arrived, and the Basilica authorities noted that more than half of them were women—some of them in mini-skirts! Only then did the Columbia people learn that not in nine hundred years had a woman set foot in the sacristy, and women had never been permitted in the building after sundown. But the recording sessions were scheduled between 8:00 P.M. and 2:00 A.M., and it was necessary for both singers and personnel to be able to move freely about the building. The solution concocted by the Columbia people was pretty ludicrous, but it mollified the authorities: the women were allowed to stay in the building at night if they were garbed in hastily procured long-sleeved, chin-to-ankle surgical gowns.

The first night was spent recording unaccompanied music and adjusting microphones. During the day rehearsals were held in a room at La Fenice, where tempi were settled, mistakes were corrected, and revisions were made. Then, as John McClure related,

Hours later in a dark cathedral after the tourists had been cleared away, we would engage a whole new set of problems which were probably routine to the house group four hundred years earlier. Since Gabrieli had written for every combination from single six-part chorus to two or three five-part choruses . . . our corresponding groups were placed in separate galleries eighty feet apart on either side of the main altar. This was as exciting for us as it was for the awed visitors in olden days, but it also meant that each group would hear the other a split second late, making for fearsome problems in ensemble. Poor Vittorio Negri had to train himself to ignore the evidence of his ears since when the ensemble was perfect for the microphones, the "other" group would necessarily sound late to him. As an added annoyance, any performance hints he had for the exiles [in the galleries] had to be shouted across the void slowly in several languages through cupped hands to surmount the relentless beast of reverberation which coiled around us all.

McClure figured that Gabrieli himself must have had to put up with some of these problems, but he presumably had the support of the church. The present authorities seemed to regard the twentieth-century musicians who were trying to reconstruct a part of Venice's musical heritage as little more than a nuisance. They considered suspect even such innocent breaches of decorum as Peggy's shedding her shoes in order to tiptoe silently on some errand. But in the end, as McClure noted, even they seemed slightly softened by the magic of Gabrieli's music, "full of the love of God, but fuller of the love of life and quite free of all false piety."

For nine nights *The Glory of Gabrieli* wound onto the tape reels, and when they stopped turning McClure, Biggs, Negri, and all the rest knew that they had captured something worth all their work and frustration. On the final night of recording the chorus finished early and descended on a local *trattoria* for a victory feast while Biggs and the instrumentalists completed a few final Canzonas. "By two we were through," recalled McClure, "Biggs, as usual, fresh as lettuce, the rest of us bleary-eyed and drooping."

Biggs and Peggy swung home via England, stopping briefly to discuss the forthcoming English tour with Quita Chavez of CBS's London office. Biggs seems hardly to have slowed down. He showed up at the New York office in October to listen to the tapes, and he was so enthusiastic about the results that he telephoned the choral directors to share his elation. By the end of the month he was off for two recitals on a new Bosch tracker-action organ in St. Mark's Church of Portland, Oregon—almost halfway around the world from St. Mark's in Venice.

Somewhere during the busy year of 1967 Biggs found time to act as program chairman for a mid-winter conclave held by the Boston chapter of the American Guild of Organists. He appeared on the program himself, in a concert at the Museum featuring both the organ and the pedal harpsichord and including a Handel gamba sonata in which his old friend Alfred Zighera was

Rehearsal at St. George's Church, New York, ca. 1967

soloist. The conclave ended December 29, on New Year's Eve Biggs played a concert at St. George's Church in New York, and on New Year's day he finally took his doctor's prescription and flew off for a quiet three weeks in Curacao. Not that he spent all his time loafing on the beach—he had arranged to practice on the Flentrop organ in the Fortkerk, and, as was his usual practice, he gave the church a free recital to express his appreciation.

The first of the Venice albums, entitled *The Glory of Gabrieli,* consisted of choral music interspersed with organ intonations. It appeared in January 1968, simultaneously with the recording of the Copland Symphony. A second Gabrieli album (containing Canzonas and Sonatas for organ and instruments) came out in July, and the Christmas record, *What Child Is This,* appeared in October. For some reason the third Gabrieli disc (more choral works and intonations) did not reach the public until late in 1971.

Reviews of the initial Gabrieli release were almost unanimous in their praise. *High Fidelity* called it "the greatest marriage of music and acoustics in history," and everyone seemed impressed with the stereo effects and the sheer opulence of the sound, except for a reviewer in *The Gramophone,* who wrote the whole project off as a "vast publicity stunt." Frank Cunkle in *The Diapason* objected mildly to the use of modern brass instruments by Edward Tarr's players, but admitted that they did "little to lessen the impressive and exciting results." He praised conductor Negri for his grasp of the musical style and observed that "Mr. Biggs is heard alone on a small Rieger in six intonations but his presence is felt throughout." Cunkle also had good words for Biggs's Copland release, suggesting that the record "should serve to rekindle interest in this original version with its effective organ part"—a reference to the fact that Copland later rewrote this youthful Boulanger-influenced opus, without the organ part, as his Symphony No. 1.

But it was the second Gabrieli release, the album of Canzonas and Sonatas played by Biggs with the Edward Tarr Brass Ensemble and the string players from La Fenice, that won the coveted Grammy award of the National Academy of Recording as the best chamber music performance of 1968. Strangely, this quite beautiful recording was glossed over fairly lightly by most of the reviewers, who had perhaps expended all their best adjectives on its predecessor. Vernon Gotwals in *Music* declared it "indeed a prize winner, a marvelous record!" On this disc Biggs is involved in all the ensemble music and makes one solo appearance in a crisp and spirited Ricercare.

In the 1930s Biggs had performed and recorded on the then new Aeolian-Skinner organ in Harvard's Memorial Church. Because of its chambered location in an acoustically dead building and orders from organist Archibald T. Davison to suppress the upperwork, the instrument had never given complete musical satisfaction. By the 1960s its electro-pneumatic action was deteriorating alarmingly, and organist John Ferris formed an advisory committee, of which Biggs was a member, to study the alternatives. Eventually they recommended that the acoustics be improved and that the Aeolian-Skinner organ be sold and replaced by a new four-manual Fisk mechanical-action organ, encased and free-standing in the front of the room. Early in 1968, shortly after his return from Curaçao, Biggs played the first of a series of inaugural recitals on the new organ; included in his program was the premiere of Daniel Pinkham's *A Prophecy*.

Following the Harvard concert, Biggs devoted himself to the editing of the Gabrieli Canzonas and to the preparation of a successor to the original "talking dog" record, to be called *The Organ in Sight and Sound*. Accompanied by an illustrated booklet and an article on organ design by Flentrop, it followed a completely new script. It contained numerous new musical examples, many of them especially recorded in Arlesheim, Zurich, and on the new Harvard organ, plus others culled from recent recording expeditions. The album, issued late in 1969, is a monument to Biggs's meticulous editorial skills, and as a layperson's guide to the organ it has not been equalled.

Columbia declared March 1968 E. Power Biggs Month and released six Biggs albums with appropriate publicity. Only two were new, however: *Bach Organ Favorites, Vol. 3,* and *Historic Organs of Spain.* The rest were reissues of previous Bach and Handel albums, plus a "sampler" disc called *A Biggs Festival,* consisting of excerpts from several earlier recordings. Reissues and reshufflings of this sort became a fairly regular thing after this time, despite the fact that Biggs continued a heavy recording schedule. A year later another potpourri entitled *E. Power Biggs Greatest Hits* was released, the only new item on it being Ives's Variations on "America," recorded on the new Fisk organ at Harvard.

Biggs seems to have liked these collections. The *Greatest Hits* album was put together by Peter Munves of the Columbia staff, and it afforded Biggs the opportunity to record the popular Ives work on a good-sized modern organ. "How wonderful of you to cook up this special round-up record!" he wrote Munves in January 1969. "And I'm delighted to have this opportunity to pop in the new Ives *Variations on America.* It is bright and gay, far better than the previous version." He also gave his opinion of Schuman's orchestral transcription, first setting the scene with the sixteen-year-old Ives "having a devil of a good time" on a hot Fourth of July. "Personally, I don't think that William Schuman's recent orchestral version catches all this. This Ives belongs on the organ, just as much as JSB."

In the early summer of 1968 Biggs again went abroad. The hectic schedule of the Gabrieli sessions had precluded doing the planned *Historic Organs of Italy* recordings on the same trip, but Biggs had his itinerary mapped out, as well as plans for a *Historic Organs of France* tour. There were some problems with arrangements for the former, but the way seemed clear for a short excursion to the Andreas Silbermann organs of Alsace in May, despite the fact that engineer Kolbe was hobbling around on crutches as the result of a skiing accident. The Italian recording tour became a part of a second trip in the fall, and the organs recorded were the cream of historic Italian instruments. Frescobaldi is heard on the almost magical sound of the twin organs—one from the fifteenth, the other from the sixteenth century—in the acoustically perfect Basilica of San Petronio in Bologna. Instruments by Antegnati, Callido, and Serassi, dating from the sixteenth to the nineteenth centuries, round out the album.

The fall trip included concerts in Switzerland—at Vevey and at the Montreux Festival—but the largest part of it was spent in England. Most of Biggs's appearances there were with orchestras—three with the London Philharmonic and three with the Royal Liverpool Philharmonic. Save for an Elgar work, most of the pieces were drawn from the repertoire of Biggs's recent American orchestral appearances. Two solo programs were given, one on a new Mander organ in London's Merchant Taylors' Hall; the other, in which Biggs was assisted by oboist Leon Goossens, on the recently restored "Handel" organ in Great Packington, where Biggs had previously recorded the Handel Concertos.

The year 1968 ended with another round of domestic concerts, and 1969 began with a tour in completely new territory: Australia. Biggs's recordings had been selling well "down under" (although Biggs claimed that he did not understand how they could play them upside down!), and it began to look as though an Australian tour would be worthwhile. Early in February Biggs and Peggy packed their bags and departed wintry New England for the summery antipodes.

The tour, sponsored by the Australian Broadcasting Commission, occupied the entire month. Biggs played his way from one end of the country to the other, one of his first appearances being at the Perth Festival of the Arts. A good part of the time he was wrestling with some of Australia's famous (or infamous) town hall organs. He made no appearances in churches and played no large tracker-action organs, although he did play part of one of his Sydney Town Hall concerts on a little tracker-action organ positive by Ronald Sharp, the rising young Australian builder who was soon to begin work on a mammoth instrument for the new Sydney Opera House.

Biggs made something of a hit in Australia, not only with his audiences, but with the press. When his commitments made him unavailable to reporters, they sought out Peggy and plied her with questions about her background, her work, and, of course, what it was like to be married to a busy concert artist. She complied with information about her part-time work with foreign visitors in the Harvard University Protocol Office, human interest bits about their country farmhouse retreat and how she met Biggs while singing in his church choir, and anecdotes about copying music and bandaging ailing organs on recording tours. She conceded that things were pretty hectic much of the time, but that,

> Biggs is fortunate. His work is his hobby—not like a lot of people whose lives begin at five o'clock. It does mean that Biggs's work begins when we get up and stops when we go to bed, that letters and things come to meals and there are no holidays.

Biggs himself had plenty of press coverage, of course. His encounter with what one reviewer called "that dear old superannuated noise machine," the Sydney Town Hall organ, was not, by either his or the reviewers' accounts, an unmitigated success. What saved the day was his imaginative programing and insistence on using the Broadcasting Commission's Ronald Sharp positive for a group of delicate early works. Thus, while the critics tended to disagree on the effectiveness of works by Bach, Franck, and Hindemith rendered on the huge organ, they all (in contrast to the Canadians) loved the irreverent Ives Variations, were favorably disposed toward Pinkham's *Prophecy,* and were clearly charmed by Biggs's performances on the little positive organ, which included, as an unprogramed bonus, the Anna Magdalena pieces rejected by the Londoners.

Unfortunately there was no clear-voiced positive to give relief from the Town Hall organ in Melbourne. A reviewer there blamed the instrument's "blunt attack and foggy tone" for hindering Biggs's music making and contrasted the "pallid and monochromatic" effect of Soler's *Emperor's Fanfare* played on the Melbourne organ and the brilliant impact of the same piece on Biggs's *Historic Organs of Spain* disc. At a party following the concert, when someone asked Biggs what ought to be done with the organ, he offered three options: "Burn it. Have it thrown in the sea. Or give it to anyone willing to take it away." Biggs usually did not make such blunt statements within earshot of the press, and when his comments were published, they stirred up a fairly predictable response. A letter to the *Melbourne Herald* from seven young organists enthusiastically endorsed Biggs's dictum and called on the City Council to replace the old instrument with a "new mechanical action, well-made instrument of eclectic design." It was quickly followed by one from an older organist defending the Town Hall organ and caustically putting down the young upstarts.

Another recalcitrant Town Hall organ faced Biggs for one of his final concerts in Adelaide. When he was told that the organ had first been used at a governor's swearing-in ceremony in 1877, Biggs expressed the hope that his concert would be its "swearing-out" and admitted that working out registrations on the instrument had caused a certain amount of swearing on his own part. But the situation in Adelaide was more hopeful than in Melbourne, for the instrument was already scheduled for a major rebuilding. The Adelaide reviewers were divided in their opinions of the concert. One disliked the Ives and was generally a bit bored with it all; the other called it a "popular success," thought that Biggs had worked wonders with the decrepit organ, and noted that the audience in the sold-out house had asked for three encores.

It was a successful tour, and despite the difficult instruments he had to work with, Biggs liked Australia and its inhabitants. Certainly the Australians liked Biggs, and perhaps found Biggs in person to be something different from Biggs on records. Meredith Oakes in the *Sydney Daily Telegraph* summed up this impression nicely:

> He has been brought here as a "heavy," when in fact he is something different and, in a way, more appealing. He is, in fact, an extremely musical man who loves to play the organ.

19 | *Bach and Handel*

> Handel was born in 1685, a circumstance he shared with
> J. S. Bach. The two are often compared, usually to the benefit of
> neither. Both were prolific composers, but Bach composed for
> his own satisfaction, for a relatively small group of hearers.
> Handel composed on a grand scale for the largest of audiences.

Biggs generally wrote his own jacket notes, and while he was working on a recording it was his habit to jot down random ideas for them in spiral-bound student notebooks from the Harvard Coop. The above quotation, written around 1970, is from one of these notebooks. Bach and Handel had been Biggs's musical companions from his student days; their music dominated the content of his earliest recordings and is woven in an unbroken thread through a lifetime of recitals, radio broadcasts, and records.

Perhaps it was the very differences between these two masters that fascinated Biggs: "Bach lived his life in a succession of German towns. Handel ranged throughout Europe, and took the British nation by storm." But their differences transcended geography: "Bach's mind was in the clouds, oriented to the hereafter. . . . Handel's heaven is more earthly—here and now." Such statements crop up repeatedly throughout these notes, as though Biggs could not resist turning over in his mind the paradox of these two composers who appealed to him so strongly, yet in such different ways. "But one turns from the complexities of Bach to the more frank and outgoing melodies of Handel. And then, refreshed, one listens again to Bach with renewed. . . ." Biggs apparently could not find the right word to complete the sentence, but the key thoughts are there: Handel "refreshed"; Bach "renewed." Both were good for a musician's soul.

Bach got his due in 1969 with the recording of *Bach Organ Favorites, Vol. 4* (in a letter to John McClure, Biggs suggested that this album might be "the most punchy and varied of the series"), as well as the pieces from the *Anna Magdalena Book*, intended for the still unfinished *Biggs Bach Book* (which was not released until 1971). The year 1969 also saw the release of *Bach's Greatest Hits*, another Columbia assortment drawn from a variety of sources and including Biggs's arrangement of "Jesu, Joy of Man's Desiring." But Handel was also very much in Biggs's plans.

With the European and Australian tours as well as a full recital schedule, Biggs had been burning the candle at both ends for the past two years. His health broke down shortly after his return from Australia, and he was hospitalized with pneumonia. By late spring, however, he was back on his feet and rested, ready to plunge into his usual activities. His concert calendar continued to be full, and it included a dedication recital on the rebuilt organ in Emmanuel Church, Newport, Rhode Island, where he had found his first employment in the United States. A major recording tour, scheduled for the fall, was to include two new Handel recordings with orchestra at Great Packington and a *Historic Organs of England* album.

The "tempest in a teapot" over the Great Packington organ refused to be laid to rest. A Dutch reviewer had tried to stir it up again in the December 1966 issue of *Luister*. His worst allegation was that the pitch of the organ had been raised an entire half-step. This morsel was quickly siezed upon and quoted in the jacket notes of a rival Handel Concerto album issued by Deutsche Grammaphon Archiv as proof that their recording was more "authentic." Noel Mander and Dirk Flentrop came to Biggs's rescue by examining the pipes of the organ and determining that the actual pitch difference between the old and new tunings was considerably less than a half-step. Columbia demanded a retraction, but it did not appear in print until nearly eight years later.

The retuning and repairs made to the Great Packington organ in 1957 were, of course, "first aid" to make the organ usable for recording, as was the electric blower that Biggs had donated to the church. By 1968 it was discovered that the instrument was critically damaged by woodworm, and, under a grant from the Pilgrim Trust, a full-scale restoration was carried out by Noel Mander, who kept the altered pitch. Biggs played the reopening concert, and the organ was once more in the public eye. A new rash of letters pro and con the restoration appeared in the *Times* (London), *Musical Opinion,* and *Musical Times.* The "cons" were mostly those who had criticized the 1957 retuning; the "pros" included Sir William McKie and Cecil Clutton of the Organs Advisory Committee of the Anglican Church, and the organ builders H. John Norman and Cuthbert Harrison. *The Diapason,* looking for a circulation booster, reprinted this correspondence, much to the annoyance of Biggs, who was just then deep into preparations for another recording session with the organ in question. Subsequent letters to *The Diapason* were largely supportive of the restoration, however, and included one from McKie, who noted that the Great Packington church authorities were "entirely satisfied with the integrity of the treatment given to the organ and the way in which the work has been carried out."

At the suggestion of Peter Munves, Biggs had begun early in January 1969 to dig out material for some new Handel recordings. A re-recording of the Concertos had been decided against, so Biggs ensconced himself in Harvard's Widener Library to search for other suitable pieces. While the Organ Concertos are almost the only works scored specifically for orchestra with obbligato organ, Biggs found a plethora of other material for orchestra and continuo buried in the scores of Handel's many operas and oratorios: overtures, marches, curtain tunes, ayres, sinfonias, and a Sonata from *The Triumph of Time and Truth,* which, with its obbligato organ part, seems almost a prototype for the later Concertos.

Nor were Handel's more-familiar melodies neglected. Two orchestral concertos containing instrumental versions of choruses from *Messiah* were included, along with such popular favorites as "Where'er you walk" from *Semele* and the ubiquitous *Largo.* All of this was grist for Biggs's programmatic mill and resulted in two nicely varied albums, released in 1970 and 1972 under the title of *The Magnificent Mr. Handel.* Biggs found that, with a few exceptions, it was feasible to use Handel's own instrumentations for the music. "Where'er you walk" and the *Forest Music* were tastefully arranged for organ and orchestra by Daniel Pinkham. With his briefcase filled with useful scores, Biggs departed for England in September 1969.

John McClure and Hellmuth Kolbe were on hand in Great Packington to take care of the technical end of things. They were snugly if a bit damply ensconced in the crypt of St. James's Church, where McClure, who probably thought he had seen everything in Venice, was startled by a visit from some curious sheep. A visitor of another sort was Anthony Hicks of *Musical Times,* who interviewed the musicians, later reporting that

> Biggs emphasized that he was not out to prove anything by his choice of programme; he had simply picked out of the H[andel]-G[esellschaft] some numbers which he thought too good to lie gathering dust, and which he wanted to put on record.

Considering that Biggs had spent most of the spring sifting through material, discussing it with associates, and sketching out innumerable program combinations, this statement was certainly an oversimplification. Hicks liked Biggs's choice of conductor: "Like Biggs's previous partner, Sir Adrian Boult, [Charles] Groves is able to bring out the nobility inherent in Handel's music. . . ." He hoped that the earlier Concerto recordings would be re-issued (they already had been, in 1968, but apparently only in the United States) and mused, "How odd that it takes an American (albeit British born) to remind us what fine Handelians two of our conductors are!"

After wrapping up sufficient material for the two *Magnificent Mr. Handel* albums, Biggs stayed at Great Packington long enough to record seven short selections from Handel's little-known *Aylesford Pieces*—a highly appropriate choice for this organ since the church housing it stands on the estate of the Earl of Aylesford, in whose home, Packington Hall, the music had originally been discovered, and where the organ itself had once been located. These pieces became part of the *Historic Organs of England* album. Biggs and the recording crew set off to do the rest of it in places like Adlington Hall in Cheshire, where an important seventeenth-century organ had recently been restored by Noel Mander.

The English recording tour ended with a London dinner party for Biggs, the CBS staff, and reporters, and Biggs returned to America and to a busy concert schedule. In less than a week he was making his appearance in the familiar Poulenc and Saint-Saëns works with the Milwaukee Symphony Orchestra, playing the recently completed Aeolian-Skinner organ in the Music Hall. Early December found him following a northerly route, which included another orchestral program in Cedar Rapids, Iowa, and a solo recital in Regina, Saskatchewan. By New Year's Eve he was back at St. George's Church in New York for his annual program.

"The parallel lives of Bach and Handel . . . mark the height of the baroque, but their music is as contrasted as the poles of a magnet, and must be enjoyed in different ways." Biggs had been having a thoroughly good time with Handel, but by 1970 he was ready for Bach again. Ever since his first European tours in the 1950s he had wanted to record in Bach's own church in Leipzig, yet thus far all his attempts even to cross the East German border had been frustrated. But with the gradual thawing of travel restrictions to Communist countries, plus the extra pull the European CBS affiliates could muster, it began to look as though his plans might at last be realized. Biggs hardly dared to hope. At the bottom of a memorandum sent to McClure in May 1969 regarding projects in the works, is "LEIPZIG, 1970—if they let us in. Repertoire as previously listed, or as modified. And . . . how about thinking of using the St. Thomas Choir?! One could do a fully authentic 'Jubilee' type record."

In July Biggs wrote to McClure again, noting that another record company had gotten onto the "historic organs" bandwagon, something Biggs was not going to take lying down: "The fact that Telefunken copies our ideas and even our titles makes me want all the more to try to prevent them from getting ahead of us!" He then listed Columbia's Swiss, Spanish, and Italian albums already out, plus the soon to be issued French and English ones, noting that the *Golden Age* set had already covered northern Germany and Holland. "*And* if we are lucky enough to get to East Germany next summer, 1970, we would have the finest Gottfried Silbermann at Freiberg." In Biggs's opinion, the repertoire on the Telefunken releases was a bit on the pedestrian side anyway—"let's hope our records are more cheerful and interesting!"

By November 1969 things appeared promising, and at the top of Biggs's "McClure Monster List" was "Bach at Leipzig," all neatly timed and scheduled for late August 1970, followed by a tentative program for Freiberg.

In early 1970 things were looking very rosy indeed for the East German project. Hans Stracke and his colleagues in the West German CBS office had received a *bona fide* invitation from VEB Deutsche Schallplatten of East Berlin. Biggs could record in Leipzig and Freiberg with the understanding that two master tapes would be made, one for the East German firm, the other for CBS and Columbia. In a six-page autobiographical outline he wrote for publicity purposes in 1974, Biggs listed under the heading of "Honors" his various honorary doctorates and fellowships and added at the end, "Though it is not something with a ribbon around it, I regard as a very great honor the spontaneous invitation from VEB Deutsche Schallplatten . . . to visit Leipzig and Freiberg to make recordings."

Even with the East German invitation Biggs still had to have approval from the State Department in Washington, and by the time he had completed a round of domestic concerts in March it still had not come through. He finally got some action after writing to Massachusetts senators Kennedy and Brooke ("I am sure you will understand that an invitation to record in Bach's own church is the very highest honor for an organist . . .").

A brief rest in Curaçao in April preceded Biggs's first European jaunt of the year. In May, after taking care of some recording loose ends in Switzerland (where he also did a television spot) and England, he picked up engineer Hellmuth Kolbe and crossed the East German border for a brief exploratory trip. In Leipzig and Freiberg he tried out the organs and met with Reimar Bluth, director of the Eterna division of VEB Deutsche Schallplatten, who would be in charge of the recordings. In a letter written to a CBS official late in 1976, Biggs described that occasion:

> I remember vividly our first exploratory visit to Leipzig. . . . We were met at check-point Charlie in Berlin, and driven to Leipzig. The director (Reimar Bluth) was in the front seat. As we came near the center of Leipzig, Herr Bluth turned and said, "In a moment you will see the Thomaskirche." He had sung there as a choir boy, and he knew the place inside and out, yet he could not have said it with more excitement—not even if he were proposing to show us the celestial regions.

Back in the United States at the end of May, Biggs was able to report to McClure that it had been "a very productive two weeks!" Enough material had been recorded at Arlesheim to complete *The Biggs Bach Book*, a good tape had been obtained of the historic organ in Staunton Harold to round out the

English album, and the Eurovision TV appearance had been successful. Best of all, the East Germans had proved most friendly and cooperative, and Biggs now had a good idea of what he wanted to record in August. His plans included six large Bach works on the new Schuke organ in the Thomaskirche, and the six Concerto transcriptions of J. G. Walther in Freiberg. Biggs would have liked to record Bach there as well, but was discouraged from it by the Eterna people, probably because it would conflict with their own ongoing series of Bach recordings made by German artists on all of the extant Silbermann organs.

Biggs then spent June and July editing, writing jacket notes for the English album, and pulling together loose ends. The French album, featuring two splendid Andreas Silbermann organs, was released, but it failed to make as much of a splash as the Spanish and Italian issues had. Save for the d'Aquin *Noëls,* Biggs had never really felt comfortable with the French classic literature, and there is a certain uncharacteristic stiffness in some of the playing on this disc.

In August Biggs finally realized his long-held ambition to record Bach in Bach's own church. A year later he wrote in *Music,*

> One enters the historic Thomaskirche of Leipzig with an intuitive sense of having been there before. . . . The scene is already in one's imagination, a picture gained even before a first visit from the writings of Bach's biographers and from old engravings.

Today the church and a few of the older buildings surrounding it are isolated in a kind of historic district, appearing much as it did in Bach's day, although it is but a few blocks from modern business buildings and one of the busiest railroad stations in all Europe. Bach, whose final resting place is beneath a simply inscribed stone slab in the middle of the chancel floor, would not recognize either of the two organs now in the Thomaskirche, but somehow that is not really important:

> This is the place, you feel. This is where so much happened. This is where Bach's auditors, privileged beyond their comprehension, experienced the first hearing of the powerful music that has encircled and convinced the world.

Later Biggs was to remark that just experiencing the same acoustics that Bach knew—and they are indeed wonderful for music—was worth all the waiting.

The recordings, made on the modern three-manual mechanical-action organ by Alexander Schuke of Potsdam, went smoothly, and every night Leipzig police rerouted the traffic in the streets leading to the church to ensure quiet recording conditions. Although Kolbe assisted, the recordings in both Leipzig and Freiberg were made on East German equipment from Deutsche

Schallplatten, since Kolbe could not bring in his own. Biggs did bring his camera, though, and spent some of his spare time photographing the church, the Bach window, and the bronze statue of Bach outside the south door of the church.

Returning to Cambridge in September, Biggs reported back to McClure at Columbia:

> As you know, there are two excellent records awaiting you in East Germany. Playing at the Thomaskirche, Leipzig, was really high drama, and I feel the record will catch this! The instrument records quite impressively and the Thomaskirche acoustics are fine. The Walther Concertos on the Silbermann at Freiberg will have lots of sparkle. . . . Though I practiced and registered all the six Bach works previously discussed, it was quickly evident that for this "special occasion" the war horses . . . were much more effective and appropriate than the alternates. . . .

There had been some problems with voltage fluctuations, but Biggs felt Kolbe could correct them in the editing. The wide Silbermann pedalboard and somewhat irregular action of the unrestored Freiberg organ had also posed minor problems, "but the sound is just fine. . . ."

Biggs's Leipzig album contains four large Bach works, the familiar Toccata and Fugue in D minor, the Passacaglia, and the Preludes and Fugues in C major ("9/8") and G major ("Great"). War horses they may have been, but Biggs had lived a lifetime with these pieces, and he could still make them run like young colts. The record was released in the summer of 1971, and in *Stereo Tape* for December 1971, Igor Kipnis wrote:

> The power of Bach's music on the instrument in these authentic surroundings is undeniably impressive. So, too, is Biggs's playing. It has real propulsion, power, and drive, and I am inclined to think that this is the American organist's finest recording of his long career.

At the conclusion of the Passacaglia Biggs employed the cadenzas first used somewhat experimentally in his pedal harpsichord recording of the same work. *High Fidelity* called this "marvellously effective," praising the freshness and warmth of all the performances on the record. "In short, there's not a thing to criticize, and Biggs has re-established himself in my mind as one of the world's foremost organists and Bach players." The review expressed concern that Biggs might be becoming something of a "lightweight," playing short, easy pieces to the neglect of the big ones that many listeners still wanted. In an earlier review, the same writer had even gone so far to suggest that Biggs was in his "twilight years." Biggs claimed not to be affected by reviews, noting that they never seemed to alter record sales and observing that "the reviewer reviews himself." But reviews are one way of feeling the pulse of the public,

Biggs at the console of the Gabler organ, Weingarten, 1955

and there are indications that Biggs was paying attention. In a list of notes on future projects sent to McClure in February 1970, he wrote, "In general, we should graduate back to large instruments—window rattlers—Trondheim, Weingarten, etc." The enthusiasm generated by the Leipzig release, coming on the heels of rather half-hearted reviews of the English record (full of short pieces played on small organs), probably confirmed the wisdom of this.

There was, however, one other reason for turning again to big organs and big pieces for recording: quadraphonic sound. Columbia had only recently begun to record quadraphonically, and the hi-fi aficionados were quickly tooling up with new playback equipment. Biggs had begun asking his friends if they knew of any churches with four organs. Recording the pedal harpsichord and the Flentrop organ at the Museum in quad had already been done. But the audiophiles were awaiting an organ spectacular to show off their new equipment. Biggs was going to give them one if he could, and they were going to hear Bach and Handel as they never had before.

20 | *The Compleat Record Man*

If there was such an award as the Compleat Record Man, you would certainly be eligible. Performer, researcher, A&R planner, recordist, mixer and editor, publicist, advertising man and now retail contact man—all of these you have done with great flair and enthusiasm.

Biggs, while on a concert trip to Atlanta in 1972, had agreed to do a small errand for Columbia. He probably thought little of it, but it prompted an effusive note of thanks from Pierre Bourdain of the Columbia Masterworks Department, in which the above testimonial appears. Biggs did indeed do all the things Bourdain lists, and in this respect he was virtually alone among recording artists. By 1972 he had been with Columbia for a quarter of a century, and it is evident that he was regarded as "one of the family" by everyone from the top executives to the secretaries and engineers.

And Biggs worked hard for Columbia, which was more and more becoming his major link with his public. Columbia, for its part, relied on Biggs's taste, judgment, and ability to generate ever fresh and creative ideas. It also trusted Biggs's instinct for knowing when an idea had had its day—and when it was time to move on to a new one.

In the late 1960s, encouraged by Hellmuth Kolbe and good record sales, Biggs had seemed ready to carry on the Historic Organs series indefinitely, and he even talked half-seriously of such esoterica as "Historic Organs of Yugoslavia." But after the pronounced success of the East German Bach and Walther albums, there appeared only two further items in that series. One, made up largely of already recorded but unreleased tapes from various tours, was entitled *Famous Organs of Holland and North Germany* and was released in January 1973. "Famous" replaced "Historic" in the title of this album because Biggs wanted to include a tape made in the 1960s of Jan Koetsier's delightful Partita for English horn and organ, a modern work recorded on a modern Flentrop organ in Breda. The other album was a Columbia editing-room assemblage of excerpts from previously released recordings with the ungainly title of *E. Power Biggs Plays 24 Historic Organs in 8 Countries Covering 7 Centuries of Music by 24 Composers,* which was released early in 1972. On its

185

four sides Biggs pulled together some of the best examples of organs and music from a dozen or so older albums, throwing in for good measure a new Bach Toccata and Fugue in D minor recorded in Arlesheim and left over from *The Biggs Bach Book* sessions.

One projected album would have combined the historic theme with the "window rattlers" in a "Historic Organs of South Germany" recording featuring the "splendid massive sound" of the large Baroque organs in Weingarten, Ottobeuren, and Ochsenhausen. Perhaps because of the notoriously difficult playing actions or the uncertain condition of these instruments, this album never materialized. With new projects beckoning and other record companies capitalizing on the "historic organs" theme, Biggs probably felt that he had made the point that he had stated in an article in the *Saturday Review* in 1968:

> Best of all, recordings (and pictures) give people a clearer sense of the *identity* of the organ. The musical public has a good appreciation of excellence in orchestral tone and other musical fields. But considering the vast variety of instruments of all shapes, sizes, and tonal aims (not to mention current electronic counterfeits) which claim to be organs, it is no wonder that many music lovers have only the fuzziest idea of what an organ is, or should be, and the way in which it can and should sound.

One is still likely to encounter organists, students, and music lovers who credit Biggs's recordings, particularly those of historic instruments, with giving them their first glimpse of the identity—and variety—of the organ.

Biggs's concert schedule was drastically curtailed in 1970. Early in the year he played a concerted program as well as solo recitals in Harrisburg, Curaçao, and the Busch-Reisinger Museum. Fortunately, not much had been scheduled for the fall, for illness struck again in November, forcing Biggs to cancel an appearance with the McGill Chamber Orchestra in Montreal. With characteristic concern, he arranged for Boston Symphony organist Berj Zamkochian to fill in for him.

In 1971 no recording tours were planned, for, as Biggs wrote Kolbe in January, "It may turn out to be a year of consolidation of various things we have in the icebox, and—for me—of building up new repertoire and program ideas (which take time!) for European recording a little later on." Thus a good portion of the year was spent in editing and planning. The church with four organs had yet to turn up, but in the meantime St. George's in New York, which had proven ideal for stereo recording, was also about as good a setting for a quad recording as one could find in the United States. The organ itself is divided into three fairly widely spaced segments, and all one needed for the fourth quadrant was a brass band.

Biggs broached the idea of a quadraphonic recording at St. George's to

McClure in one of his "idea lists," along with a Rheinberger album and another *Bach Organ Favorites*. He had recorded the Walther Concertos on the pedal harpsichord after his return from Germany and wanted to do further harpsichord work. Other ideas included some large Romantic works on the Music Hall organ in Methuen, where he had not recorded for a number of years, another Americana album (looking ahead to the Bicentennial), and more Bach works with instruments.

The *Bach Organ Favorites* series, recorded at the Busch-Reisinger Museum, continued popular with the record-buying public. The title of the series, as Biggs noted on the jacket of the fifth album, was self-explanatory:

> But how can it be justified through five record albums, with more to come? If all compositions contained therein are favorites, what *are* the favorites? Well, illogically, all are favorites. Bach's organ music is so splendid and varied that, in performance, every Bach work asserts its particular charm, and one's favorite may very well be whatever Bach one happens to be playing at the moment.

Volume 5 of the Bach series was recorded in August 1971, a punishingly hot month. Since the building was not air-conditioned, the heat had caused the organ to go badly out of tune, necessitating a complete retuning. To avoid street noises, the recordings were done late at night, with the windows closed and boarded up for additional sound insulation. Down in the basement, where the recording equipment was, it was relatively comfortable, but the TV monitor disclosed a hard-working Biggs in a sweaty tee shirt in the gallery upstairs, stopping occasionally to mop his brow with the towel slung around his neck, or to listen to a replay of something just taped. Biggs rested and practiced at home during the day, but he was the original night owl and displayed incredible stamina during these sessions, which usually ran for four or five nights. Finally Biggs would turn and announce over the monitor, "I think we have it!" As the engineers and producer shut down their machines and stretched, Peggy produced a bottle of champagne.

With another *Favorites* album finished, Biggs turned his attention to what he called "the St. Georgy Orgy." He had recently engaged a publicity agent, Audrey Michaels, "in an effort to get some good publicity stories, on the wave of the Leipzig and Freiberg releases," he reported to McClure, "but also about all our records and the unique meaning records have for organs and organ music (sounds stuffy, doesn't it!)." Unfortunately the agent could not understand why Biggs did not want to "rush around playing all possible concerts." But, "the fact is, as you know, the recording projects take more and more time, and one must make a choice." Although Biggs greatly disliked talking—or, presumably, even thinking—about it, he was neither as young nor as strong as he once was, and he was finding it necessary to slow down and husband his energies more.

As "live bait for publicity," Michaels suggested doing a duplicate of the St. Thomas, Leipzig, program at St. Thomas's Church in New York. Biggs added the idea of a follow-up organ and brass program at St. George's, where he traditionally played a New Year's Eve concert anyway. From this the plans for the quadraphonic recording at St. George's rather quickly ripened, in order to take full advantage of the players and practice required by the concert. Early plans included some standard baroque numbers, but the final program consisted almost entirely of nineteenth- and twentieth-century pieces, some of them arranged from the solo organ repertoire and almost all of them "window rattlers." Biggs had sensed the initial seismic rumblings of a Romantic revival and intended, as usual, to get there first with the most.

Audrey Michaels did her job well. When Biggs arrived in New York during the holiday season, there were feature articles in several papers on Biggs and his recordings and forthcoming concerts, and the *New York Times* ran a half-page interview. On December 22 Biggs began his "St. Thomas at St. Thomas" program, only to have it interrupted by a bomb threat. According to producer Andrew Kazdin, who was in the audience, "As they calmly cleared the church, Biggs played on! They had to come to get him in the loft—and he didn't want to go! Eventually my *own* nerves got the better of me, and I helped coax him down." On New Year's Eve Biggs combined a preview of the quad recording at St. George's with carol singing and James Hewitt's *Battle of Trenton,* with Edward O. Miller, the church's rector, reading Hewitt's programmatic descriptions.

As 1972 opened Biggs was still searching for European locations for his proposed Rheinberger and quadraphonic Bach recordings. Columbia again declared March Biggs Month, releasing three all-new albums (*Music for Organ, Brass and Percussion,* recorded at St. George's; the Walther Concertos, recorded in Freiberg; and *The Magnificent Mr. Handel, Vol. 2)* plus the grab-bag, *E. Power Biggs Plays 24 Historic Organs . . . ,* all on March 29, Biggs's birthday. *Bach Organ Favorites, Vol. 5,* appeared during the summer.

Spring was taken up largely with concerts, four on the West Coast and a few in the South. In April Biggs gave two recitals on the new Mander organ at Westminster College in Fulton, Missouri. This instrument, housed in eighteenth-century casework, is located in a historic church building moved from London as a memorial to Winston Churchill. Biggs was also arranging American tours for Hannes Kastner of Leipzig and Hans Otto of Freiberg, in return for their help during his East German recording tour. Illness again interfered with Biggs's plans in late spring, and in order to catch up on his editing and recording responsibilities he kept his fall schedule clear of concert commitments.

Biggs had made up his mind to record the two Rheinberger Concertos for organ and orchestra, but gave up his initial thoughts of a European site in favor of St. George's, which could if necessary also serve for the solo Romantic and "Bach in Quad" albums he was planning. But Kolbe now had quad equipment, and thus a European location for the Bach project was still hoped for. An additional Bach record appeared in Biggs's plans at this time, to consist of concerted movements from cantatas done with positive organ and chamber orchestra. A gimmicky quad recording in which the four voices of a fugue would be recorded separately on the pedal harpsichord and then put together never materialized. Plans for the updated Americana album were being formulated, and Biggs was actively preparing for some of the higher-priority projects. One was Rheinberger; the other Bach. "What I'd like to do this coming summer," he wrote Tom Frost of Columbia, late in 1972, "is to establish a beachhead in Quadraphonic Bach. . . ."

The Rheinberger Concertos were recorded at St. George's Church in late November with a good pick-up orchestra directed by Maurice Peress, who had also collaborated on the earlier brass album. The timing was fortuitous, for a month later, the very day after Biggs's New Year's Eve concert, St. George's Church was severely damaged by fire, and the organ was put out of commission for several months.

Early in 1973 Biggs began planning another exploratory excursion to Europe. He also increased his concert activity with spring performances scheduled in Montreal, Washington, and on the new Danish-built Frobenius organ in the First Congregational Church of Cambridge. In March he took part in a bizarre midnight concert at Radio City Music Hall in New York, really a Columbia publicity stunt, billed as "Keyboard Colossus." It ran two hours without intermission and included everything from one of Bach's Brandenburg Concertos to the *Thunder and Lightning Polka* of Johann Strauss, Sr., played by ten pianos. At intervals Biggs served up two serious pieces (by Bach and Soler) and two not-so-serious ones (Ives's Variations on "America" and Hewitt's *Battle of Trenton*) on the Music Hall's "Mighty Wurlitzer," spiced with appropriate commentary. For the finale he joined the ten pianos, harpsichord, and everything else available in Sousa's *Stars and Stripes Forever* while flags waved, lights twinkled, and the ten pianos went slowly around on the revolving stage. "I've always felt that Biggs would rather have been somewhere else that night," Andrew Kazdin later observed, "but like the good trouper he was he carried it off with great charisma and wit."

In June Biggs, having made inquiries of European friends, went to Europe in search of a quad recording site. In the Cathedral of Freiburg-im-Breisgau (Baden) he found what he was looking for: "There are FOUR independent organs in the Münster," he reported to Columbia, "each playable at its own console, and all together from a central console. *The Quad and Stereo*

Rehearsing with the orchestra, St. George's Church, 1972. Photo by Edward O. Miller, Jr.

possibilities are absolutely unique!" Biggs had already chosen four big Toccatas and Fugues ("In all these Toccatas, the antiphonal phrases can 'run all around the church' quite logically") and was all set to book the Cathedral for a fall recording session.

Biggs was still planning more Bach and Handel on the pedal harpsichord, but a chance suggestion from a friend led to a very different sort of album. The great ragtime composer Scott Joplin had caught the public fancy, and his music was being played by everything from synthesizers to brass bands. Why not Joplin on the pedal harpsichord? Why not indeed, responded Columbia. "I think the Ragtimes would be a fun record," said Biggs, who, with his usual industry, began researching and arranging a program, which he recorded at the Columbia studio early in August.

A few weeks later, in September 1973, Biggs wrote to Kazdin, "Joplin is a forgotten dream, and now I'm full of Freiburg!" With Kazdin and Peggy, he met Kolbe there at the end of the month and got right to work. Recording four widely separated organs in a mammoth reverberant building raised problems not anticipated by Biggs, whose only other quad experience had been in the much smaller St. George's Church. In the Freiburg Cathedral there is a Marcussen organ high on the north wall of the nave in a Gothic "swallow's nest" position. Located almost exactly between two Rieger organs (in the choir and at the left of the crossing) and a Spaeth organ in the west end gallery, it was a crucial link in the overall quadraphonic picture. While all four organs have their own consoles, they may also be played simultaneously from a central console, but Biggs discovered that the critical nave (Marcussen) organ could only be played from the bottom manual of the central console, which also controlled one of the front organs. This prohibited the two from being played separately in any overlapping situation and threatened the full realization of some of Biggs's quad effects. His old friend Josef von Glatter-Götz of the Rieger firm came to the rescue by rewiring the nave organ to the third manual. On his return, Biggs wrote to him,

> I've never played a *quartet* of organs before! Balancing, and so on, introduced many problems, and I suppose we took two or three times as long as normal for the recording. "Marcussen on the third manual" made many interweaving antiphonal effects possible. In fact, without this the project would not have been possible.

Biggs recorded sufficient material for two albums at this session, one of which, his "Bach beachhead," was released exactly a year later. The second, released two years later, in August 1975, was the quad showpiece the hi-fi enthusiasts had been waiting for, a rather hoked-up mélange of familiar Baroque transcriptions, mostly by Handel and Purcell, which played all manner of tricks with four speakers and was effective even in stereo. " 'Proclamation' was the idea," stated Biggs in the jacket notes.

The Rheinberger album was released shortly after Biggs's return from Freiburg, in August 1973. In a full-page review in *The Diapason,* Robert Schuneman hailed it as a sign that the Romantic revival was "more than surface deep," praised the balance, but criticized the uncharacteristic brilliance of St. George's "American classic" organ. The review by Vernon Gotwals in *Music* was briefer but even more enthusiastic: "BUY this record; BUY it!!" he exhorted his readers. But he too felt that the Möller organ was not "Romantic" enough in tone-color to do full justice to the music; perhaps that is why the idea of recording a solo album of Romantic works at St. George's was never realized.

Two months later the very different Joplin record appeared in the stores. Reviewers generally put it in the category of an aural coffee-table book—a well-produced "party record." *FM Guide* for April 1974 subjected it to a careful comparison with other Joplin releases, and while admitting that it might lack something in authenticity, praised the "vitality and rhythmic sassiness" of Biggs's interpretations. Columbia pushed the Joplin and Rheinberger issues, plus the earlier Leipzig Bach release, in their pre-Christmas advertising: "From Rags to Rheinberger and Bach again!" In the summer of 1974 Biggs recorded a second album of Joplin rags; this time he thought up his own tongue-in-cheek publicity hype: "After 25 years with Columbia Records, E. Power Biggs is in Rags!" Many of his organist colleagues liked the Joplin rags well enough to want Biggs's arrangements of them, and eventually two sets were published, by G. Schirmer and by Hansen.

Biggs, unlike most other recording artists, always took a major part in the editing of his own tapes. Andrew Kazdin, his last producer, wrote in 1983, "You must understand that NONE of Biggs's personal involvement in the editing process was asked of him by anyone at Columbia Records. He just liked to do it himself." When a minor illness forced Biggs to leave before finishing a splicing task with engineer Ed Michalski, he very apologetically asked Kazdin to complete the job—which, Kazdin noted, was really the producer's duty anyway. Editing was not the only "gift" Biggs routinely bestowed on Columbia, and so Kazdin also became his self-appointed watchdog, to prevent Biggs from overextending himself on the company's behalf. He discovered that Biggs was using his own funds (including royalty checks) to pay for record release flyers and advertisements in the organ journals. "I tried to sniff out these cases," recalled Kazdin, "and get the appropriate party at Columbia to take over Biggs's (well thought out) plan and, of course, intercept the bill just in time to pay it."

Autographing records in the Harvard Coop, 1975. Photo by Jet Commercial Photographers.

Few who listen to the finished product have any conception of the amount of work that goes on between the capturing of the final cadence of a piece of music on tape and the pressing of the completed record. Andrew Kazdin has summarized what normally occurs—"in the vast majority of cases":

> After the recording sessions, the producer would gather all the original tapes together and start a careful listening process. During this period, all sorts of minute details can be found. Slight errors of performance which went undetected in the recording session can be noted and, hopefully, slated to be replaced by healthier counterparts. When the many hours of listening are completed, the producer's score is marked with an exact splicing plan—a roadmap which shows precisely how to construct the final edited tape so that it will contain the best and cleanest performance of which the artist is capable.
>
> Next, the producer takes this plan into an editing room—usually at Columbia Records and usually manned by an engineer familiar with the niceties of "Classical" Music. Here many days of painstaking splicing can ensue. The splicing plan contained in the producer's score is now turned into reality. The final result is a tape which exhibits the sought-after performance. Then the third step takes place. The spliced tape very often consists of more than 2 tracks and so the producer must then go about the job of mixing the spliced, multi-track tape into the final 2-track master which will be the one used to generate the records themselves.

That Kazdin explains, is what the post-production task *usually* consists of, but, "NOT WITH BIGGS!"

> I don't know when his unique working method became adopted because it was in full swing when I began my association with him. The first part of his system is occasionally shared by other recording artists. At the time of the sessions (or sometime just afterward) an extra tape is made of all the "takes" that were recorded. Biggs would take this tape home . . . and do all the listening and choosing himself. As I said, some artists prefer to make up the written splicing plan themselves.
>
> However, this is where the similarity ends. After the plan was written into the score, Biggs would then actually splice together his copy-tapes just to see if the plan would work. Naturally, this tape was not actually used to make the record. It became merely a prototype to verify the plan itself.
>
> Then, as if the previous involvement were not enough, Biggs would come to New York (very often, I believe, at his own expense) and go to work in Columbia's editing rooms—usually with an engineer called Ed Michalski—and supervise the splicing of the original tapes to conform to his prototype. Finally, he would turn over this spliced tape to his producer who would do whatever mixing was necessary.

In August 1973 Andrew Kazdin received some tapes of Biggs's "home work" and surmised from them that Biggs's equipment was not in the best of condition. Well aware of the many favors Biggs continually did for Columbia, he saw an opportunity for Columbia to do one in return. Kazdin learned that it had indeed been some time since Biggs's machines had received even routine maintenance. In an interoffice memo he cited the "enormous amount of work which [Biggs] does using this equipment for the benefit of the Masterworks Department" and requested that one of Columbia's technicians be sent to Cambridge at company expense to service it. "It would be a very nice gesture on our part and would, in a sense, partially express our appreciation and gratitude for the 'extracurricular' work which Mr. Biggs constantly performs for the benefit of his product."

Biggs's veteran Ampexes apparently gave the Columbia technicians more trouble than they anticipated, and some of the problems eluded them until late September. Biggs, meanwhile, had invested in a pair of new Sony machines, so that when the two Ampex machines finally did get put back in good order, he was able to edit in quad as well as in stereo.

By December Biggs was well into his editing chores again. In that month he sent Columbia a "What's Next" list in which he outlined work in progress:

1) Am editing "Bach Organ Favorites" Volume VI
2) You have in Ice Box:
   Walther Six Concertos played on the Pedal Harpsichord (needs about one day
   of final editing)

3) "Bach in Quad" *The Four Toccatas and Fugues* on the Quartet of Organs at Freiburg (to be edited)
4) "Quadraphonic Spectacular"—well, let's hope—at Freiburg (to be edited)
5) "Multiple D minor record" (becomes possible when Freiburg material is edited.)

Am working on:
1) Joplin Volume II   When would you wish to record this?
2) Bach "Six Cantata Concertos" for Leipzig, June 1974.

As if editing, advertising, and sending out his own flyers were not enough, Biggs was also willing to pitch in with public relations jobs for Columbia. In the summer of 1974 Biggs and Peggy attended a company convention in Los Angeles by express invitation from Columbia's president, Goddard Lieberson. Afterward Biggs thanked Lieberson for his "most generous introduction at the Saturday festivities," and Pierre Bourdain thanked Biggs for upholding the honor of the Columbia Masterworks Department: "Your participation lent a note of elegance and musical authority to what would otherwise have been dominated by decibels and primitive rhythms."

Biggs still bent his literary talents to his work as well. Not only did he continue to write jacket notes, but his research into his subject matter often resulted in interesting articles for the trade magazines. The European tours, the historic organs, the glass armonica, the pedal harpsichord, the Handel recordings, Leipzig—all became subjects for his concise and pithy writings. Typical are the articles on Rheinberger that appeared in *The Tracker* and *Music* in 1973 and 1974 respectively. Biggs went straight to the source for his historical information and graphics: Rheinberger's birthplace in Vaduz, Liechtenstein. Along with his profuse thanks to the Vaduz authorities for their aid, he sent copies of the Rheinberger recording as soon as it was pressed. Biggs was habitually generous with copies of his albums, which he had to procure at his own expense. All individuals in any way connected with a recording always received a copy, from the proprietor of a Freiburg hotel where Biggs had stayed during a recording session to reviewers, concert hosts, friends, and even an occasional fan (often a young one) who had written a particularly sincere letter.

While some recording artists do take a certain amount of interest in the editing and marketing processes, and a few like to write their own jacket notes, many more record with a fundamentally "take it or leave it" attitude and show little interest between the completion of the recording session and the issuance of their album. But Biggs, "the Compleat Record Man," found all aspects of the recording and producing process genuinely interesting. He saw the phonograph record as a complex art form, no part of which could be neglected if the result was to have excellence. When a reviewer criticized a "smudgy" spot on a recording, Biggs took this remark as an affront not to his playing but to his *editing*.

Yet when a record was done, it was done. When a copy of the finished release arrived from Columbia, Biggs usually played it once, to make certain that everything was as he expected it to be. He would already be immersed in another project that demanded all his attention. As with any art form, some records were bound to be better than others, but Biggs could be satisfied that he had done all that was humanly possible to realize the maximum potential of each one.

21 | *Elder Statesman*

All art exacts its price, certainly much hard work and possibly economic hardship. But whatever pressure you have— you must, as I'm sure you do—*enjoy* your profession. Fight the good fight!

Biggs addressed these words to a group of organ builders in 1975, and they applied as much to his own life work as to theirs. Now in his sixties, he continued with undiminished enthusiasm to work hard, fight for his ideals, and, certainly, to enjoy his chosen profession.

Biggs's last engagement in 1973 was an appearance with the Symphony Orchestra of Corpus Christi, Texas, conducted by his friend Maurice Peress. On the program were three works for organ and brass and a Rheinberger concerto, all of which Biggs had previously recorded at St. George's with Peress, plus the perennially popular Saint-Saëns Organ Symphony. He began 1974 by playing Strauss and Rheinberger with the Minnesota Orchestra, along with two solo works. Roy M. Close of the *Minneapolis Star,* who seems to have been lukewarm to Rheinberger's music in general, found the Organ Concerto No. 2 a cut above his expectations:

Biggs's interpretation was thoughtful and appropriate. . . . His playing was sufficiently warm to convey the spirit of nobility so many of Rheinberger's themes seem designed to evoke. But it was also attentive to nuances and became admirably lyrical when the score called for it.

Biggs gave several concerts in California at the end of January, but he had to cancel a March engagement when he slipped and broke his arm. This was not his first fracture, although it was the first to necessitate the cancellation of a scheduled appearance. Biggs's physicians advised him to call off the few remaining spring concerts, but the form letter sent by Johanna Giwosky in reply to inquiries concerning concerts stated only that because of "the pressure of various recording commitments" Biggs was not accepting any more engagements in 1974.

Biggs did in fact have a heavy load of work to do for Columbia. Although

197

he did no actual recording in 1974, there were jacket notes to be written for the Freiburg and the second Joplin releases, a great deal of editing to be done (some of which had been delayed by the repairs to his equipment), and much correspondence to be carried on with regard to future projects. Clearance had been received to record in Leipzig again, and a firm date was set in 1975. This album was not to be another solo performance, but the Bach cantata sinfonias that Biggs had been recommending to Columbia for some time. As the American bicentennial was just around the corner, another Americana album was also high priority, and Biggs began making exploratory trips to potential recording sites in the fall of 1974.

Of the six Biggs albums released in 1974, three were reissues. The other three were the Freiburg Bach album, Walther on the pedal harpsichord, and *Bach Organ Favorites Vol. 6*, which was really a piecing together of some previously recorded but unreleased Trio Sonatas and Concertos. Whether new or reissued, all received favorable reviews, the Freiburg quadraphonic recording drawing the most attention. It was so successful that Biggs was already rounding up material for a second Freiburg foray. By November Biggs's "idea lists" included more Rheinberger, possibly done in the composer's own church in Vaduz, and some of his favorite Sowerby and Piston pieces, including two major works with orchestra: "I'm listing these but not urging them, for costs would be pretty steep. However the Piston [Prelude and Allegro] would fit very well on an 'organ and strings' record." In the way of new recording sites, Biggs was casting interested glances in the direction of Washington's Shrine of the Immaculate Conception, a spacious building with a large Möller organ, and New York's Alice Tully Hall, with its new Kuhn instrument.

Although Biggs had said he would accept no further recital engagements in 1974, he did take part in the dedication of a rebuilt tracker-action organ in the small town of Sharon, Connecticut, in October. And, although he did not perform, he was present at the dedication of the new Flentrop organ in Oberlin College's Warner Hall on November 22, where he participated in a symposium on "The Organ in the Twentieth Century." Numerous presubmitted questions were discussed by the panel, which included Biggs, Fenner Douglass, Charles Fisk, Marie-Claire Alain, George Taylor, Harald Vogel, Hans Steketee of the Flentrop firm, and the writer. The subject of electronic instruments was raised, giving Biggs the opportunity to deliver, in no uncertain terms, his opinions on what he called "the carnage at Carnegie"—an allusion to the refusal by New York's Carnegie Hall of the gift of a large Flentrop organ and the subsequent installation of an unimpressive electronic instrument. Asked his opinion of swellboxes (possibly not a totally serious question), Biggs shot back, "Why, there ought to be a law against them!"

As part of the ceremonies at Oberlin, Biggs was awarded an honorary doctorate. As a trustee slipped the hood over Biggs's head, Peggy muttered, *sotto voce,* "He's already got a closetful of those at home!" The Biggs closet did indeed already contain tokens of honorary doctorates bestowed by Acadia University, Coe College, and the New England Conservatory. Other honors accumulated during his career included fellowships in the Royal Academy of Music, the Royal College of Organists, and the American Academy of Arts and Sciences; citations for service from the Handel and Haydn Society and the National Association of American Composers and Conductors; and the title of Knight-Commander of the Order of Isabella the Catholic, bestowed by the Spanish government in recognition of Biggs's work on behalf of historic Spanish organs.

Good reviews and honors were the bright side of the fall of 1974, but in September a very dark shadow fell across Biggs's path with the death of the harpsichord maker John Challis. Challis, just one year Biggs's junior, had succumbed to a long and debilitating illness, although he had managed to work almost to the end. Biggs, who felt a strong debt of gratitude to Challis for building and maintaining his pedal harpsichord, as well as for his support and willingness to assist in research projects, was moved to write a short but appreciative account of Challis's life and work, which appeared in *Harpsichord* the following spring.

As an almost exact contemporary of Challis, Biggs could identify strongly with the harpsichord maker's efforts to popularize "old music, played on appropriate instruments" back in the 1930s and 1940s. He himself had been working toward that same end, at a time when most keyboard performers still unquestioningly accepted the modern grand piano and the romantically voiced electric-action organ as suitable vehicles for the keyboard works of the Renaissance and the Baroque.

Other parallels emerged in Biggs's account. Challis had returned from his four years of apprenticeship with Dolmetsch in 1930, the same year that Biggs became a permanent resident of the United States. In the late 1930s, when Biggs was encouraging G. Donald Harrison to build more organs of classical tonal design, Challis was making clavichords and harpsichords over his father's jewelry shop in Ypsilanti and barely selling enough instruments to make ends meet. In the 1940s and 1950s, when Biggs's career as a performer was reaching its peak and the type of instrument he advocated was becoming more popular, Challis had to move to a much larger workshop in order to serve his growing clientele. Biggs and Challis finally met in the 1960s, when their paths crossed over the pedal harpsichord. Both were committed nonconformists who loved their work and believed strongly in what they were doing; their mutual respect was instantaneous and enduring. The loss of this kindred spirit affected Biggs quite deeply, but it was not in his nature to brood long over such events when there was work to be done.

A number of plans were in the formative stage for 1975, but first there was another medical problem to be taken care of. Biggs had been having problems with cataracts, and his left eye was operated on only a few weeks before his Oberlin appearance. He had been concerned that he might have to wear an eye patch, but he showed up patchless if a bit bloodshot. Shortly afterward he wrote to Dr. Alfred Scott, his surgeon, "I'm delighted with my bright new eye! Thank you very much! The January 17 and 19 concerts in Los Angeles appear quite possible." However, he was eager to have the surgery on the other eye as soon as convenient ("My objective would be to try to be all right for some special events—New York on April 13th, and recording in Leipzig later . . ."). The second operation was scheduled for early February. Biggs was thus able to perform in Los Angeles—two concerts with orchestra at First Congregational Church—and to give a late-January recital at the Busch-Reisinger Museum.

By this time Biggs had cut back rather substantially on concert tours. He was always willing to schedule concerts close to home, however, including the Museum event and another in March at King's Chapel, in which he performed some of the Bach Sinfonias he planned to record at Leipzig. He also made an appearance, as he had for several years, during the annual "Bach Birthday Bash" of the local National Public Radio station, WGBH. In 1975 he gave only two performances away from home, but they were major events, with orchestras.

Of greatest import to Biggs, perhaps, was his part in the inauguration of the new mechanical-action Kuhn organ in Alice Tully Hall, part of the Lincoln Center complex. Some of its significance for Biggs had to do with his outspoken stand concerning pipe organs in New York's concert halls. A few years earlier the organ world had been stunned to learn that the generous gift of a Flentrop organ to Carnegie Hall had been refused for suspiciously vague reasons. Officially, it was said that the organ would spoil the acoustics, but no scientific authority was ever cited to support this premise, and, as Biggs and many others had pointed out, most of the acoustically finest halls in the world already contained organs. To add insult to injury, the large Aeolian-Skinner organ, which had caused its builders such misery, and which Biggs had dedicated, had been removed from Avery Fisher (formerly Philharmonic) Hall during the most recent of a seemingly interminable series of remodelings. This left New York bereft of organs in any of its major halls, but thanks to the generosity of arts patron Alice Tully, a good-sized organ from the Swiss firm of Th. Kuhn had recently been installed in one of the smaller halls. Biggs and most of the other organists hastened to put their stamp of approval on it.

Four concerts were given to open the new organ; two solo recitals (by André Marchal and by Karl Richter) and two concerted ones. Biggs took part in the second of these, performing a Haydn concerto and one of the Bach sinfonias with the Musica Aeterna Orchestra. Reviewer Allen Hughes, commenting on the "professionalism and integrity" of Biggs's performance, thought his presence on the program especially fitting "to celebrate this symbol of triumph of the cause he has served so well for so long." Biggs, who was quoted in the *New York Times* as proclaiming that "This is the way God intended organs to be built," shared honors in this concert with two other organists, Catherine Crozier and Thomas Schippers. Afterward, he wrote appreciative letters to the builders, commending their work, and to Alice Tully, to whom he predicted that "This organ is going to cast a long shadow—an illuminating shadow."

Biggs's next concert was to have been on May 14, with the Kansas City Orchestra under Maurice Peress. Biggs flew out, began preparing for the concert, collapsed, and had to be hospitalized. His appearance with the orchestra was cancelled; and the Leipzig trip, scheduled for the first week in June, seemed in jeopardy. But within a few days he was allowed to return home, where he rested and carried on his correspondence and trip preparations as though nothing had happened.

With Peggy, Biggs departed for Leipzig on May 29, 1975. Rehearsals with the Gewandhaus Orchestra under Thomaskantor Hans-Joachim Rotzsch began the next day, and the following seven evenings were given over to recording. Biggs played on a five-stop Schuke positive organ instead of the large instrument he had recorded on in 1970, and the music represented a very different facet of Bach's genius, one perhaps even more closely linked to the Thomaskirche. It was music Biggs had been wanting to record for some time, the six Cantata Sinfonias having an obbligato organ part. These works are unique in the literature of the period. "In effect, they are one-movement organ concertos," wrote Biggs, who wondered if Bach might even have intended them to form an independent set of pieces. To fill out the remaining space on the record, Biggs added the beloved "Jesu, Joy of Man's Desiring" and the ebullient Sonata to Cantata 31 (the Easter Cantata).

As usual, Biggs provided his own articulate jacket notes. There he ventured the opinion that these unique works might have been designed as display pieces for the organist, either Bach himself or one of his sons or students. The organ parts are indeed quite extraordinary. They sparkle and laugh their way through the orchestral fabric; they are heartbreakingly happy and full of the juice of life. Of one of them, Biggs wrote, "Though the title 'We must through great tribulation enter the kingdom of heaven' is formidable, the music of Sinfonia 146 is pure joy."

Biggs always appreciated the work of his collaborators in concerted programs, but a greater than usual empathy developed between him and the East German performers on this particular occasion. "They could not have

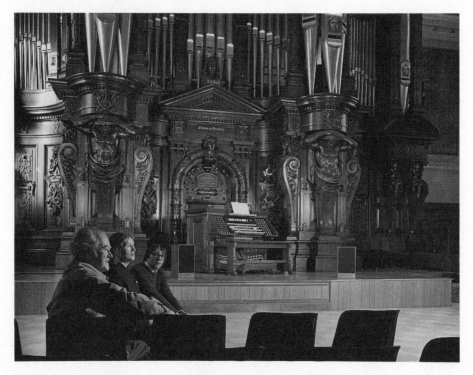

Biggs's last recording session, Methuen Memorial Music Hall, 1975

been more cooperative throughout, nor made us more welcome," Biggs wrote afterward to Pamela Ilott of CBS News. "There is something deeply moving in this, and I am sure it is their basic religious feeling—unaffected by whatever politics may be." Cantor Rotzsch was singled out for special praise: "He was a tower of strength, a great chap, and an excellent conductor," wrote Biggs to Paula Scherr of CBS Records, and he insisted that Rotzsch's picture appear on the record jacket. Biggs was also moved by the "rare sense of wonder and devotion" that permeated the instrumentalists' performance. But it is also possible that these fellow musicians responded as they did partly out of admiration for Biggs's own honest devotion to Bach, as well as for his grit and enthusiasm in the face of obviously increasing frailty.

Biggs's next recording project—and, as it turned out, his last—likewise lacked nothing in the way of vitality, but it was of a definitely more rollicking and secular nature. The recording sessions for the Bicentennial album were sched-uled for late September 1975, and Biggs was winnowing out program ideas. He had decided that the public was probably getting tired of Ives's "America" (or at least would be by the time 1976 ended) and was searching for works of equal interest to replace it. A visit by the writer to the Library of Congress in the spring of 1975 turned up the lively score of *The Battle of Manassas,* composed by a popular nineteenth-century black pianist known as Blind Tom. It was added at the last moment to a stack of photocopies of other material, largely because it was certain to appeal to Biggs's sense of humor. That it did, but Biggs also saw the possibilities of rearranging it for the organ, and it made a good foil for two other large works he had already chosen—Dudley Buck's Variations on "The Star-Spangled Banner" (a quite worthy replacement for the Ives) and a transcription of John Philip Sousa's *Stars and Stripes Forever,* which gave the album its title.

Although Biggs had investigated a number of possible organs for this recording, from the Tannenbergs of Pennsylvania to a large 1876 Hook & Hastings in Buffalo which had originally been part of the Centennial Exposition in Philadelphia, the final choice boiled down to three organs that were close at hand. The small Brattle Organ, an early eighteenth-century chamber organ in St. John's Church, Portsmouth, New Hampshire (which had been unplayable at the time the first Americana record was made, but was restored by Fisk in 1965), was used for two short pieces, but everything else was played on the rebuilt Boston Music Hall organ in Methuen Music Hall or the new Fisk organ in Boston's Old West Church. Some trial and error was involved in deciding which pieces would go best on which instruments. Early in September, after a visit to the various organs, Biggs reported to Kazdin,

> As you see, the emphasis has shifted back to Methuen. Because, whatever the problems there, I believe we will obtain in Methuen more of a slam-bang concert atmosphere than in Old West Church. Old West is, however, quite ideal for the perky Colonial airs and marches, and also—curiously enough—for Manassas.

The "problems" at Methuen had to do with the organ's slow response and the difficulty of hearing its sound properly from the console. Otherwise there was a distinct advantage to this well-insulated hall: since no other uses were scheduled for the fall, recording could go on without interruption at just about any time of day. Old West Church, on the other hand, was a heavily used building, and street noise made it impossible to record there at any time other than late at night.

Stars and Stripes Forever was as different from the earlier *Organ in America* release as night from day. Biggs threw any stuffy pretense of authenticity to the winds and produced the most "slam-bang" version of *The Battle of Trenton* he had ever played. The other big pieces on the disc are in the same uninhibited vein. The little "Colonial airs and marches" are, as he said, "perky." That word might not readily have been applied to Biggs by anyone who observed him laboring up the stairs to the organ gallery at Old West

Church, yet once seated at the console he bent to his task with astonishing vigor.

The same vital spirit animated Biggs's one public speaking engagement in the fall of 1975, an address given in October at a convention of the American Institute of Organ Builders in Albany. Most of the ideas in his speech were not new, but in restating them Biggs summarized some of his own basic tenets. His theme was the absolute importance of good organs—*real* organs—to the proper realization of fine music. That good organs encourage good playing almost goes without saying, but Biggs felt also that the great organs of history were the inspiration for some of the masterpieces of organ literature. He then offered his own imaginative reconstruction of the way the young Bach, as a student in Lüneburg, might have been inspired to create his monumental Toccata in D minor:

> How did this masterpiece come into being? Certainly not by sliding down a shaft of light from above. Rather, I believe, by the young Bach sneaking up to the organ gallery of St. John's Church, where there was an organ already 150 years old, and—experimenting. He'd try that famous opening twiggle on the chief manual and enjoy the six-seconds' echoes that followed. Then, an octave lower on another manual, complete with echo—and yet another. Then, that wonderful low pedal and the spread chord, melting into major. The whole Toccata exploits in the simplest of musical language almost every grand effect of which an organ is capable, and is the most perfect instance where we may certainly believe that a great organ inspired a great composition. Of course, it's an advantage to have a great composer at hand.

Biggs warmed to his subject, bringing up the matter of the "synthetic object" in Carnegie Hall. He had attended Virgil Fox's opening concert on the electronic instrument and observed that, despite the size of the instrument and the virtuosity of the player, "the electronic sound is still pudgy, inarticulate, the flutes without character (unless you consider the tremolo to be character) and the ensemble becomes more turgid as it gets louder." If there was little for the ear, there was nothing for the eye: "Where is the symmetry of organ pipes, the beauty of an organ case, where, in fact, is any *identity?*"

Electronic science had its uses in the reproduction of musical sound, as no one with as long a history in broadcasting and recording as Biggs could possibly deny, "but not for the *creation* of sound. Synthetic sound cannot equal the richness, the complexity, the natural glory of sound emanating from rank on rank of pipes. Electronically produced sound seems second hand. It quickly becomes tiring." This was not where the future of "Bach's Royal Instrument" lay. "Rather, the *past* is the *future* of the organ. . . ." By this Biggs meant not necessarily the literal copying of historic instruments but the study of them, the absorbing of the lessons they had to teach. "It means that you have a foundation of centuries to build on."

Biggs's talk was published in *Music,* and reader reaction was warmly commendatory. In a letter to the editor, Richard Ditewig of San Francisco summed up the general reaction succinctly:

> Mr. Biggs's life has been one of dedication, service, and uncompromising standards. . . . In his latest statement Mr. Biggs is challenging all who hear him to never settle back for mediocrity but to strive for artistic perfection in all we say and do.

Biggs's outspoken advocacy of the pipe organ was certainly not new, but at a time when massive advertising campaigns were being aimed at convincing potential organ purchasers that a counterfeit was as good as the real thing, his words gave heart to colleagues who shared his convictions but lacked his visibility. He was invited to give a similar talk to the New York chapter of the American Guild of Organists in June 1976. The Manhattan organists made a gala event of it by following Biggs's address with a dinner to which Alice Tully, critic Allen Hughes, Guild of Organists President Roberta Bitgood, and other dignitaries were invited.

In his New York speech Biggs again delivered his opinions on the Carnegie Hall situation, but not without a liberal touch of humor. Having related an anecdote about a village Strawberry Festival in which a shortage of strawberries had caused prunes to be substituted, Biggs demanded to know "WHAT WAS THIS PRUNE DOING IN CARNEGIE HALL?"

Again, Biggs willingly admitted the usefulness of electronic science in the reproduction of musical performance. "Electronics with attached keyboards," as he called them, might even be handy "for occasional purposes, such as opening the World Series, for taking on a concert trip to Timbuctoo, and they are said to be prevalent and popular in cocktail bars." But, "In Carnegie Hall we are dealing with *music* and the *integrity of music.*" He backed up his views on the integrity of the organ with a technically knowledgeable comparison of the manner in which pipe organs and "electronic devices" produce their respective sounds, effectively countering the few shopworn arguments against organs in concert halls, and concluding with the warning that "imitations have a very short shelf life."

Allen Hughes reported the event in the *New York Times* for June 9, quoting Biggs at length and referring to him as "an elder statesman of the music world, whose indefatigable labors over nearly half a century have made his name synonymous with organ playing." He also noted that Biggs was cutting back considerably on his concert activities. "I'm not averse to recitals," Biggs had told Hughes, "but I'm gradually dropping that. I want to communicate now through recordings."

22 | The Measure of a Musician

In March 1976, when Biggs turned 70, Daniel Pinkham and other friends arranged a private (but "full house") concert in his honor at King's Chapel in Boston, followed by a reception at King's Chapel House on Beacon Street. Biggs was his usual genial self, but seemed more than a little touched by this surprise party. Some of the Columbia people came up from New York; others sent telegrams. "Wish we could be there to shake the hand that shook the establishment," cabled John McClure. Andrew Kazdin wished him "the happiest of birthdays—with overlaps" (a reference to Biggs's method of recording sectional takes to facilitate splicing). One, recalling the title of a recently recorded Joplin rag, read, "Congratulations and best wishes to our favorite 'entertainer' on your 70th birthday. Love from the Columbia crew."

The Bicentennial album, *Stars and Stripes Forever*, was released early in June and generated enthusiastic reviews. Vernon Gotwals, writing in *Music*, called it "a whole packet of firecrackers, ranging from little snappers to noisy aerial bombs and breathtaking star-spangled rockets." He praised the engineering and observed that Biggs played "superlatively well." Biggs, who seems never to have lost his small boy's enjoyment of a celebration, still had another Bicentennial-connected event ahead of him.

In 1950 a major American Guild of Organists convention had been held in Boston. It coincided with the bicentennial of J. S. Bach's death, and an impressive program with a strong Bach emphasis had been put together by dint of considerable hard work on the part of Biggs, Peggy, and a few others. In 1976 Boston was again the site of a national convention. The Guild had grown in membership, the Boston chapter had become the largest in the country, and its 1976 convention, attended by a record 2,400 people, was an extravaganza with a distinctly American emphasis. Biggs was appointed honorary program chairman (the actual chairman being John Ferris of Harvard), and he attended many of the meetings and offered valuable suggestions. A feature of the 1950 convention had been an "A. G. O. Night at the Pops" in Symphony Hall, with Biggs as soloist with the famed Boston Pops Orchestra under the baton of

Arthur Fiedler. The convention committee agreed quite early that it would be unthinkable not to feature the same team at the 1976 event.

Boston's Symphony Hall seats over two thousand people, even with the informal table arrangements that replace the orchestra seats for the "Pops" season, and the conventiongoers filled nearly every seat on the night of June 25. The program featured Rheinberger's Organ Concerto No. 2 and one of Mozart's "Epistle" Sonatas, with Biggs as soloist, plus some purely orchestral numbers and the traditional "Pops extras." One of these, which could never have been attempted with an ordinary audience, was the impromptu performance—necessarily from memory—of Handel's Hallelujah Chorus from *Messiah* by the entire audience. But the Biggs-Fiedler team was clearly the major attraction, as much for the younger generation of organists, for whom these two senior musicians were already approaching legendary status, as for those old enough to remember nostalgically the 1950 concert.

There was, however, one little complication. Two days before the concert Biggs had broken his left elbow. His doctor wanted him in the hospital, but Biggs would not hear of it. Instead, he kept the injury a closely guarded secret and strode onto the stage of Symphony Hall on June 25 with the wounded limb inconspicuously strapped into a position that would allow him to play as scheduled. As Peggy later observed, "If the elbow was stiff, the fingers were not." The console was placed squarely before the podium so that Biggs could see Fiedler, but the audience could not really see Biggs. Somehow he managed to give a polished performance of the two concerted works and even stay for the reception that followed, where Peggy and a few friends hovered around him to fend off any well-wishers who appeared bent on an overly physical greeting. The next morning Biggs went straight to the hospital. In a review of the program in the August issue of *Music,* Wilma Salisbury wrote, "The beloved artist played with distinction, showing a sure ear for balance in his choice of registration and a good instinct for audience appeal in his choice of repertoire. After the Rheinberger Concerto, the soloist was cheered by the crowd." And those who knew about the elbow cheered the loudest.

The night before the performance, Biggs had been made an honorary member of Boston's venerable Handel and Haydn Society, then in its 162nd year of continuous existence. Before the ceremony, when asked by conductor Thomas Dunn what he would like said about him, Biggs replied, "Ah, just say that I play the organ." Dunn, elaborating slightly, neatly summarized Biggs's career:

> E. Power Biggs plays the organ. Countless listeners having their first love affair with music, cherish that fact in their hearts. Few in the history of performance leave indelible marks on their art; of them, none rivals him in the affection and respect of layman and colleague alike. He is the rollicking forward scout of scholarship, and, while busy these fifty years restoring the noble classics of the

instrument to health, with prodigal generosity he has cultivated a garden of musical flowers and brought several generations of budding composers to bloom.

Not even Biggs could have suspected that the Boston program would be his last public performance, for he had in fact already signed up for fall concerts in New York and Chicago. In September he made a nonperforming appearance before the Merrimack Valley chapter of the American Guild of Organists at Methuen Music Hall, giving a carefully prepared and well-received program of taped examples and spoken commentary on the subject of historic organs. Biggs probably planned to do more programs of this kind, for shortly afterward he agreed to present a similar one for the Harvard-Radcliffe Organ Society in the spring.

In October Biggs suffered a broken leg, and his fall concerts had to be cancelled. But the month was marked by the first American showing, on the TV program "Lamp unto My Feet," of a documentary he had made the previous year for CBS. Part of it had been videotaped in Leipzig following the 1975 recording sessions, and the rest had been done in Cambridge. Earlier in his career Biggs had on more than one occasion tried to stir up interest in a motion picture on the life of Bach, and he had even roughed out a tentative script. Nothing ever came of it, but in this short television production Biggs had at last made good his objective of bringing Bach to the public in sight as well as in sound. The *New York Times* called it "a quiet, civilized half-hour, done with taste and dignity. An inspiring way to start a Sunday—or any day."

In the fall of 1976 Biggs was interviewed by Bruce Morgan of Cambridge's *Real Paper,* an "underground" journal gone more or less respectable. To Morgan Biggs restated his conviction that great organs precede great organ music and affirmed his stance "pro" tracker action and reverberant acoustics and "con" electronic imitations. He also related some of his experiences and observations regarding broadcasting and recording ("I consider that I've been awfully fortunate in that the right machines came along at the right time") and cited his invitation to play at Bach's church in Leipzig as the "most satisfying" experience of his long career.

In November the Bach Sinfonia recording was released, and Biggs gave away numerous copies as Christmas gifts. Friends and reviewers marveled at its freshness and vitality. Arthur Lawrence, in *The Diapason,* was of the opinion that the album represented some of Biggs's finest playing—"The performances are all that one might hope for, and more"—and considered it one "to be treasured by any admirer of Bach or Biggs."

Biggs continued to generate ideas for future recording projects. A list scrawled out longhand in April 1976 was headed "Ideas Ideas 1976–2076 (but leave 2076 for a while)" and included another quadraphonic spectacular at Freiburg, "Arch-Romantics" (Liszt, Franck, Rheinberger) at Methuen,

Handel on the pedal harpsichord, more Bach in East Germany, and another Christmas disc. By fall he was seriously mapping out the Methuen album and thinking that he might like to do some Pachelbel as well. A fall "idea list" added an organ and violin album (something Biggs had not yet done); something English for organ, trumpets, and kettledrums (always a favorite Biggs combination); and, with orchestra, the Sowerby, Piston, and Porter concertos. Along with everything else, he kept a sharp eye on developments in the organ world, noting that the large new Flentrop organ at Duke University and the soon-to-be-restored dual organs in Mexico City Cathedral might have possibilities for future recordings. The Duke instrument, on which Biggs's advice had been asked in the early stages, was dedicated in 1976; and the monumental Mexico City project, also being done by Flentrop, was to be completed by the fall of 1977. As usual, Biggs wanted to be the first to record them.

In January 1977 Biggs presented Columbia with still another unique idea for an album tentatively entitled "In Praise of Bach." It was conceived as a cooperative effort between Columbia and Eterna that would dovetail chorale preludes played by Biggs in New York's St. Thomas's Church with chorales and cantata movements sung by the choir of St. Thomas's Church in Leipzig— "the reverberation of 3,000 miles," exclaimed Biggs, with characteristic enthusiasm. "In addition to Bach's magnificent music, I think the Greetings from St. Thomas to St. Thomas will lend this record a unique distinction!" Columbia was sufficiently interested in the idea to initiate correspondence with Eterna about it.

Biggs concurred with Robert Schumann's dictum that "we are never finished with Bach." In his later years he returned with increasing frequency to the composer who occupied the uppermost place in his pantheon of musical saints, finding ever new inspiration for his own work in Bach's timeless music. At the conclusion of his CBS Bach telecast, he affirmed the continuing relevance of the great composer: "The mind, the genius, the music, the discipline of Bach's whole life stand as a challenge to us today." Biggs shared the discipline and wholeheartedly accepted the challenge.

During January and February 1977, in addition to correspondence concerning recording plans, Biggs corrected proofs for an edition of Rheinberger's Organ Concerto in F and a collection of short early American keyboard pieces, both to be issued by McAfee Music Corporation. Uwe Pape of Berlin, in the process of writing a book on the "organ reform" movement in America, asked Biggs for some recollections of the two Busch-Reisinger Museum organs, and Biggs cheerfully complied. He seemed more than willing to respond to requests of this nature. His own account of his recording career had appeared in *The Tracker* and the *Schwann Catalog* during 1976; and a request in 1975 from Jean Rizzo, who was doing research on Biggs's teacher G. D. Cunningham, elicited a long letter which was virtually an article in itself and was in fact published as one in the March 1978 issue of *Music*. A similar request from a Colorado researcher early in 1977 for material pertaining to Biggs's work with Koussevitzky resulted in some extensive notes that Biggs himself reworked into the last article he ever submitted to *Music*.

During the last fifteen years of Biggs's life, his health gradually declined. Yet, as Peggy observed, "He found the whole idea of giving in to physical infirmity ridiculous. Of course one must go on. Every time a physician said 'you ought not to,' he replied 'but I must.' " Biggs's physical problems did nothing to dampen his sense of humor—he was always amused by the perplexed expressions of airline security guards when the pins in his knees set off the alarm in the detector gate.

Biggs had good reasons for not wanting his public to know the state of his health, and, since he was not the least interested in sympathy, even his friends had little inkling of it. Peggy, of course, was fully aware of his physical condition, and her account gives a clear picture of Biggs's difficulties during the 1960s and 1970s, when some of his finest recordings were made:

> In 1958 Biggs developed Rheumatoid Arthritis—a cruel disease for any musician, but particularly so for an organist. Only constant practice despite pain kept his hands and feet limber. He was most grateful to his orthopedic surgeon, Dr. Theodore Potter—a "man of action" whose continued surveillance made the impossible possible—and the supportive roles of his physicians Carey Peters, Tillman McDaniel, Peter E. Barry, and Ahmed Mohuiddin. In later years surgery was scheduled after, between, and far enough away from, recording sessions. Once, when Dr. Potter showed X-rays of his hands, and pointed out the new joints that constant practice had worn in, Biggs quipped that that picture would make an interesting record sleeve cover. . . .

From the mid-1970s on Biggs suffered additional problems, and in the spring of 1977 emergency surgery became necessary. But his weakened constitution was unequal to the stress, and despite heroic efforts on the part of the operating team, death came on March 10, 1977. Biggs had been busy with his editing, writing, and planning right up to the time he left for the hospital a week earlier.

Biggs's death sent shock waves of disbelief through the musical world. Like his friend Arthur Fiedler, who died two years later, he had (although he probably did not care for the idea) become an institution. His youthful affinity for lively, happy music and his continuing involvement in all aspects of his art kept his audiences from learning of his infirmities. The music on his two last recordings gives no hint that it is being played by a very sick man who—because he was above all a realist—probably knew he had little time left. He had been unobtrusively putting his affairs in order, while at the same time optimistically planning for the future on the very slim chance that things might improve.

A private burial service was conducted in Cambridge's Mount Auburn Cemetery, the final resting place of many another notable from the greater Boston area, and on March 27, two days before Biggs would have turned 71, a memorial service was held in Harvard's Memorial Church. It was planned by Peggy, with the willing assistance of many friends, and music occupied a prominent place. It began with a Biggs favorite, "My Spirit Be Joyful" from Bach's Easter Cantata, and included Bach's "Sheep May Safely Graze"—the old broadcast sign-off music—and "Now Thank We All Our God," plus Telemann's *Heroic Music*. The players were all members of the Boston Symphony Orchestra and included some of Biggs's old collaborators: Alfred Zighera, Louis Speyer, and Roger Voisin. Daniel Pinkham directed, and Thomas Dunn was the accompanist. Two anthems were sung by John Ferris's Harvard University Choir, fortified by a liberal infusion of "friends"; and readings were given by Edward O. Miller, Rector of St. George's Church in New York; Peter Gomes of Memorial Church; and Biggs's cousin Murray Biggs, director of the Shakespeare Ensemble of the Massachusetts Institute of Technology. Members of the Harvard-Radcliffe Organ Society and young organ builders from Charles Fisk's workshop were the ushers.

Memorial Church is a sizable building, and it was filled to capacity. The atmosphere was subdued, yet the occasion was more for remembering than for mourning. Edward Miller, taking his cue from the titles of the Telemann pieces, offered a prayer of thanksgiving for his friend's life and work: "For his quiet devotion, his playfulness, gentleness, and unobtrusive generosity we give thanks. . . . With humor, with gaiety gladdened by goodness, he transmitted serenity to make our spirits rejoice." Miller had known Biggs well enough to be aware of the odds Biggs had been fighting during his last few years: "We thank you for this example of a brave man of hope whose indomitable will refused to succumb to handicap, but remained always on the side of life, with vigor and charm."

Letters of condolence poured in from all over the world. They came from friends, fans, students, and fellow musicians; from the Earl of Aylesford, the President of Harvard, and the United Parcel Service delivery man. Many mentioned the positive influence Biggs had had on the sender's life or career, and others expressed gratitude for favors done many years earlier. Biggs's colleagues at Columbia expressed their feelings in an advertisement in the *New York Times:*

> E. Power Biggs became an artistic legend in his own lifetime. He was a man cherished for his great warmth and wit, his indefatigable spirit. He found a home not only in the small town of Cambridge, Massachusetts, but also at the seat of any organ, and in the hearts of people everywhere.
>
> We rejoice in the life of E. Power Biggs.

Almost immediately Andrew Kazdin began planning a commemorative release that would document Biggs's entire career as a recording artist, from 1938 to 1976. Since Peggy was often the only one who could answer a question or find something among the hundreds of reels of tape in the house, she too became involved in this project and proved her own merit as a writer by contributing an article to the jacket booklet. In addition, she began the sad and monumental task of sorting out a lifetime accumulation of papers, programs, correspondence, and scores. "Time is very much out of joint for me," she wrote Hellmuth Kolbe in midsummer. "Last March seems a hundred years away, yet our last trip to Leipzig is so near that I can put out my hand and touch it."

The spring and fall of 1977 saw a nationwide proliferation of memorial concerts, many of which made a point of including music Biggs had edited or that was associated with his recordings. They ranged from a program given by the Handel and Haydn Society in Boston's Old West Church (where Biggs had made portions of his last recording) to the first of what would become a series of annual events organized by the San Francisco chapter of the American Guild of Organists. That concert, in which six organists and a chamber orchestra participated, was free, and its promoters hoped to attract an audience of two thousand. But Biggs had a lot of friends and admirers on the West Coast. "3,000 Jam Biggs Tribute," ran the headline of a review in the *Oakland Tribune* for September 27:

> People were standing on seats, sitting on kneelers, and very nearly kneeling atop standees. It was the largest Bay Area audience in over a decade for a classical pipe-organ concert, and it didn't even need a light show for a drawing card. Biggs deserved every bit of the adulation. . . .

And Biggs would have approved—not of the adulation, which seemed to have less effect on him than on many other musicians—but of the fact that three thousand people had come to listen to fine organ music. In this regard it was indeed a high tribute to Biggs's life work.

Obituaries reached the wire services and appeared throughout the country—routine coverage, perhaps, for conductors, prima donnas, and rock stars, but somewhat rare in the case of organists. Tributes abounded. The *New York Times* devoted a feature article to Biggs's life; and an article in the *Boston Globe* by Daniel Pinkham praised Biggs's championship of new music and recalled that whenever Pinkham had substituted for him on a radio broadcast, Biggs had encouraged him to perform his own compositions. The Boston Symphony Orchestra devoted a section of one of its program booklets to its "old and cherished friend"; and critic Michael Steinberg, in the *Newsletter* of the Handel and Haydn Society, declared his indebtedness to Biggs for having introduced him to many musical works for the first time. "We do and shall miss him painfully, this friend, companion, champion."

The *Harvard Crimson* printed a snapshot of an exuberant Biggs in a Popeye tee-shirt and celebrated his "Warmth, wit, and wisdom." Richard Buell wrote an insightful appreciation in *The Phoenix,* giving Biggs credit for launching into currency "many of the historically accurate notions about organ playing that we now take for granted." Buell seemed somewhat awe-struck by the scope of Biggs's recorded *oeuvre,* which ranged from "impressive, continent Bach" to "some rather silly Scott Joplin. . . . His was so energetic, useful and imaginative a life that our sorrow at his passing has surprisingly little disappointment in it."

The musical community was acutely aware that it had sustained a serious loss. Virtually every professional journal, down to the humblest Guild chapter newsletter, paid tribute in its own way. The Organ Historical Society's quarterly, *The Tracker,* catalogued Biggs's many contributions to the Society's cause (including free recitals and his continuing to pay dues even after having been elected an honorary member) and urged members to donate copies of Biggs's records to their local libraries as a memorial. The two "trade" journals, *The Diapason* and *Music* (soon to be renamed *The American Organist*), each devoted special issues to Biggs and his work. Charles Henderson, editor of the latter, expressed the feeling of many of his colleagues when he wrote, "The organ world has lost one of its strongest men." Even the American Theatre Organ Society gave Biggs an extensive writeup, in which it was noted that he had once been instrumental in obtaining a recording contract for a gifted young theatre organist.

In a way, Biggs created his own memorial in the records he made, the music he edited, the students he helped, and the untold number of organs his influence helped to save or to bring into being; not the least of these is the instrument still heard regularly in the Busch-Reisinger Museum in Cambridge. He would probably be pleased with some of the memorials created in his name. Throughout the country churches, colleges, and American Guild of Organists chapters have established annual memorial concerts. Scores and recordings have been given to libraries to help further Biggs's educational work. A fund established by the Organ Historical Society assists younger members to attend the Society's conventions. And at Boston University a room bearing Biggs's name houses an organ research library founded by the Boston chapter of the American Guild of Organists. Its holdings include all Biggs's scores, books, recordings, and papers.

Early in 1979 Andrew Kazdin's painstakingly researched memorial album was finally released, to laudatory reviews. The four discs present excerpts from nearly forty years of Biggs recordings, from the Technichord and Victor 78s through the long years of Biggs's association with Columbia, plus some pedal harpsichord recordings of Handel works discovered in Columbia's "ice box." The well-illustrated booklet accompanying the album contains a delightful account of Biggs's early years by Peggy, an overview of his recording career by Kazdin, and a discography that underscores the impressive scope of Biggs's recording achievements.

In March 1979, *The Diapason* published some recollections of Biggs by Larry Palmer, who, like many other musicians of his generation, benefited from Biggs's supportiveness. His closing words undoubtedly echoed the feelings of a large portion of his readers: "Thanks, EPB, for all you did for the organ, for the harpsichord, for music in this country. We miss you."

Appendix A
The Biggs Instruments

Germanic Museum, Cambridge, Massachusetts
Aeolian-Skinner, 1937

HAUPTWERKE

Quintade 16'
Principal 8'
Spitzflöte 8'
Principal 4'
Rohrflöte 4'
Quint 2 ⅔'
Super Octave 2'
Fourniture IV (1 ⅓')

POSITIV

Koppelflöte 8'
Nachthorn 4'
Nasat 2 ⅔'
Blockflöte 2'
Terz 1 ⅗'
Sifflöte 1'
Zimbel III (½')
Krummhorn 8'

PEDAL

Bourdon 16'
Principal 8'
Gedeckt Bass 8'
Nachthorn 4'
Blockflöte 2'
Mixtur III (4')
Posaune 16'
Trumpete 8'
Krummhorn 4' (Pos.)

4 Couplers
8 General Combinations
Crescendo Pedal

The Cambridge Portative
Schlicker Organ Company, 1953

GREAT

Gedeckt 8'
Quintadena 8'
Octave 4'
Rohr Floete 4'
Nasat 2 ⅔'
Principal 2'
Rohr Floete 2'
Mixture III
Krummhorn 8'

POSITIV

Gedeckt 8'
Quintadena 8'
Rohr Floete 4'
Rohr Floete 2'
Quintadena 2'
Larigot 1 ⅓'
Siffloete 1'
Cymbal II

PEDAL

Untersatz 16'
Gross Gedeckt 8'
Gedeckt 8'
Octave 4'
Bourdon 4'
Quintadena 4'
Rohr Floete 2'
Nasat 1 ⅓'
Mixture II
Ranket 16'
Krummhorn 8'

2 General Combinations

This is a unified organ, all stops being derived from the following ranks: Untersatz 16', Gedeckt 8', Quintadena 8', Octave 4', Rohr Floete 4', Nasat 2 ⅔', Mixture III, Cymbal II, Ranket 16', and Krummhorn 8'.

Busch-Reisinger Museum, Cambridge, Massachusetts
D. A. Flentrop, 1958

HOOFDWERK	RUGPOSITIEF	BORSTWERK
Prestant 8'	Holpijp 8'	Zingend Gedekt 8'
Roerfluit 8'	Prestant 4'	Koppelfluit 4'
Octaaf 4'	Roerfluit 4'	Prestant 2'
Speelfluit 4'	Gemshoorn 2'	Sifflet 1'
Nasard 2 2/3'	Quint 1 1/3'	Cymbel I
Vlakfluit 2'	Mixtuur II	Regaal 8'
Terts 1 3/5	Kromhoorn 8'	
Mixtuur IV		

PEDAAL	COUPLERS
Bourdon 16'	Hoofdwerk-Pedaal
Prestant 8'	Rugpositief-Pedaal
Gedekt 8'	Borstwerk-Pedaal
Fluit 4'	Rugpositief-Hoofdwerk
Mixtuur III	Borstwerk-Hoofdwerk
Fagot 16'	
Trompet 8'	

The Pedal Harpsichord
John Challis, 1964

MANUAL I	MANUAL II	PEDAL
16'	8'	16'
8'	Harp on 8'	8'
8'		4'
4'		Harp on 16'
Harp on 8'		Harp on 8'

"Full Harpsichord" Pedal
Venetian Swell (Pedal only)

Appendix B
E. POWER BIGGS EDITIONS

Associated Music Publishers

J. S. Bach. *Two Christmas Chorales and Doxology* (organ with two trumpets)
————. *Three Wedding Chorales* (organ with two trumpets)
————. *Two Fanfares and Chorale* (organ, three trumpets, and timpani)
W. Selby. *A Lesson*
A. Soler. *Concerto No. 3 in G Major* (arranged for organ solo)
J. P. Sweelinck. *Balleto del Granduca*
Festival Anthology (collection)
Manuals Only (collection)

H. W. Gray Company

J. S. Bach. *The Art of the Fugue*
————. *Jesu, Joy of Man's Desiring* (organ)
————. *Jesu, Joy of Man's Desiring* (organ and strings)
————. *Jesu, Joy of Man's Desiring* (organ and piano)
————. *Sheep May Safely Graze* (in B flat)
————. *Sheep May Safely Graze* (in G)
————. *Sheep May Safely Graze* (organ and piano)
————. *Sheep May Safely Graze* (organ, strings, flutes)
————. *Two Sinfonias* (Cantata 106, Cantata 156)
————. *Concert-Overture and Alleluia* (Cantata 142)
————. *Sinfonia, Chorale and Variations* (Cantata 4)
————. *A Solemn Prelude* (Cantata 21)
Couperin/Dandrieu. *Two Pictorial Pieces: "The Trophy" and "The Fifers"*
J.-F. Dandrieu. *Offertoire for Easter*
L.-C. D'Aquin. *The Cuckoo*
W. Felton. *Concerto in B Flat* (organ solo)
————. *Andante* (from Concerto in B Flat)
G. F. Handel. *Royal Fireworks Music*
————. *The Faithful Shepherd*
————. *Concerto in F Major, No. 13* "The Cuckoo and the Nightingale" (for organ solo, or with instruments)
F. J. Haydn. *The Musical Clocks*, A Suite of 7 Pieces
F. Liszt. *The Christmas Tree*

217

W. A. Mozart. *Adagio* (for the Glass Harmonica or Musical Glasses)
———. *Prelude on the Ave Verum*
A. Soler. *The Emperor's Fanfare*
G. Valentini. *Christmas Pastorale*
A. Vivaldi. *Concerto in D Minor* (organ solo)

Charles Hansen

S. Joplin. *E. Power Biggs Plays Scott Joplin*

McAfee Music Corporation

D. Buck. *The Star Spangled Banner* (Concert Variations)
W. A. Mozart. *Adagio and Rondo*
J. C. Oley. *Eleven Chorale Preludes*
J. Rheinberger. *Organ Concerto in F Major, No. 1* (full score and parts)
———. *Organ Concerto in G Minor, No. 2* (full score and parts)
C. Saint-Saëns. *Fantasia in E flat*
Antiphonal Music for Two Keyboard Instruments (collection)
A Collection of Easy Marches and Airs from Early America

Mercury Music Corporation

J. S. Bach. *My Spirit Be Joyful* (Cantata 146) (organ and trumpets)
———. *Now Thank We All Our God* (Cantata 79) (organ and trumpet)
J. Brahms. *Eleven Chorale Preludes*
A. Corelli. *Trio Sonata*, Op. 1, No. 1 (organ and strings)
———. *Trio Sonata*, Op. 3, No. 2 (organ and strings)
L.-C. D'Aquin. *New Book of Noëls* (2 volumes)
———. *Noël X*
C. Ives. *Variations on "America"* and *Adeste Fideles*
W. A. Mozart. *17 Sonatas for Organ and Orchestra* (5 volumes)
———. *Fugue in G minor*
H. Purcell. *Ceremonial Music* (organ with optional trumpets)
F. Schubert. *Fugue in E minor* (originally for piano duet)
R. Schumann. *Four Sketches* (originally for pedal piano)
Treasury of Early Organ Music (collection)
Treasury of Shorter Organ Classics (collection)

Music Press

W. F. Bach. *Complete Organ Works*
Frescobaldi/Homilius. *Ricercare* and *Prelude*
J. L. Krebs. *Fugue in C Major* ("Postilion")
———. *8 Chorale Preludes* for Organ with Trumpet (or Oboe)
W. A. Mozart. *Adagio and Rondo*, K. 617 (organ with string quartet)

Theodore Presser Company

J. S. Bach. *Suite for Organ from the Little Notebook of Anna Magdalena Bach*
J. Hewitt. *The Battle of Trenton*
J. P. Sousa. *The Stars and Stripes Forever*

G. Schirmer, Inc.

L. C. D'Aquin. *Noel We Sing* (SATB with organ interludes)
S. Joplin. *Scott Joplin for Organ*

B. F. Wood Company

J. S. Bach. *Fugue in C Major* ("Fanfare")
———. *Chorale: All Glory Be to God on High*

N.B. As of 1986, Mercury and Music Press editions are available from Theodore Presser Co.; and McAfee, H. W. Gray, and B. F. Wood editions are available from Belwin-Mills Publishing Co.

Appendix C
E. POWER BIGGS DISCOGRAPHY

COMPILED BY ANDREW KAZDIN

Items 1-29 are all 78 rpm. Items 30-148 are 33⅓ rpm except where otherwise stated. Items 1 and 2 are both on the Technichord Label; 3-28 and 33 are R.C.A. Victor; 29-32 and 34-148 are all Columbia Masterworks.

1. Handel, The Cuckoo and the Nightingale—Allegro; Daquin, Variations on a Noël. Germanic Museum, Cambridge, Mass. (1938) 1139-A/B.

2. **A Bach Organ Recital:** Concerto in A Minor after Vivaldi; Wachet auf; Sonata #1; Prelude and Fugue in E-flat. Germanic Museum, Cambridge, Mass. (1938) T1.

3. Handel, Concerto #10 in D Minor, with Fiedler Sinfonietta, Arthur Fiedler, cond. Germanic Museum, Cambridge, Mass. (10/39) M 587.

4. **Organ Music (Bach and Daquin):** Bach, Wachet auf; In Dulci Jubilo; Nun freut euch; Nun komm' der Heiden Heiland. Daquin, Noël grand jeu et duo; Noël sur les flûtes. Germanic Museum, Cambridge, Mass. (12/39) M 616.

5. Handel, Concerto #2 in B-flat, with Fiedler Sinfonietta, Arthur Fiedler, cond. Germanic Museum, Cambridge, Mass. (1/40) 15751.

6. **Bach: The Little Organ Book, Vol. 1.** Chorale Preludes Nos. 17 to 32. Germanic Museum, Cambridge, Mass. (4/40) M 652.

7. Handel, Concerto #11 in G Minor (Beginning), with Fiedler Sinfonietta, Arthur Fiedler, cond. Germanic Museum, Cambridge, Mass. (9/40) 2009.

8. Handel, Concerto #11 in G Minor (Conclusion), with Fiedler Sinfonietta, Arthur Fiedler, cond. Germanic Museum, Cambridge, Mass. (9/40) 2100.

9. **Bach: The Little Organ Book, Vol. 2.** Chorale Preludes Nos. 33 to 45 and Nos. 1 to 4. Germanic Museum, Cambridge, Mass. (10/40) M 697.

10. **Bach: The Little Organ Book, Vol. 3.** Chorale Preludes Nos. 5 to 16. Germanic Museum, Cambridge, Mass. (12/40) M 711.

11. Handel, Organ Concerto No. 13 in F Major, with Fiedler Sinfonietta, Arthur Fiedler, cond. Germanic Museum, Cambridge, Mass. (2/41) M 733.

12. Beethoven, Missa Solemnis. Boston Symphony Orchestra, Serge Koussevitsky, cond. Symphony Hall, Boston, Mass. (4/41) M 758/759.

Originally published in *Music—The AGO-RCCO Magazine,* March 1978.

13. Bach, Toccata and Fugue in D Minor. Germanic Museum, Cambridge, Mass. (7/41) 18058.

14. **Bach, The Art of Fugue, Vol. I.** Contrapunctus I-VII. Germanic Museum, Cambridge, Mass. (11/41) M 832.

15. **Bach, The Art of Fugue, Vol. 2.** Contrapunctus VIII-XIV; Wenn wir in höchsten Nöthen sein. Germanic Museum, Cambridge, Mass. (11/41) M 833.

16. Bach, Jesu, Joy of Man's Desiring. Brahms, Lo, How a Rose e'er Blooming, Opus 122. Memorial Church, Harvard University, Cambridge, Mass. (12/41) 18292.

17. Felton, Concerto #3 in B-flat, with Fiedler Sinfonietta, Arthur Fiedler, cond. Germanic Museum, Cambridge, Mass. (3/42) M 866.

18. Sowerby, Symphony for Organ in G Major. Memorial Church, Harvard University, Cambridge, Mass. (5/42) DM 894.

19. Corelli, Concerto in C Major, with Fiedler Sinfonietta, Arthur Fiedler, cond. Germanic Museum, Cambridge, Mass. (6/43) DM 924.

20. Gabrieli, Processional and Ceremonial Music for Voices, Organ and Brass. Symphony Hall, Boston, Mass. (10/43) DM 928.

21. Reubke, Sonata for Organ in C Minor on the 94th Psalm. Memorial Church, Harvard University, Cambridge, Mass. (3/44) DM 961.

22. Corelli, Sonata for Organ and Strings in F Major, with Fiedler Sinfonietta, Arthur Fiedler, cond. Germanic Museum, Cambridge, Mass. (9/44) 10-1105.

23. Bach, Prelude and Fugue in E Minor ("The Cathedral"). Germanic Museum, Cambridge, Mass. (1/45) 10-1121.

24. Mozart, Sonatas for Organ and Orchestra, K. 144, 244, 245, 278, 328, 366, with Fiedler Sinfonietta, Arthur Fiedler, cond. Symphony Hall, Boston, Mass. (12/45) M 1019.

25. **Bach Organ Music:** The "Little" G-Minor Fugue; Ein' feste Burg; Fugue in C Major ("Fanfare"); Sheep may safely graze; Passacaglia and Fugue in C Minor. Memorial Church, Harvard University, Cambridge, Mass. (5/46) M 1048.

26. Dupré, Variations on a Noël. Memorial Church, Harvard University, Cambridge, Mass. (12/46) 11-9329.

27. Piston, Prelude and Allegro for Organ and Strings, with Boston Symphony Orchestra, Serge Koussevitzky, cond. Symphony Hall, Boston, Mass. (3/47) 11-9262.

28. Mozart, Adagio and Rondo, K. 617, for flute, oboe, viola, cello and celesta. Symphony Hall, Boston, Mass. (6/47) 11-9570.

29. **Organ Music of Bach:** Prelude and Fugue in E-flat; Fugue in D Minor ("Giant"); Fantasia and Fugue in G Minor; Toccata in F Major. (3/8/48) M/MM 728.

30. Re-issue of #29. (12/6/48) ML 4097.

31. **French Organ Music:** Widor, Toccata from Symphony No. 5; Marche Pontificale. Vierne, Final from Symphony No. 1. Alain, Litanies. Boëllmann, Suite Gothique. Dupré, Antiphon II. Gigout, Grand Choeur dialogué. St. Paul's Chapel, Columbia University, New York City. (1/10/49) M-MM 802.

32. Simultaneous issue of "Boëllmann" from #31. (1/10/49) 72737-D.

33. **Haydn: The Musical Clocks.** Germanic Museum, Cambridge, Mass. (7/49) 49-0419 (45 rpm); 10-1471 (78 rpm).

34. **French Organ Music.** Re-issue of #31. (8/1/49) ML 4195.

35. **Mendelssohn and A Bach Recital.** Mendelssohn, Sonata VI. Bach, Prelude in G Major (Fugue à la Gigue); Sinfonia to Cantata 106; Erbarm' dich mein, O Herre Gott; Sinfonia to Cantata 156; All Glory be to God on High. (11/7/49) ML 2076.

36. Re-issue of Mendelssohn from #35. (11/21/49) MX 324.

37. **Bach's Royal Instrument.** Toccata, Adagio and Fugue in C Major; Six Chorale Preludes (Schübler); Prelude and Fugue in G Major ("The Great"). Symphony Hall, Boston, Mass. (4/10/50) M/MM 899.

38. **Bach's Royal Instrument, Vol. 1:** Simultaneous issue of Toccata, Adagio and Fugue and Six Chorale Preludes (Schübler), from #37. (4/10/50) ML 4284.

39. **Bach's Royal Instrument, Vol. 2:** Prelude and Fugue in B Minor ("The Great"); Trio Sonatas #1, 2; Prelude and Fugue in G Major (from #37). Symphony Hall, Boston, Mass. (4/10/50) ML 4285.

40. **E. Power Biggs Recital.** "A Westminster Suite": Dunstable, Byrd, Purcell. Symphony Hall; Boston, Mass. Wesley, Air and Gavotte. Mozart, Adagio for Glass Harmonica (K. 356). Mulet, Toccata from "Byzantine Sketches." Mozart, Prelude on the Ave Verum Corpus (K. 618). Purcell: Fanfare, Trumpet Tune I and II. Voluntary on the Doxology. St. Paul's Chapel, Columbia University, New York City. (10/16/50) M/MM 954.

41. **Westminster Suite and E. Power Biggs Recital:** Simultaneous issue of #40, plus Milhaud, Pastorale; Couperin, Chaconne. (10/16/50) ML 4331.

42. Poulenc, Concerto in G Minor for Organ, String Orchestra and Timpani, with Columbia Symphony Orchestra, Richard Burgin, cond; plus re-issue of Milhaud from #41. Symphony Hall, Boston, Mass. (12/11/50) M/MM 951.

43. **Music of César Franck:** Pièce héroïque: Prelude, Fugue and Variation. Symphony Hall, Boston, Mass. (12/11/50) MX 350.

44. **Poulenc, Organ Concerto, and Music of César Franck.** Re-issue of #42 and 43, without Milhaud. (12/11/50) ML 4329.

45. **Music of Jubilee.** Bach, Sinfonia to Cantata 29, etc., with Columbia Chamber Orchestra, Richard Burgin, cond; Chorale Preludes, Chorales. (10/19/51) ML 4435.

46. **Bach's Royal Instrument, Vol. 3:** Toccata and Fugue in D Minor; Concerto in D Minor after Vivaldi: Fugue in C Major ("Fanfare"); Fugue in G Minor ("Little") Passacaglia and Fugue in C Minor. Symphony Hall, Boston, Mass. (10/21/51) ML 4500.

47. **Cathedral Voluntaries and Processions.** Purcell, Trumpet Voluntary; Voluntary in C Major ("Fanfare"). Vaughan Williams, Chorale Prelude: "Rhosymedre." Walond, Introduction and Toccata. Parry, Chorale Prelude: "Melcombe." Murrill, Postlude on a Ground. Marcello, Psalm 19. Buxtehude, Chorale Prelude: "Nun bitten wir den Heiligen Geist." Bach, "Komm süsser Tod." Anonymous, Verses from the Te Deum. Mattheson, Aria in E Minor. Schubert, Litany. Strauss, Procession for Festival Occasions. (10/13/52) ML 4603.

48. **A Bach Festival,** with brass ensemble. Bach, Chorales and Chorale Preludes. Krebs, Prelude for Trumpet and Organ. Homilius, When Adam Fell. Symphony Hall, Boston, Mass. (2/16/53) ML 4635.

49. Re-issue of Bach: Jesu, Joy of Man's Desiring; Sheep May Safely Graze; Now Thank We all Our God, from #45. Symphony Hall, Boston, Mass. (4/6/53) A-1641.

50. Julius Reubke, Sonata in C Minor on the 94th Psalm. Liszt, Fantasia and Fugue on B-A-C-H; Credo and Gloria, from an Organ Mass. Methuen Memorial Music Hall, Methuen, Mass. (1/18/54) ML 4820.

51. Re-issue of Bach, Toccata and Fugue in D Minor; Fugue in G Minor ("Little"), from #46. (9/20/54) A-1882.

52. Re-issue of Widor and Vierne from #31. (10/18/54) A-1883.

53. **Bach, Toccata in D Minor (A Hi-Fi Adventure).** 14 performances (14th with Fugue). 14 locations, 14 organs. (2/5/55) ML 5032.

54. **The Art of the Organ.** Purcell, Sweelinck, Pachelbel, Buxtehude, Bach, recorded on organs of England, Holland, Germany, Denmark and Sweden. (2/21/55) KSL 219.

55. **Bach: Eight Little Preludes and Fugues;** Fantasia in G Major. Various organs of Alsace, Germany and Austria. (4/2/56) ML 5078.

56. **A Mozart Organ Tour.** Mozart: 17 Festival Sonatas for Organ and Orchestra, with the Camerata Academica, Bernard Paumgartner, cond., and organ solos. Various organs in Germany and Austria. (7/16/56) K3L 231.

57. **Organ Music of Spain and Portugal.** Pasquini, Cabezon, Seixas, Carreira, Jacinto, Santa Maria, Casanovas, Valente, Carvalho, Cruz, Cabanilles. Various organs in Spain and Portugal. (3/57) KL 5167.

58. **Hindemith:** Concerto for Organ and Chamber Orchestra, Op. 46, No. 2, with Columbia Chamber Orchestra, Richard Burgin, cond., Symphony Hall, Boston, Mass. **Rheinberger:** Organ Sonata No. 7 in F Minor, Op. 127, Deutsches Museum, Munich, Germany. (9/30/57) ML 5199.

59. **Saint-Saëns:** Symphony No. 3, Op. 78, with Philadelphia Orchestra, Eugene Ormandy, cond. Symphony Hall, Boston, Mass. (11/11/57) ML 5212.

60. **Bach at Zwolle.** Bach, Prelude and Fugue in E-flat ("St. Anne"); Prelude and Fugue in C Minor ("Arnstadt"); Prelude (Concertato) and Fugue in D Major ("The Great"). Zwolle, The Netherlands. (4/28/58) KL 5262.

61. Stereo counterpart of #55. (7/14/58) KS 6005.

62. **The Organ.** 125 recorded musical illustrations performed on 35 notable organs dating from 1521 to 1958 with commentary by EPB. (8/25/58) DL 5288.

63. **Handel Organ Concertos.** Handel, Organ Concertos 1-6, with London Philharmonic Orchestra, Sir Adrian Boult, cond. St. James Church, Great Packington, England. (10/20/58) K2L 258, K2S 602.

64. **Handel Organ Concertos.** Handel, Organ Concertos 7-12, with London Philharmonic Orchestra, Sir Adrian Boult, cond. St. James Church, Great Packington, England. (4/6/59) M2L 261, M2S 604.

65. **E. Power Biggs Plays Mendelssohn in St. Paul's Cathedral.** Mendelssohn, Sonatas 1 and 6. St. Paul's Cathedral, London, England. (10/12/59) ML 5409, MS 6087.

66. **Handel Organ Concertos.** Handel, Organ Concertos 13-16, with London Philharmonic Orchestra, Sir Adrian Boult, cond. St. James Church, Great Packington, England. (12/14/59) M2L 267, M2S 611.

67. **E. Power Biggs Concierto en Mexico:** Campra, Rigaudon. Banchieri, Dialogo. Clarke, Trumpet Voluntary. Balbastre, Noël with Variations. Bach, Allein Gott in der Höh' sei Ehr. Karg-Elert, Lobet den Herrn mit Pauken und Zimbeln. Widor, Toccata. Dupré, Variations sur un Noël. Jaime Nuno, Mexican National Anthem. Released *only* in Mexico. DCO 3001.

68. **Music for Organ and Brass.** Canzonas of Gabrieli and Frescobaldi, with the Boston Brass Ensemble, Richard Burgin, cond. (2/15/60) ML 5443, MS 6117.

69. **The Organ in America.** Anonymous Tunes from Colonial America, Phile, Billings,

Selby, Moller, Hewitt, Michael, Brown, Yarnold, Shaw, Ives. Recorded on various historical organs of America. (8/1/60) ML 5496, MS 6161.

70. **Joyeux Noël.** Daquin, Noëls. Busch-Reisinger Museum, Cambridge, Mass. (9/5/60) ML 5567, MS 6167.

71. **Six Double Concertos for Two Organs.** Soler, Concertos 1-6, with Daniel Pinkham. Busch-Reisinger Museum, Cambridge, Mass. (1/16/61) ML 5608, MS 6208.

72. **Hindemith: Three Sonatas for Organ.** Busch-Reisinger Museum, Cambridge, Mass. (4/3/61) ML 5634, MS 6234.

73. **Bach Organ Favorites:** Toccata and Fugue in D Minor; Passacaglia and Fugue in C Minor; Toccata, Adagio and Fugue in C Major; Fugue in G Minor ("Little"); Fugue in G Major ("Jig"). Busch-Reisinger Museum, Cambridge, Mass. (7/31/61) ML 5661, MS 6261, MQ 435.

74. **Festival of French Organ Music:** Widor, Toccata (5th Symphony); Saint-Saëns, Fantasia in E-flat Major; Franck, Pièce Héroïque; Gigout, Scherzo in E Major; Vierne, Final (1st Symphony); Alain, Litanies; Dupré, Variations on a Noël. St. George's Church, New York City. (1/2/62) ML 5707, MS 6307.

75. **Don Gesualdo, Prince of Madrigalists:** Gagliarda. (1/29/62) KL 5718, KS 6318.

76. **Variations on Popular Songs:** Sweelinck. Busch-Reisinger Museum, Cambridge, Mass. (5/14/62) ML 5737, MS 6337.

77. **Heroic Music for Organ, Brass and Percussion:** Clarke, Handel, Croft, Purcell, Telemann, with the New England Brass Ensemble. Busch-Reisinger Museum, Cambridge, Mass. (7/16/62) ML 5754, MS 6354, MQ 486.

78. **Music for Organ and Orchestra:** Strauss, Festival Prelude, Op. 61, with New York Philharmonic, Leonard Bernstein, cond., at Philharmonic Hall, Lincoln Center, New York City. Barber, Toccata Festiva, Op. 36; Poulenc, Concerto in G Minor, with Philadelphia Orchestra, Eugene Ormandy, cond., at Academy of Music, Philadelphia, Pa. (12/17/62) ML 5798, MS 6398.

79. **The Cuckoo and the Nightingale—Four Favorite Organ Concertos:** Handel, Concertos 2, 5, 13 and 16. (4/15/63) Re-issued from #63 and #66. (4/15/63) ML 5839, MS 6439.

80. **Saint-Saëns, Symphony No. 3, Op. 78,** with Philadelphia Orchestra, Eugene Ormandy, cond. Academy of Music, Philadelphia, Pa. (7/15/63) ML 5869, MS 6469, MQ 573.

81. **Music for a Merry Christmas:** Carols with Columbia Chamber Orchestra, Zoltan Rozsnyai, cond. Stadtpfarrkirche of Eisenstadt, Austria. (10/63) ML 5911, MS 6511, MQ 601.

82. **The Golden Age of the Organ:** Bach, Pepping, Schein, Cimello, Vivaldi, Walther. Various organs of Germany, The Netherlands and Austria. (2/17/64) M2L 297, M2S 697.

83. **Music of Jubilee:** Bach, with Columbia Chamber Symphony, Zoltan Rozsnyai, cond. Stadtpfarrkirche, Eisenstadt, Austria. (8/10/64) ML 6015, MS 6615, MQ 637.

84. **Haydn—The Three Organ Concertos,** with Columbia Symphony, Zoltan Rozsnyai, cond. (12/21/64) ML 6082, MS 6682.

85. **Bach Organ Favorites, Vol. 2:** Prelude and Fugue in E-flat Major; Pastorale in F Major; Prelude and Fugue in A Minor ("The Great"); Schmücke dich, o liebe Seele; Toccata in F Major. Busch-Reisinger Museum, Cambridge, Mass. (7/19/65) ML 6148, MS 6748, MQ 740, 16 11 0218.

86. **Bach on the Pedal Harpsichord:** Passacaglia and Fugue in C Minor; Toccata and Fugue in D Minor, BWV 565; Fantasy and Fugue in G Minor ("The Great"); Prelude in D Minor, BWV 539; Prelude and Fugue in G Major ("The Great"). Columbia Records Studio, New York City. (2/14/66) ML 6204, MS 6804, MQ 790.

87. **E. Power Biggs Plays Mozart for Solo Organ:** Fantasia in F Minor, K. 608 and K. 594; Adagio and Fugue in C Minor, K. 546; Adagio for a Glass Harmonica, K. 356; Andante with Variations, K. 616; Prelude on the Ave Verum, K. 508a. Great Church of St. Bavo, Haarlem, The Netherlands. (4/18/66) ML 6256, MS 6856.

88. **E. Power Biggs Plays Mozart—The 17 Festival Sonatas for Organ and Orchestra,** with Columbia Symphony, Zoltan Rozsnyai, cond. Eisenstadt, Austria. (4/18/66) ML 6257, MS 6857, MQ 799.

89. **Holiday for Harpsichord:** Schubert, Mozart, Haydn, Beethoven, De Falla, Chopin, Weber, Boccherini, Brahms, Grieg, Saint-Saëns, Tschaikovsky. Columbia Records Studio, New York City. (7/18/66) ML 6278, MS 6878, MQ 804.

90. **Buxtehude at Lüneburg:** Prelude and Fugue in G Minor; Chorale Preludes; Prelude, Fugue and Chaconne; Partita; Toccata and Fugue in F Major; Chaconne in D Minor; Fugue in C Major ("Jig"). Johannes Kirche, Lüneburg, Germany. (1/16/67) ML 6344, MS 6944.

91. **E. Power Biggs Plays the Historic Organs of Europe.** Various composers and organs. (5/29/67) ML 6255.

92. **Bach: Six Trio Sonatas played on the Pedal Harpsichord.** Also Bach-Ernst, Concerto No. 1 in G Major and Bach-Vivaldi, Concerto No. 2 in A Minor. Columbia Records Studio, New York City. (8/28/67) M2L 364, M2S 764.

93. **Reel-to-Reel Tape Counterpart of #92,** excluding the two Concertos. MQ 975.

94. **The Glory of Gabrieli,** with the Gregg Smith Singers, the Texas Boys Choir of Fort Worth, the Edward Tarr Brass Ensemble, Vittorio Negri, cond. Basilica San Marco, Venice. (1/24/68) MS 7071.

95. **Copland,** Symphony for Organ and Orchestra, with New York Philharmonic, Leonard Bernstein, cond. Philharmonic Hall, Lincoln Center, New York City. (1/24/68) MS 7058.

96. **Bach Organ Favorites, Vol. 3:** Prelude and Fugue in C Minor ("Arnstadt"); Prelude and Fugue in D Minor, BWV 539; Prelude and Fugue in E Minor, BWV 533; The Six Schübler Chorales. Busch-Reisinger Museum, Cambridge, Mass. (4/22/68) MS 7108, MQ 990.

97. **Historic Organs of Spain:** Soler, Angles, Cabanilles, Pasquini, Dandrieu, etc. Various Spanish organs. (4/22/68) MS 7109.

98. **Bach on the Pedal Harpsichord: The Six Trio Sonatas, Vol. 1.** Re-issue of Sonatas 1, 2, 3 and Bach-Ernst Concerto No. 1 in G Major, from #92. (4/22/68) MS 7124.

99. **Bach on the Pedal Harpsichord: The Six Trio Sonatas, Vol. 2.** Re-issue of Sonatas 4, 5, 6 and Bach-Vivaldi Concerto No. 2 in A Minor, from #92. (4/22/68) MS 7125.

100. **A Biggs Festival.** Various works from previous recordings. (4/22/68) EPB-1.

101. **Handel: The Sixteen Organ Concertos, Vol. 1.** Re-issue of #63, and Concertos 7, 8, 9 from #64. (4/22/68) D3S 777.

102. **Handel: The Sixteen Organ Concertos, Vol. 2.** Re-issue of #66, plus Concertos 10, 11, 12 and Six Little Fugues for Organ, from #64. (5/1/68) D3S 778.

103. **Gabrieli Canzonas,** with Edward Tarr Brass Ensemble, and the Gabrieli Consort. La Fenice, Vittorio Negri, cond. Basilica, St. Mark's, Venice. (7/15/68) MS 7142.

104. **What Child Is This:** Christmas Carols, with Gregg Smith Singers, Texas Boys Choir, New York Brass and Percussion Ensemble. St. Michael's Church, New York City. (10/2/68) MS 7164.

105. **Six Double Concertos for Two Organs.** Re-issue of #71. (12/23/68) MS 7174.

106. **Bach's Greatest Hits,** including re-issue of Jesu, Joy of Man's Desiring, from #83. (4/21/69) MS 7501.

107. **E. Power Biggs Greatest Hits:** re-issues of Bach, Handel, and Widor, Toccata; new recording of Ives, Variations on "America" on Fisk organ, Harvard University. (5/19/69) MS 7269.

108. **Our Best to You,** including re-issue of Bach Toccata and Fugue in D Minor, from #73. (9/69) MGP 13.

109. **Historic Organs of Italy:** Frescobaldi, Gesualdo, Trabaci, Gabrieli, etc. Various organs of Italy. (10/27/69) MS 7379.

110. **Bach Organ Favorites, Vol. 4:** Prelude and Fugue in D Major (the "Great"); Now come, Saviour of the Gentiles, BWV 659; Rejoice greatly, good Christians, BWV 734; Prelude and Fugue in C Minor (the "Great"); Jesus, my sure Defense, BWV 728; Blessed Jesu, see us here, BWV 731; A mighty fortress is our God, BWV 720. Busch-Reisinger Museum, Cambridge, Mass. (2/24/70) MS 7424.

111. **Handel's Greatest Hits,** including re-issue of Awake the Trumpet's Lofty Sound, from #77; The Cuckoo and the Nightingale (Allegro only), from 66; Where'er You Walk, from #114. (4/6/70) MS 7515.

112. **Historic Organs of France:** Couperin, Le Bègue, Balbastre, Clérambault, Dandrieu. Abbey Church, Marmoutier, Alsace; and Abbey Church, Ebersmünster, Alsace. (5/25/70) MS 7438.

113. **Bach's Greatest Hits, Vol. 2,** including In Dulci Jubilo, from #91. (6/29/70) MS 7514.

114. **The Magnificent Mr. Handel.** Various works, with Royal Philharmonic Orchestra, Charles Groves, cond. St. James Church, Great Packington, England. (8/24/70) M 30058.

115. **Saint-Saëns Greatest Hits,** including last movement of Symphony No. 3, from #80. (9/25/70) MS 7522.

116. **Historic Organs of England:** Dunstable, Tallis, Tye, Byrd, Dowland, Purcell, Holborne, Clarke, Handel, Stanley. Various organs of England. (2/22/71) M 30445.

117. **The Biggs Bach Book,** from The Little Music Book for Anna Magdalena Bach, plus arias, chorales and chorale preludes. Busch-Reisinger Museum, Cambridge, Mass. and Arlesheim, Switzerland. (4/19/71) M 30539, MT 30539, MA 30539.

118. **Bach at the Thomaskirche:** Toccata and Fugue in D Minor; Passacaglia and Fugue in C Minor; Prelude and Fugue in G Major ("The Great"); Prelude and Fugue in C Major (9/8). Thomaskirche, Leipzig, East Germany. (7/21/71) KM 30648, MT 30648, MA 30648.

119. **The Glory of Venice.** Various works with the Edward Tarr Brass Ensemble, the Gregg Smith Singers, the Texas Boys Choir, Vittorio Negri, cond. Basilica of San Marco, Venice. (10/20/71) M 30937.

120. **Music for Organ, Brass and Percussion,** by Gigout, Dupré, Campra, Widor, Strauss, Purcell, Karg-Elert, Clark. St. George's Church, New York City. (3/29/72) M 31193, MT 31193, MA 31193, MQ 31193, MAQ 31193.

121. **Walther: Six Concertos for Organ, after Italian Masters.** Cathedral of Freiberg, Germany. (3/29/72) M 31205.

122. **The Magnificent Mr. Handel, Vol. 2.** Various works with Royal Philharmonic Orchestra, Charles Groves, cond. St. James Church, Great Packington, England. (3/29/72) M 31206.

123. **E. Power Biggs Plays 24 Historic Organs in 8 Countries Covering 7 Centuries of Music by 24 Composers.** Bach, Toccata and Fugue in D Minor, played at Arlesheim, Switzerland, plus works of various composers on various organs; re-issued from #82, #84, #88, #90, #91, #92, #97, #109, #114, #116. (3/29/72) MG 31207.

124. **Bach Organ Favorites, Vol. 5:** Fantasy and Fugue in G Minor; Jesu, meine Freude, BWV 753; Prelude and Fugue in B Minor; Wir glauben all' an einen Gott, BWV 680; Prelude and Fugue in C Major, BWV 545. Busch-Reisinger Museum, Cambridge, Mass. (7/26/72) M 31424, MT 31424, MA 31424, MQ 31424, MAQ 31424.

125. **Best of Bach:** Re-issues of Toccata and Fugue in D Minor; Passacaglia and Fugue in C Minor; Fugue in G Minor ("Little"), from #73; Prelude and Fugue in E-flat Major, from #85. (5/73) M 31840, MT 31840, MA 31840.

126. **Famous Organs of Holland and North Germany:** Bach, Scronx, Telemann, Sweelinck, Buxtehude, Paumann, Cornet, Koetsier. Various locations and organs. (1/73) M 31961.

127. **Bach's Greatest Hits:** Quad counterpart of #106. (4/2/73) MQ 32054.

128. **Rheinberger: Two Concertos for Organ and Orchestra,** with Columbia Symphony Orchestra, Maurice Peress, cond. St. George's Church, New York City. (8/73) M 32297, MT 32297, MA 32297.

129. **Quad counterpart of #128.** (7/73) MQ 32297, MAQ 32297.

130. **A Mini-Discourse by E. Power Biggs.** A Bonus Disc packed with #128 and #129. (8/73) BTQ.

131. **Heroic Music for Organ, Brass and Percussion.** Re-issue of #68 and #77. (8/73) MG 32311.

132. **E. Power Biggs Plays Scott Joplin on the Pedal Harpsichord.** Columbia Records Studio, New York City. (10/73) M 32495, MT 32495, MA 32495.

133. **Joplin: Maple Leaf Rag and Cleopha.** Stereo "Single" re-issued from #132. (10/25/73) 4-45941.

134. **Quad counterpart of #132.** (9/73) MQ 32495, MAQ 32495.

135. **Book of Noëls.** Re-issue of #70. (1/74) M 32735.

136. **Bach Organ Favorites, Vol. 6:** Concerto in G Major, after Johann Ernst: Trio Sonata, No. 5: Trio Sonata, No. 1; Concerto in A Minor, after Vivaldi. Busch-Reisinger Museum, Cambridge, Mass. (3/74) M 32791, MT 32791, MA 32791, MQ 32791, MAQ 32791.

137. **Walther: Six Concertos after Italian Masters.** Same repertoire as #121, but played on pedal harpsichord. (5/74) M 32878.

138. **Charles Ives, the 100th Anniversary.** Including re-issue of Variations on "America," from #107. (6/74) M4 32504.

139. **Bach: The Four "Great" Toccatas and Fugues on the Four Antiphonal Organs of the Cathedral of Freiburg.** Toccata and Fugue in D Minor; Toccata and Fugue in F Major; Toccata and Fugue in D Minor ("Dorian"); Toccata, Adagio and Fugue in C Major. (9/74) M 32933, MQ 32933, MT 32933, MA 32933, MAQ 32933.

140. **Mozart: The 17 Festival Sonatas; Haydn, The 3 Organ Concertos.** Re-issue of #84 and #88. (9/74) MG 32985.

141. **E. Power Biggs Plays Scott Joplin on the Pedal Harpsichord, Vol. 2.** Columbia Records Studio, New York City. (2/75) M 33205, MT 33205, MQ 33205.

142. **The Four Antiphonal Organs of the Cathedral of Freiburg.** Handel, Mozart, Buxtehude, Purcell, Krebs, Banchieri, Soler, Campra. (8/75) M 33514.

143. **Bach Organ Favorites.** Re-issues of #73, #85 and #96. (9/22/75) D3M 33724.

144. Re-issue of #101 and #102, excluding Six Little Fugues for Organ. (10/75) D3M 33716.

145. **E. Power Biggs.** Promotional disc—not for sale. (11/75) AS 186.

146. Re-issue of 8 Little Preludes and Fugues and Concerto in D Minor after Vivaldi, from #82. (3/76) M 33975.

147. **Stars and Stripes Forever.** Works by American composers played on various historical American organs. (6/76) M 34129, MT 34129, MA 34129.

148. **Bach: The Six Organ Concerto Sinfonias** from Cantatas 29, 35, 169, 146, 49 and 31, with Gewandhaus Orchestra of Leipzig, Hans-Joachin Rotzsch, cond. Thomaskirche, Leipzig, Germany. (11/76) M 34272, MT 34272.

BIBLIOGRAPHY

Reviews are not cited unless they are of feature-article length or of unusual pertinence. In addition to the material cited, major sources for this book were the correspondence, notebooks, programs, and other papers of E. Power Biggs, now in The Organ Library of the Boston chapter, American Guild of Organists, at Boston University.

Aeolian-Skinner Organ Company. Sales brochure, ca. 1955
———. Shop files on organs in Germanic Museum, Tanglewood, and Symphony Hall.
Affelder, Paul. "More Organ Lore." *Newark Sunday News,* October 5, 1958.
"An Organ Tour with E. Power Biggs." *American Record Guide,* Vol. 21, No. 9 (May 1955).
"Back Aloud." *The New Yorker,* June 7, 1958.
Baker-Carr, Janet. *Evening at Symphony.* Boston: Houghton Mifflin Co., 1977.
Banta, Lorene. "E. Power Biggs Teaches." *The American Organist,* Vol. 16, No. 4 (April 1982).
Barden, Nelson. "Edwin H. Lemare." *The American Organist,* Vol. 20, No. 1 (January 1986); Vol. 20, No. 3 (March 1986).
Barnes, William H. *My Recollection of Church Musicians.* Evanston: Arlee/Todd Ltd., 1976.
"Baroque Organ of 1937." *The American Organist,* Vol. 20, No. 5 (May 1937).
Belt, Byron. "E. Power Biggs and Organ Revival." *Long Island Press,* December 19, 1971.
"The Biggs Complete Bach." *The American Organist,* Vol. 20, No. 1 (November 1937).
Biggs, E. Power. "Address at AIO Convention." *Music,* Vol. 10, No. 4 (April 1976).
———. "Bach's Thomaskirche." *Music,* Vol. 5, No. 11 (November 1971).
———. "Basic Principles of Classic Organ Ensemble Defined." *The Diapason,* Vol. 47, No. 4 (March 1956).
———. "The Case for the Pedal Harpsichord, Or, A New Look at the Bach Trio Sonatas." *The Diapason,* Vol. 58, No. 12 (November 1967).
———. "Dr. Schweitzer's Intuition Confirmed." *Saturday Review,* August 31, 1968.
———. "European Organs Prove Virtue of Classic Models." *Musical America,* February 15, 1955.
———. "The Flentrop Organ in Cambridge, Mass., U.S.A." *The Organ,* Vol. XLII, No. 168 (April 1963).
———. "Gabrieli in San Marco." *Records and Recording,* June 1968.
———. "G. D. Cunningham, My Teacher." *Music,* Vol. 12, No. 3 (March 1978).
———. "Handel in the Forest of Arden." *Philips Music Herald,* Vol. IV, No. 2 (May 1959).
———. "Historic Organs of Switzerland." *Music Journal,* Vol. XXIV, No. 10 (December 1966).

———. "Important Music for Organ and Orchestra." *Musical America,* March 25, 1945.

———. "Impressions of Europe, 1954." *Organ Institute Quarterly,* Vol. 4, No. 4 (Autumn 1954).

———. "John R. Challis." *The Harpsichord,* Vol. 8, No. 1 (February-March-April, 1975).

———. "Josef Rheinberger, the Master from Liechtenstein." *Music,* Vol. 8, No. 1 (August 1974).

———. "The King of Instruments Returns." *Horizon,* Vol. 11, No. 4 (March 1960).

———. "Koussevitzky and Concert Hall Organs." *Music,* Vol. 12, No. 3 (March 1978).

———. "Modern Organ—Renaissance or Retrogression." *The Musical Digest* (March 1948).

———. "A Modern Renaissance of the Organ." *Music,* Vol. 12, No. 3 (March 1978).

———. "Mozart and the Organ." *A. G. O. Quarterly,* Vol. 1, No. 4 (October 1956).

———. "Mozart's Sonatas for Organ and Orchestra." *RCA Record Review,* December 1945.

———. "Music on the Cuff." *Recordings,* February 1948.

———. "The New Aeolian-Skinner Organ in Symphony Hall, Boston." Aeolian-Skinner publicity flyer ca. 1950; reprinted from a Boston Symphony Orchestra Program.

———. "A 19th Century Genius." *The Tracker,* Vol. 18, No. 2 (Spring 1973).

———. "Notes on a Recording Trip." *The Diapason,* Vol. 55, No. 12 (November 1964).

———. "The Organ Comes into Its Own." *RCA Victor Record Review,* July 1944.

———. "Organ Designed by Handel Stirs a Teapot Tempest." *The Diapason,* Vol. 50, No. 2 (January 1959).

———. "The Organ in the Concert Hall." *A. G. O. Times,* Vol. 1, No. 5 (June 15, 1976).

———. "The Organ in the Concert Hall." *The Tracker,* Vol. 23, No. 4 (Summer 1979).

———. "Organ in the Germanic Museum." Typescript of an interview tape made in January 1973 for the Division of Musical Instruments, Smithsonian Institution.

———. "The Organ—King of Instruments." *Journal of Church Music,* Vol. 1, No. 11 (December 1959).

———. "The Organ Music of Bach." *Germanic Museum Bulletin,* Vol. 1, No. 6 (March 1938).

———. "Organ Music—from 'Hydraulis' to Bach." *RCA Victor Record Review,* June 1946.

———. "Organ Renaissance." *Church Music Review,* June 1945.

———. "Organ Renaissance: Music Old and New." *Modern Music,* Vol. XXI, No. 4 (May-June 1944).

———. "The Organs of Arp Schnitger." *Journal of Church Music,* Vol. 7, No. 1 (January 1965).

———. "The Pedal Harpsichord: Two in One." *Music Journal,* Vol. XXVI, No. 2 (February 1968).

———. "Right on, Mr. Edison." *The Bicentennial Tracker.* Wilmington, Ohio: Organ Historical Society, 1976.

———. "Some Ageless Instruments." *Journal of Church Music,* Vol. 13, No. 1 (January 1971).

———. "Some Comments from an Organist Turned Slightly Harpsichordist." *Music,* Vol. 11, No. 1 (January 1977).

———. "The Story of Benjamin Franklin and the Armonica." *Music Clubs Magazine,* Vol. XXXV, No. 5 (May 1956).

————. "Thrilling Recital Tour of Fine Organs in European Lands." *The Diapason,* Vol. 45, Nos. 11, 12 (October, November 1954).

————. " 'To God Alone be Glory.' " *Christian Science Monitor,* July 29, 1950.

————. "25 Years of Recording." *Music,* Vol. 12, No. 3 (March 1978).

————. "200 Years Alive—George Frederick Handel." *High Fidelity Magazine,* Vol. 9, No. 4 (April 1959).

————. "Welcome Back American Trackers." *The Diapason,* Vol. 51, No. 10 (September 1960).

————. "What Is Good Music?" *New York Herald Tribune,* February 5, 1961.

————. "Why I Play 'Organ Music' on the Harpsichord." *Harpsichord,* Vol. III, No. 3 (August-September-October 1970).

Biggs, Margaret Power. Jacket insert notes to *A Tribute to E. Power Biggs.* Columbia Records, 1979.

Briggs, John. "An Organ Lecture." *New York Times,* October 26, 1958.

Brush, Gerome. *Boston Symphony Orchestra.* Boston: Merrymount Press, 1936.

Buell, Richard. "E. Power Biggs: 1906–1977; The King of the King of Instruments." *The Boston Phoenix,* March 22, 1977.

Challis, John. "The Pedal Harpsichord." Program notes for a concert by E. Power Biggs, May 11, 1965.

Clapp, Stephen C. "The Music Makers." *Harvard Crimson,* September 27, 1958.

Conly, John M. "Vox Humana Fortissimo." *The Reporter,* September 24, 1964.

Coolidge, Elizabeth Sprague. Correspondence in Library of Congress.

"Copy of Bach Organ Is Placed at Harvard." *The Diapason,* Vol. 28, No. 6 (May 1937).

Covell, William King. Correspondence in Organ Library, Boston University.

Dickson, Harry Ellis. *Arthur Fiedler and the Boston Pops.* Boston: Houghton Mifflin, 1981.

————. *Gentlemen, More Dolce Please!* Boston: Beacon Press, 1969.

"E. Power Biggs." *Current Biography,* November 1950.

Ervin, Horace. "Notes on Franklin's Armonica and the Music Mozart Wrote for It." *Journal of the Franklin Institute,* Vol. 262, No. 5 (November 1956).

"European Recording Tour—General Story." Texas Boys' Choir publicity release, 1967.

"Famed Handel Organ Restored by Mander Reopened by Biggs." *The Diapason,* Vol. 60, No. 2 (January 1969).

Ferguson, John Allen. *Walter Holtkamp, American Organ Builder.* Kent, Ohio: Kent State University Press, 1979.

Fesperman, John. *Flentrop in America.* Raleigh: Sunbury Press, 1982.

————. *Two Essays on Organ Design.* Raleigh: Sunbury Press, 1975.

Fisk, Charles. Jacket notes for *J. S. Bach, Clavierübung Part III.* Titanic Records, 1983.

Flint, Edward W. "The Fisk Organ at Harvard." *The Organ,* Vol. XLVIII, No. 190 (October 1968).

————. *The Great Organ in the Methuen Memorial Music Hall.* Methuen, Mass.: Methuen Memorial Music Hall, 1950.

Freeman, Andrew. "The Organ in Great Packington Church near Meriden." *Musical Opinion,* November 1936.

————. "Organs at Salzburg." *The Organ,* Vol. XV, No. 60 (April 1936).

Gammons, Edward B. "Making Organ History in Boston." *The American Organist,* Vol. 34, No. 1 (January 1951).

————. "Recitals on Baroque Organ at Harvard Raise Enthusiasm." *The Diapason,* Vol. 28, No. 6 (May 1937).

Gehring, Philip. "E. Power Biggs." *The Cresset,* Vol. XL, No. 5 (March 1977).

"Germanic Museum Said to Have First Classical Organ in the U.S." *Christian Science Monitor,* March 27, 1937.

Harrison, G. Donald. "The Classical Organ in the Germanic Museum." *Germanic Museum Bulletin,* Vol. 1, No. 6 (March 1938).

———. Correspondence with W. King Covell in Organ Library, Boston University.

"Het Händel-orgel van Great Packington." *Luister,* Vol. 22, No. 257 (February 1974).

Hicks, Anthony. "Recording at Great Packington." *Musical Times,* December 1969.

Holden, Dorothy J. *The Life and Work of Ernest M. Skinner.* Richmond, Va.: Organ Historical Society, 1985.

Hughes, Albert D. "Bach Tone and Touch of Biggs Make Harvard's Organ Unique." *Christian Science Monitor,* August 21, 1943.

Hughes, Allen. "Biggs and His Pipe Organ Renaissance." *New York Times,* December 22, 1968.

———. "Electronic 'Pipe Organs' Distress Biggs." *New York Times,* June 9, 1976.

———. " 'Perfect' Tully Hall Organ Is No Trifle." *New York Times,* April 9, 1975.

Hummel, Carolyn F. "Old North Church Gets 'New' Organ." *Christian Science Monitor,* July 29, 1958.

Hunt, Eileen. "E. Power Biggs: Legacy of a Performing Artist." D. M. A. diss., Boston University, 1986.

Johnson, H. Earle. *Symphony Hall, Boston.* New York: Da Capo Press, 1979.

Johnson, Harriett. "Organ with Charisma." *New York Post,* April 10, 1975.

Jongepier, Jan. *Flentrop Orgelbouw 75 Years.* Raleigh: Sunbury Press, 1978.

Kazdin, Andrew. Jacket insert notes to *A Tribute to E. Power Biggs.* Columbia Records, 1979.

Kennedy, T. R., Jr. "Triple Keyboard Expert." *New York Times,* August 5, 1945.

Kimball, George. "A View of Pipe Organs from E. Power Biggs." *Rochester Times-Union,* January 7, 1970.

Lawrence, Arthur. "The Redoubtable Mr. Biggs." *The Diapason,* Vol. 68, No. 5 (April 1977).

Ledbetter, Stephen. "A Brief History of the Boston Symphony Orchestra." B. S. O. program booklet, October 10–11, 1980.

"Leo Sowerby: A Symposium of Tribute." *Music,* Vol. 2, No. 10 (October 1968).

"Letters to British Editors Reveal a Curious Story." *The Diapason,* Vol. 60, No. 4 (March 1969).

McClure, John. "How We Taped the Sound of San Marco." *High Fidelity Magazine,* Vol. 18, No. 2 (February 1968).

McCord, David. "More E. Power Biggs to You." *The New Yorker,* April 1948.

McCurdy, Alexander. "E. Power Biggs on Performing Bach's Music." *Etude,* (July 1950).

Martin, H. Winthrop. "A History of the American Guild of Organists in Boston, Massachusetts." M. S. M. thesis, Union Seminary, 1954.

Miller, Margo. "Widow to Open Library Dedicated to 'Biggsie.' " *Boston Globe,* November 22, 1985.

Moe, Lawrence. "A Tribute to E. Power Biggs." *The Diapason,* Vol. 68, No. 6 (May 1977).

Morgan, Bruce. "The Organ Master of Brattle Street." *The Real Paper,* October 23, 1976.

"New Organ in Boston Hailed at Premiere." *The Diapason,* Vol. 40, No. 12 (November 1949).

"Night at Pops." *Music,* Vol. 10, No. 5 (May 1976).

Noble, T. Tertius. "T. Tertius Noble's Fifty Years' Career as Church Musician." *The Diapason,* Vol. 22, No. 4 (March 1931).

Ochse, Orpha. *The History of the Organ in the United States.* Bloomington: Indiana University Press, 1975.

O'Connell, Charles. *The Other Side of the Record.* New York: Knopf, 1949.

"Organ Revivalist." *Time,* May 10, 1954.

Owen, Barbara. "E. Power Biggs: A Profile." *Music,* Vol. 5, No. 6 (June 1971).

———. "Flentrop Tracker on Harvard Campus Described." *The Diapason,* Vol. 49, No. 1 (December 1958).

———. "Hail and Farewell: The Biggs Memorial Service." *The Diapason,* Vol. 68, No. 6 (May 1977).

———. "So Let Us Now Praise Famous Men." *Journal of Church Music,* Vol. 23, No. 3 (March 1981).

———. "The Symphony Hall Organ and Poulenc's Concerto." *Handel and Haydn Magazine,* Vol. 1, No. 2 (Winter 1982).

"Paaah, Chaaah, Aaah." *Newsweek,* August 18, 1958.

Palmer, Larry. "E. Power Biggs: An Affectionate Remembrance." *The Diapason,* Vol. 70, No. 4 (March 1979).

———. "The Pedal Harpsichord." *The Diapason,* Vol. 65, No. 1 (December 1973).

Pape, Uwe. *The Tracker Organ Revival in America.* Berlin: Pape Verlag, 1978.

Pierce, Edward F. "Ben Franklin's Harmonica." *Think,* Vol. XXII, No. 5 (May 1956).

Pinkham, Daniel. "Favorite Memories of a Great Organist." *Boston Globe,* March 20, 1977.

"Pope of Instruments." *Newsweek,* April 22, 1946.

"Portrait of a Builder: John Challis." *The Harpsichord,* Vol. 11, No. 3 (August-September-October, 1969).

"Rich Tones of Rare Old Boston Organ Heard Once More." *Christian Science Monitor,* July 15, 1936.

Richards, Emerson. "Tanglewood's Berkshire Organ and Festival." *The American Organist,* Vol. 23, No. 10 (October 1940).

———. "That Baroque Organ at Harvard." *The American Organist,* Vol. 21, No. 3 (March 1938).

Riley, John W. "What went into the Building of Symphony Hall's New Organ." *Boston Daily Globe,* November 9, 1949.

Schiller, Jonathan. "The Great Organ." *Musical America,* February 15, 1954.

Schonberg, Harold C. "A Portion of Fryed Snake." *New York Times,* October 13, 1963.

Schuneman, Robert. "Oberlin Dedicates New Organ." *The Diapason,* Vol. 66, No. 2 (January 1975).

Sly, Allan. "New Organ in Cambridge." *Christian Science Monitor,* October 7, 1958.

Smith, Moses. "Germanic Gets Organ Built on Plan of Bach's." *Boston Evening Transcript,* March 27, 1937.

Thomson, Virgil. "The Organ." *New York Herald Tribune,* August 5, 1945.

Thorpe, Day. "Rare Tones from New Organ Give Recital Classic Quality." *Washington Evening Star,* March 6, 1954.

Webb, Stanley. "A Handel Organ Restored." *Musical Times,* December 1968.

Whitworth, Reginald. "G. D. Cunningham and the Organ in the Town Hall, Birmingham." *The Organ,* Vol. XIII, No. 49 (July 1933).

Williams, Alexander. "The New Classical Organ: A Victory for Bach." *Boston Herald,* April 26, 1937.

Wimbush, Roger. "Here and There." *The Gramophone,* January 1966.

Zeuch, William E. "Sowerby Concerto First Heard in Boston." *The Diapason,* Vol. 29, No. 6 (May 1938).

INDEX

235

EDITOR: *Natalie Wrubel*
BOOK DESIGNER: *Matthew Williamson*
JACKET DESIGNER: *Matthew Williamson*
PRODUCTION COORDINATOR: *Harriet S. Curry*
TYPEFACE: *Sabon*
PRINTER: *Haddon Craftsmen, Inc.*
BINDER: *Haddon Craftsmen, Inc.*

BARBARA OWEN is internationally known as a writer and lecturer on the history of the organ, its music, and its players. She is a past president of the Organ Historical Society and the author of *The Organ in New England* and numerous articles for *Grove's Dictionary of Music and Musicians*.